Join the Celebration!

A COLLECTION OF FAVORITE RECIPES

Women's Board of the Union League Boys and Girls Clubs

Edited by Lee Karton and Barbara Barker

Hillsboro Press
PROVIDENCE PUBLISHING CORPORATION
FRANKLIN, TENNESSEE

All proceeds from the sale of *Join the Celebration! A Collection of Favorite Recipes* will benefit the Union League Boys and Girls Clubs.

To order additional cookbooks, use the order form at the back of this book or contact:

Women's Board
Union League Boys and Girls Clubs
65 W. Jackson Boulevard
Chicago, IL 60604
Telephone: (312) 588-1863
Fax: (312) 583-0320
Web site: www.ulbgc.org
E-mail: cookbook@ulbgc.org

This cookbook is a collection of favorite recipes, which are not necessarily original.

About the cover and illustrations: A grand ball at the Union League Club of Chicago is depicted in internationally known artist Guy Buffet's painting, Grand bal dans la grande salle, 2001. A member of the Union League Club, Buffet graciously contributed the use of the painting for the cover and created the charming line drawings that introduce each chapter especially for the cookbook. The painting is part of the Union League Club's permanent art collection.

Illustrations by Guy Buffet

Cover design by Hope Seth

Printed in the United States of America

08	07	06	05	04	1	2	3	4	5

Library of Congress Control Number: 2004112139

ISBN: 1-57736-290-X

HILLSBORO PRESS
an imprint of
Providence Publishing Corporation
238 Seaboard Lane • Franklin, Tennessee 37067
www.providence-publishing.com
800-321-5692

Dedicated to
the Union League Club of Chicago
in commemoration of its 125 years of commitment
to the community,
and to
the Union League Boys and Girls Clubs
for 85 years of service to the youth of Chicago.

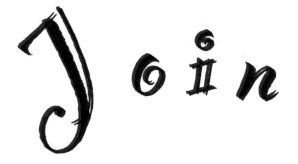

Join the Celebration!

A COLLECTION OF FAVORITE RECIPES

Menu

Starters

Specialties of the House

A La Carte

INTRODUCTION

THANK YOU FOR JOINING THE CELEBRATION! BY PURCHASING THIS COOKBOOK, YOU HAVE ASSISTED the Women's Board of the Union League Boys and Girls Clubs in its ongoing effort to serve the needs of over seven thousand disadvantaged inner-city children in Chicago.

From its inception, the mission of the Union League Boys and Girls Clubs has been "to provide a healthy, safe, and productive alternative to the streets." Our four clubs are located in areas where gangs, drugs, and violence are a terrible reality of everyday life. Often, hard-working parents have no choice but to leave their children to fend for themselves after school. The clubs are safe havens, places where children can go to learn and have fun, places where they feel safe, secure, and accepted. Each club is supervised by a professional staff and offers a range of activities tailored to the special needs of its members. Tutoring, dance, art classes, craft projects, athletics, computer labs, field trips, and team sports are among the many activities offered. Special programs for teens, career education, and educational scholarships are available. Particular emphasis is given to promoting academic excellence, building self-esteem, and developing leadership and social skills. Each summer, almost five hundred children attend our Wisconsin summer camp. Perhaps most important of all, these youngsters receive the guidance and support many of them need to remain drug free, out of gangs, and in school.

The Union League Foundation for Boys' Clubs was created in 1919. During the 1970s, the then all-male Board of Trustees undertook the task of raising funds through an annual ball. Many of the trustees' wives were drafted to help plan the event. On June 1, 1978, the trustees approved the formation of the Women's Board of the Union League Foundation for Boys' Clubs to formalize their activities. The first meeting of the Women's Board was held on the same day, and the ladies wasted no time getting to the business at hand. All of the items on the agenda were fund-raising projects, including the upcoming annual ball, now the exclusive project of the newly formed board. In a bit of déjà vu, one of the items up for discussion was the *Centennial Cookbook*, later published by the Women's Board to commemorate the 100th anniversary of the Union League Club of Chicago.

Much has changed in the twenty-five years since that initial meeting. There have been many new faces, ideas, and projects. One thing, however, has remained unchanged: The unwavering dedication of the members of the Women's Board to raise funds to help meet the needs of the clubs. To that end, the board has raised over three million dollars. The annual benefit ball has become a major fund-raising event, and other efforts, such as this cookbook, bring in additional funds. With the support of the Board of Trustees and the Union League Club Board of Directors, the Women's Board has become a full partner in the development activities of the organization.

Join the Celebration! was undertaken to commemorate two significant events: the 25th anniversary of the Women's Board of the Union League Boys and Girls Clubs and the 125th anniversary of the Union League Club of Chicago. Good food is important to any celebration, and favorite dishes make the celebration even more special. With that in mind, we asked the four thousand members of the Union League Club located throughout the world to send us their favorite recipes. Those included in this collection run the gamut from family favorites to regional specialties, from exotic to homestyle, from ethnic to All-American comfort food. There are simple recipes that are well within the capabilities of the novice cook and sophisticated recipes to challenge the accomplished cook. Most of the chefs represented in the Chefs' Favorites section have participated in benefits held at the Union League Club, such as the annual Share Our Strength event supporting hunger awareness. Others are known for their philanthropic activities.

We hope this cookbook provides you with many hours of enjoyment and that this collection of favorite recipes inspires you to create your own celebrations!

Women's Board directors at the board's gala Silver Anniversary Ball (2002).

HISTORY

O N A JUNE NIGHT IN 1862, ELEVEN MEN MET IN SECRET IN THE SMALL TOWN OF PEKIN, ILLINOIS. They had come together in this troubled time to form a new patriotic organization, the Union League of America, and they took an oath to dedicate themselves to the preservation of the Union. Union League Clubs based upon this patriotic principle were subsequently formed throughout the country and gave rise to the Union League Club of Chicago.

The Chicago Club of the Union League of America, later known as the Union League Club of Chicago, was founded in 1879. Throughout its 125-year history, the Club's activities have largely been directed toward non-partisan participation in public affairs. One of the four standing committees formed at the outset was the Committee on Political Action which became a real force in the civic development of the city. True to its original purpose, particular emphasis has been given to participation in patriotic activities and the improvement of government at the local and state levels. Stamping out corruption in government, fair elections, judicial reform, and merit selection of judges are among the many ongoing civic issues championed by the Union League Club. Over the years, the scope of the Club's activities has been enlarged, and the Club has become identified not only with civic causes, but also with the development of Chicago's social and cultural life.

Ferdinand Wyeth Peck, a former president of the Club, is credited with bringing permanent opera to Chicago in the 1880s and was joined by other members in spearheading the drive to build the Auditorium Theatre in which to house it. Now a registered landmark, the theatre was designed by members Dankmar Adler and his brilliant young associate, Louis Sullivan. Boxes for the first season in 1889 were auctioned off. Member George Pullman paid the top bid of sixteen hundred dollars, and three other members, Marshall Field, Samuel Allerton, and Robert T. Crane, each paid one thousand dollars. The founding of the Chicago Symphony Orchestra also involved Union League Club members. All but one of the incorporators of the Chicago Orchestral Association were members of the Club, and other members, including Daniel Burnham, helped raise the funds necessary to endow the orchestra and build Orchestra Hall. Club members were instrumental in bringing the World's Fair to Chicago in 1893, and three members, including Daniel Burnham, served as successive presidents of the World's Fair Association. Determined to make the great collection exhibited in the fair's Columbian Museum permanently available, Club members approached Marshall Field who gave one million dollars toward the founding of a new museum, now known worldwide as the Field Museum. Other members were prominent donors. Union League Club members also promoted the founding of Chicago's incomparable Museum of Science and Industry. It was known for many years as the Rosenwald Museum in honor of Club member Julius Rosenwald who donated three million dollars for its establishment. Member John G. Shedd provided three million dollars for the construction of the aquarium bearing his name. Architect Daniel Burnham's Montauk Building was the world's first skyscraper, and much of his acclaimed Chicago plan for the city is still being followed. Among other notable projects influenced by Union League Club members are the construction of the Lawson YMCA, Northwestern University's Patten Gym, Wilmette's Gillson Park, Grant Park, the University of Chicago's Eckhart Hall, and the Harold Washington Library.

The Club has been located at 65 W. Jackson Boulevard for 118 years. The original clubhouse, built in 1886 complete with "new-fangled electric lights," was an imposing structure of brick and terra cotta. Its two-story main dining room on the fifth floor was said to offer a magnificent view of Lake Michigan. In need of repairs and enlargement, the old clubhouse was demolished in 1924. Over one thousand members attended a farewell banquet at the Club the night before demolition was scheduled to begin. The grand opening of the new clubhouse was held on May 21–22, 1926. Today, its twenty-three floors house public areas, dining facilities, meeting rooms, a business center, athletic and spa facilities, a swimming pool, hotel rooms and suites, and administrative offices. The library boasts thirteen thousand volumes, including a fine

The original Union League Club of Chicago building, built in 1886

collection of rare books and manuscripts, and is administered by a professional librarian and staff. The Club's important collection of fine art is displayed throughout the building and is overseen by a full-time art curator and a conservator. A professional archivist maintains the vast collection of historical documents, photographs, and other memorabilia. Approximately twenty-two hundred of the Union League Club's four thousand members and privilege holders live or work in the greater Chicago area. Others live all over the world and use the clubhouse as their home away from home. Members of the Union League Club founded and support three separate philanthropic organizations. Created in 1949, the Civic and Arts Foundation funds scholarships and grants for individuals and groups involved in the visual and performing arts and in civic and community endeavors. The Engineers Foundation provides scholarships and grants to engineering students. The third organization is the Union League Boys and Girls Clubs.

During World War I, the Club created the War Committee, which immediately became active in supporting American servicemen. The Club was opened to all army and navy men, and the committee helped establish a canteen for all servicemen in the city. Equally important, the committee became deeply involved in building public morale for the war effort and in educating citizens, particularly immigrants, about the American position in the war. In 1919, during the post-war period, the Club looked for a new vehicle through which it could participate in matters of public concern. The decision was made to merge the highly successful War Committee with the Committee on Public Action, and the Public Affairs Committee was born.

In its first year, 995 boys joined Club One and the juvenile deliquency rate in the district dropped by 80 percent.

For many years, the Club had been concerned about the problem of delinquency among underprivileged boys, and several members had been investigating the possibility of establishing a boys' club. In 1919, representatives from the Boys' Clubs Federation were invited to speak at a dinner held to discuss the issue. They told that "66 per cent of boys in the city were of the underprivileged class; that is boys who had little or no home life and who, from supper until bedtime, were accustomed to playing in the streets and running in gangs." Members who had served on the War Committee knew that many of the young recruits had been delinquents prior to being inducted into the service. They knew about the low literacy rates among these young men and their pervasive feeling that the future held nothing for them except poverty and hopelessness. A meeting of the Public Affairs Committee was called. The representatives from the Boys' Clubs Federation spoke, as did two judges present who reported that sixteen thousand boys had appeared in their two courtrooms on various offenses during the prior year. The Public Affairs Committee moved quickly, and the Union League Foundation for Boys' Clubs was incorporated on December 26, 1919. Forty-three charter members of the foundation gave one thousand dollars each, and others subscribed in amounts that brought the total to forty-five thousand dollars. The Public Affairs Committee gave ten thousand dollars left over from the operation of the servicemen's canteen toward opening the first boys' club.

In seeking a site for Club One, the trustees looked for a community where property values were low and delinquency was high. By February 1920, the foundation had purchased the Chopin Club, a three-story brick building at 19th and Leavitt Streets in the area known today as Pilsen. The area was not known for its gentility. It was a congested neighborhood of some eighty thousand people crowded into one square mile. Of the twenty-two nationalities represented, most were immigrants from Poland, Bohemia, Germany, and Czechoslovakia. Among other things, the building had housed a dance hall and a saloon, and had one of the worst reputations for rowdiness on the West Side. The police had recorded seven murders in or around the Chopin Club, and it had come to be known as the "Bucket of Blood." The building was purchased for eighteen thousand dollars and was entirely renovated to include a gymnasium, library, game room, meeting and study rooms, and a "moving picture" room. The structure was later

Lunch at Club Two (1933)

raised to allow for the installation of a swimming pool in the basement. The building's dedication on May 29, 1920, was a festive occasion. The Chicago Newsboys Band provided music, and Chicago Mayor William Hale "Big Bill" Thompson gave the address.

The parents of the 995 boys who became members of Club One in its first year were frugal, law-abiding, hard-working people who adhered to old-world customs. Their children, however, were seeking a new American way of life. The club's programs soon improved the social life of the neighborhood's young people and helped the boys to spend their spare time constructively and to develop a sense of responsibility and leadership. The influence of Club One on the community was remarkable. Judge Arnold of the juvenile court reported that juvenile delinquency in that district dropped by 80 percent during the club's first year of operation! By the end of the third year, there were sixteen hundred active members, and seven hundred members had qualified for positions in the business community, most of them employed by members of the Union League Club. The makeup of the community has changed over the years and is now primarily Hispanic.

These campers are among the thousands of inner-city children who have enjoyed summer fun in the country (circa 1940).

In 1924, the Union League Club purchased an eighty-acre tract of land in Salem, Wisconsin, as a summer camp. Club members dug into their pockets and raised sixty-five thousand dollars for the construction of the first permanent buildings. Located just sixty miles from Chicago, the camp now covers some 250 rolling acres and includes a lake for swimming, fishing, and boating, tennis courts, baseball diamonds, basketball courts, nature trails, and plenty of open spaces for outdoor activities. Younger campers are

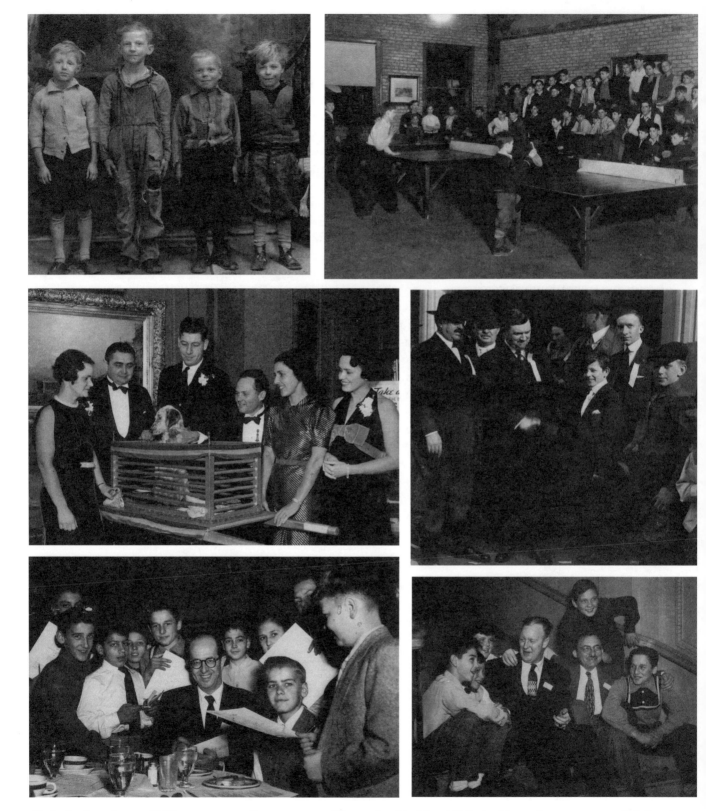

Clockwise from the top: Children as young as five were accepted for membership (circa 1920); A table tennis tournament at Club Two draws a crowd of onlookers (circa 1935); The Hon. George F. Barrett, Judge of the Cook County Circuit Court, congratulates "Mike" Lebanowski, the first member of the Union League Boys' Club (May 29, 1920); Jack Brickhouse, "The Voice of the Chicago Cubs," was a guest at one of the Boys' Clubs celebrity luncheons at the Union League (circa 1955); "Sgt. Bilko," actor-comedian Phil Silvers, signing autographs for Boys' Clubs members (circa 1955); This winsome puppy was a raffle prize at an early Boys' Clubs fundraiser held at the Union League Club (circa 1935).

taught to swim in the large pool near the lake shore. A playground for younger children was installed and equipped with funds raised by the Women's Board. Among its twenty-five permanent buildings are a newly remodeled kitchen and mess hall, a recreation center, living cottages, a hospital, and a chapel. More than fifty staff members are employed each summer, and almost five hundred children attend camp in four two-week sessions.

Club One was such an unqualified success that the trustees moved to open a second facility at Wolcott and Race Streets in Chicago's West Town area. The neighborhood was a melting pot of some twenty-five nationalities, predominately Italian and Polish. Union League Club members donated $168,543 for the property and building, and ground-breaking ceremonies were held amidst much public fanfare and excitement in the neighborhood. Opened in April 1926, Club Two was designed and built as a boys' club and, like Club One, was well-equipped to serve the interests of its young members. Today, most of Club Two's members are Hispanic.

The riots of the late 1960s in Chicago's Humboldt Park area provided the impetus for the third club. Barreto Club, located at 1214 N. Washtenaw, was originally known as Club Three. In 1968, the foundation agreed to supervise the operation of the Latin American Boys' Club which had been organized by Puerto Rican immigrants. The foundation contributed funds and organizational assistance for several years. After much discussion about assuming the responsibility for a third club, the foundation purchased the clubhouse in 1970. One of the original club's founders, Miguel Barreto, continued to serve on the neighborhood board of directors. Returning home one evening, Barreto was robbed and murdered. Club Three was renamed Barreto Club in his memory, and his death has served as a symbol of the importance of directing the youngsters of the community away from gangs and violence. In the late 1970s, Barreto was the first of the clubs to open its activities to girls. The other clubs and camp soon followed, and the organization's name was officially changed to the Union League Boys and Girls Clubs in 1988. Ultimately, the decision was made to demolish the Barreto clubhouse and construct a new one. The new Barreto Club was dedicated in June 2004. The majority of its members are African-American and Hispanic.

Lafayette Club was established in 2002 and is the organization's first outreach endeavor. Located at 2714 W. Augusta Boulevard in the Humboldt Park area, the club is staffed and operated by the Union League Boys and Girls Clubs, but is housed in the Jean de Lafayette public school. The location was chosen to make the club available to children who would otherwise be at risk by having to cross boundaries drawn by rival gangs. Its members are largely African-American and Hispanic.

In 1978, the Board of Trustees approved the formation of the Women's Board which has become an important fund-raising arm of the organization, primarily through its annual benefit ball. In a desire to become involved in the work of the organization, younger members of the Union League Club formed the Associate Board and provide mentoring and special activities for children such as holiday parties, bowling, and trips to the ball park.

Celebrities and well-known sports figures have often visited the clubs to meet the youngsters and offer encouragement. Boxing great Jack Dempsey was a frequent visitor. The legendary Babe Ruth and Lou Gehrig attended the tenth anniversary celebration of the

Clockwise from the top: Pom Pom Squad's performances are a highlight at Club Two functions; organized team sports beat hanging out on street corners; arts and crafts programs are among the most popular activities; little ones get a head start with schoolwork and discover that learning can be fun; 42 percent of Union League Boys and Girls Clubs members are girls; several members of LaFayette Club participate in the Boys and Girls Clubs Merit Music Program, which defrays the cost of music teachers and instruments.

Clockwise from the top: The clubs opened their doors to girls in the 1970s; airing on Saturday afternoons, "Club Kids on the Radio" is a collaboration with Loyola University's WLUW-FM radio station; a modern day pilgrim enjoys the annual Thanksgiving dinner served by members of the Board of Trustees, Women's Board, Associate Board, and staff; Club One's Dance Squad performs at numerous events; the clubs provide a positive environment where talents and abilities are encouraged; computer labs are available for computer skills training, homework and scheduled recreation. *Center:* JROTC members form an Honor Guard at Lafayette Club's Awards Night.

Boys' Clubs in 1929. Joint events with members of the Union League Club—often referred to by club kids as the "big kids' club"—have been held almost from the beginning. For many years, members hosted Men and Boys Celebrity Luncheons in the Club's Main Dining Room. Among the many guests were Ernie Banks, Tony Zale, Dick Butkus, Gayle Sayers, Johnny Morris, George Halas, U.S. Supreme Court Justice Byron "Whizzer" White, Hugh O'Brien, Basil Rathbone, Robert Alda, Irv Kupcinet, Jack Brickhouse, Johnny Desmond, and Forrest Tucker. The clubs' annual Awards Nights are much anticipated, and Union League Club members join in the festivities. A special effort has been made to expand the horizons of the girls. Many members of the Union League Club's Women's Initiative Networking Group invite club girls as guests to their annual Take Your Daughter To Work Luncheon which features career education and inspirational speakers.

Baseball legends Babe Ruth and Lou Gehrig help celebrate the tenth anniversary of the founding of the Union League Boys' Clubs.

The Union League Boys and Girls Clubs currently serve some seven thousand children. Its offices and administrative personnel are located at the Union League Club. Full-time professionals, part-time workers, and volunteers staff the clubs and administer the fine programs for which the clubs have become known. Tutoring, computer labs, competitive and recreational sports, arts and crafts, educational field trips, and organized outings are among the many activities offered. The clubs provide a focal point in each community and are a stabilizing influence.

Well over 200,000 youngsters have been served by the clubs over the past eighty-five years. Many have matured into community leaders. Some have joined the Union League Club as members, including a former member of Club One who was elected Union League Club president in 1969. Many have come back to tell the membership how influential the clubs were at a critical point in their young lives. Others have returned to their neighborhood clubs to serve as volunteers. The effort to serve Chicago's under-privileged boys and girls is ongoing. The goals of promoting academic excellence; encouraging talents and abilities; fostering the development of self-esteem, leadership, and social skills; and directing energies into constructive channels has never changed.

BIBLIOGRAPHY

Grant, Bruce. *Fight for a City, The Story of the Union League Club of Chicago and Its Times, 1880–1955*. Chicago: John S. Swift Co., Inc., 1955.
Kellman, Jerold L. *The First One Hundred Years*. Chicago: Union League Club of Chicago, 1984.

About the Illustrator

Hand-lettered recipe:

French Onion soup Gratinée
for 4 Persons

4 Medium size Onions, 3-tablespoons of butter.
6 cups of beef stock or bouillon.
Salt and Pepper. Day old French bread or
toast. Fresh grated Parmesan cheese.

Slice the onions and cook very gently in
butter until light brown. Salt and Pepper to
taste. Add Beef stock and bring to a boiling point

Reduce heat and simmer for 10 minutes, then set aside
to blend. When ready to serve, heat to popping hot
and sprinkle some cheese on it, then put in
individual casseroles. Arrange sliced bread on
top and add more Parmesan cheese. Set in the
sun long enough to brown the cheese. Make the
soup the day before and it will taste even better.
Bon appetit!

Guy Buffet

The whimsical illustrations gracing the pages of this cookbook were created especially for *Join the Celebration!* by world-renowned artist Guy Buffet. His delightful painting of a grand ball at the Union League Club of Chicago appears on the cover.

Buffet began his artistic career by sketching on napkins and tablecloths in his family's restaurant in Paris. He sold his first painting at the age of thirteen to an American tourist and soon began studying at the famed Beaux Arts de Toulon. Today, his art is in private collections and museums throughout the world, including La Musee de la Monnaie in Paris, the Honolulu Academy of Art, the Union League Club of Chicago, and the John Deere Museum. The official artist for Champagne Perrier-Jouet, his images have also been used for the Tour de France, Absolut Vodka, the Napa Valley Mustard Festival, and Aloha Airlines, among others. He was the official artist for the 2002 Winter Olympics in Salt Lake City, Utah. His signature drawings of chefs, waiters, and sommeliers appear on numerous items, including ties, note cards, calendars, and a collection of dinnerware created exclusively for Williams-Sonoma. Guy Buffet wines, with labels bearing his droll restaurant denizens, were recently introduced. A Union League Club member, Buffet divides his time between homes in Paris, Hawaii, and the French Riviera.

An accomplished cook, Buffet contributed his recipe for French Onion Soup Gratinée (page 58). With typical élan, he hand-lettered the recipe and accompanied it with one of his inimitable bistro characters. *Ah, c'est magnifique!*

Brunch & Breads

Blitz Kuchen
(Lightning Cake)

The recipe for this simple cake was handed down by a grandmother who was born in Luxembourg. It comes together in a flash—hence the name. Serve it alone or topped with fresh fruit or berries.

¾ cup unsalted butter, softened
1½ cups granulated sugar
2 cups flour
2 teaspoons baking powder

¼ teaspoon salt
¾ cup whole milk
2 eggs, lightly beaten

Preheat the oven to 350°F. Butter a 9x13-inch pan. Place the butter, sugar, and flour in a bowl and rub it together with your fingertips until crumbly. Remove ¾ cup of the mixture for the topping and set aside. Add the baking powder and salt to the bowl and stir to combine. Add the milk. Add the eggs and beat until smooth, about 1 minute. Pour the batter into the prepared pan and sprinkle with the reserved topping. Bake until a tester comes out clean, about 25 to 30 minutes. Remove to a wire rack and cool.

Serves 10 to 12

Blueberry Macadamia Nut Bread

Blueberries, macadamia nuts, and fresh orange—no wonder it's a favorite!

4 cups flour
1 tablespoon baking powder
2 teaspoons baking soda
2 teaspoons salt
½ cup butter
2 cups granulated sugar

2 tablespoons grated orange zest
2 eggs
1½ cups fresh orange juice
3 cups fresh blueberries
2 cups whole macadamia nuts

Preheat the oven to 350°F. Grease and flour 3 medium-size bread pans. Combine the flour, baking powder, baking soda, and salt in a bowl and set aside. In the bowl of an electric mixer, cream together the butter and sugar until fluffy. Beat in the orange zest and eggs. Add the orange juice and beat thoroughly. Add the flour mixture in 3 or 4 additions, beating just until each is incorporated. Gently stir in the blueberries and macadamia nuts. Divide the batter among the bread pans and bake until a tester inserted in the center comes out clean, about 1 hour. Cool the loaves in the pans for 10 minutes before turning out. Cool completely on wire racks before storing.

Makes 3 medium-size loaves

Cheese Stuffed Pumpkin-Pecan Muffins

Don't be surprised when everyone asks for this recipe!

2 cups flour
½ cup sugar
½ cup chopped pecans
1 tablespoon baking powder
1½ teaspoons pumpkin pie spice
½ teaspoon salt
2 eggs, beaten

¾ cup canned pumpkin
½ cup butter, melted
¼ cup sour cream
3 ounces cream cheese,
   cut into cubes
Cinnamon sugar

Preheat the oven to 400°F. Grease the muffin cups. Combine the flour, sugar, pecans, baking powder, pumpkin pie spice, and salt in a large bowl. In a separate bowl, whisk together the eggs, pumpkin, butter, and sour cream. Add to the dry ingredients and stir just until moistened. Fill the prepared muffin cups ⅔ full. Place a cube of cream cheese in the center of each muffin. Sprinkle the cinnamon sugar over the batter. Bake until the muffins are golden brown and a tester comes out clean, about 15 to 20 minutes. Cool for 5 minutes before turning out of the pan.

Makes 10 to 12

Cranberry Nut Bread

Serve this holiday loaf warm with sweet butter for breakfast or with an afternoon cup of tea.

2 cups sifted flour
½ teaspoon salt
½ teaspoon baking soda
1½ teaspoons baking powder
1 cup sugar
1 egg, beaten

½ cup orange juice
2 tablespoons vegetable oil
Grated zest from 1 orange
2 tablespoons hot water
½ cup chopped nuts
1 cup fresh cranberries, quartered

Preheat the oven to 325°F. Grease a 5x8-inch loaf pan. Sift the dry ingredients into a large bowl. Combine the egg, juice, oil, orange zest, and hot water in a small bowl. Add to the dry ingredients and stir just until moistened. Fold in the nuts and cranberries. Pour the batter into the pan and bake for 1 hour and 10 minutes. Transfer the pan to a wire rack and cool completely. Turn the loaf out of the pan and wrap in foil. Refrigerate for at least 12 hours before slicing.

Makes 1 loaf

Cherry Streusel Muffins

These family favorites are welcome any time. Unthawed, individually frozen cherries can be substituted.

STREUSEL TOPPING
    ½ cup flour
    ¼ cup sugar
    ½ teaspoon cinnamon

4 tablespoons unsalted butter, cut
    into small pieces and chilled

MUFFINS
    ½ cup unsalted butter, melted
    1½ cups pitted sweet or sour cherries,
        or ½ cup dried cherries
    2 cups bleached all-purpose flour
    ½ cup sugar
    1 tablespoon baking powder

½ teaspoon cinnamon
½ cup milk
2 eggs, lightly beaten
½ teaspoon vanilla
½ teaspoon almond extract (optional)

Preheat the oven to 425°F. Place the ingredients for the topping in a bowl. With your fingertips, rub in the butter until the mixture is crumbly. Set aside.

Lightly brush 12 muffin cups with a little of the melted butter. In a small bowl, toss the cherries with 2 tablespoons of the flour. Combine the dry ingredients in a large bowl. In a separate bowl, combine the melted butter, milk, eggs, vanilla, and almond extract. Add to the dry ingredients and stir just until moistened. Fold in the cherries. Fill each muffin cup ⅔ full and sprinkle with the topping. Bake for 15 to 20 minutes or until the muffins are golden and a toothpick inserted in the center comes out clean. Cool for 5 minutes before turning out of the pan.

Makes 12

Easy Strawberry Preserves

The preserves are fabulous on biscuits or scones! Use only perfectly ripe, sweet berries.

    1 quart ripe (not overripe) strawberries
    ¾ cup sugar
    1 tablespoon lemon juice

Wash the berries, drain well, and hull. Place them in a large skillet and mash lightly. Stir in the sugar and lemon juice. Bring to a boil, lower the heat, and simmer until thickened, stirring from time to time and skimming off foam. Cool and refrigerate for up to 1 week, or freeze for several months. The recipe can be doubled.

Makes about 3 cups

Lemony Blueberry Cornmeal Muffins

Buttermilk and cornmeal add great flavor and texture to these scrumptious muffins.

MUFFINS

1½ cups flour
⅓ cup yellow cornmeal
1 teaspoon baking soda
¼ teaspoon salt
Grated zest from 2 lemons
1 cup granulated sugar

½ cup vegetable oil
1 large egg
1 cup buttermilk
1 cup fresh or individually frozen
    blueberries (unthawed)

GLAZE (optional)

3 tablespoons lemon juice
1½ tablespoons sugar

Combine the flour, cornmeal, baking soda, and salt in a large bowl. In another bowl, combine the grated lemon zest with the sugar, oil, and egg and stir together with a wooden spoon. Stir in the buttermilk. Add the dry ingredients and mix just until moistened. Do not overwork the batter. Fold in the blueberries and let the batter rest for 15 minutes.

Position a rack in the center of the oven and preheat to 375°F. Grease 12 muffin cups or line with paper cups. Fill the cups ⅞ full. Bake until the muffins are lightly browned and a toothpick inserted in the center comes out clean, about 22 minutes. Cool in the pan for 5 minutes before turning out.

For the glaze, combine the lemon juice and sugar in a small bowl and stir until the sugar is dissolved. Dip the tops of the warm muffins in the glaze. Set aside until the glaze sets.

Makes 12

Flavored Butters

Unbelievably simple to make, these butters add a special touch to breakfast breads, pancakes, or waffles.

STRAWBERRY, RASPBERRY, OR ORANGE BUTTER

1 stick unsalted butter, softened
¼ cup top quality strawberry or raspberry jam, or orange marmalade

HONEY BUTTER

1 stick unsalted butter, softened
¼ cup honey
½ teaspoon cinnamon (optional)

In a bowl, beat the butter with an electric mixer until fluffy. Add jam, marmalade, or honey and combine on low speed. Add more to taste. Use immediately, or cover and refrigerate. Let soften before serving.

Makes ¾ cup

Quick Butterscotch Rolls

Nothing beats the aroma of cinnamon wafting from the oven. Leavened with baking powder, these sweet treats go together quickly. Serve them warm with sweet butter.

1 cup unsalted butter, softened	2 tablespoons granulated sugar
¾ cup packed light brown sugar	½ teaspoon salt
1 tablespoon light corn syrup	1 egg, slightly beaten
½ cup coarsely chopped pecans	1 cup milk
3 cups flour	1 teaspoon cinnamon
2 tablespoons baking powder	

Preheat the oven to 425°F. In the bowl of an electric mixer, cream together ½ cup of butter, ½ cup of brown sugar, and the corn syrup until fluffy. Spread the mixture in the bottom of a 9x9-inch pan and sprinkle evenly with the pecans.

Sift the flour, baking powder, granulated sugar, and salt into a large bowl. With a pastry blender, cut in ¼ cup of butter until the mixture looks like cornmeal. Add the egg and milk and blend thoroughly.

Turn the dough out onto a floured surface and knead for 30 seconds. Roll the dough into an 9x18-inch rectangle and spread with the remaining ¼ cup of butter. Sprinkle with the remaining ¼ cup of brown sugar and the cinnamon. Roll the dough lengthwise into a cylinder. With a thin, sharp knife, cut the roll into 16 pieces. Arrange the pieces in the pan with sides touching. Bake for 25 minutes.

Invert the rolls onto a wire rack set over a sheet of waxed paper. Spread the syrup left in the pan over the rolls. Serve warm.

Makes 16

Southern Pecan Oatmeal Cake

This moist cake has a very appealing texture and is equally good for breakfast, afternoon tea, or dessert.

CAKE

1⅓ cups flour	1½ cups boiling water
1 teaspoon baking soda	1 stick unsalted butter or margarine
1 teaspoon cinnamon	1 cup light brown sugar
¼ teaspoon salt	1 cup granulated sugar
1 cup quick-cooking oats	2 eggs

TOPPING

6 tablespoons butter or margarine	1 cup chopped pecans
½ cup granulated sugar	¼ cup evaporated milk

Preheat the oven to 350°F. Grease a 9x13-inch pan. Combine the flour, baking soda, cinnamon, and salt in a bowl. Place the oats in another bowl and add the boiling water and butter. Let stand until the butter melts and stir to combine. Stir in the brown and granulated sugars. Add the eggs and beat with an electric mixer on medium speed for 1 minute. Add the flour mixture and continue to beat for 2 minutes. Pour the batter into the prepared pan and bake for 30 to 35 minutes or until a toothpick comes out clean.

While the cake bakes, melt the butter and stir in the remaining ingredients for the topping. Set aside.

Remove the cake from the oven and turn on the broiler. Spread the topping over the cake. Watching carefully, broil until the topping is bubbly and browned. Remove the pan from the oven and cool on a rack. Serve the cake warm or at room temperature.

Serves 10 to 12

The Best Raisin Scones

Serve these light scones with English clotted cream, flavored butter, or whipped sweet butter and preserves. Cut them out the night before and enjoy them fresh from the oven in the morning.

1 egg, lightly beaten
½ cup cold whipping cream
½ cup raisins, currants, or
   dried cranberries
2¼ cups unbleached all-purpose flour
¼ cup sugar
1 tablespoon baking powder

Pinch of salt
1 stick cold unsalted butter, cut in
   1-inch cubes and refrigerated for
   at least 30 minutes
1½ teaspoons grated lemon zest
1 egg beaten with 1 tablespoon water
   or milk for egg wash

Position a rack in the middle of the oven and preheat to 400°F. Line a baking sheet with parchment. Combine the beaten egg with the cream. In a small bowl, toss the raisins with 1 tablespoon of the flour. Combine the remaining flour with the sugar, baking powder, and salt in the bowl of an electric mixer. Mix on low speed to blend. Add the butter and lemon zest and mix until the mixture looks like coarse meal. Add the egg and cream mixture and stir just until incorporated. Quickly mix in the raisins.

Turn the dough out onto a floured surface and gently knead 3 or 4 times. Flour a rolling pin and roll the dough into a ¾-inch thick circle. Cut out scones as closely together as possible with a 3-inch round cutter. Press the scraps together, roll once more, and cut out more scones. (Alternatively, roll the dough into a ¾-inch thick square, cut into 4-inch squares with a sharp knife, and cut each square into 2 triangles.) Place the scones 1 inch apart on the baking sheet. (Cover with plastic wrap and refrigerate overnight. Let stand at room temperature while preheating the oven.)

Brush the tops of the scones with the egg wash and bake until golden brown, about 20 minutes (the tops may crack). Cool on racks and serve warm.

Makes 8

Two-Cheese Muffins

These cheese and cornmeal muffins aren't only for brunch. They're also great with ham, pork, or chili.

1½ cups bleached all-purpose flour
½ cup yellow cornmeal
¼ cup sugar
1 tablespoon baking powder
¾ teaspoon salt
⅔ cup small curd cottage cheese

¾ cup shredded mild or sharp
   Cheddar cheese
1 egg, lightly beaten
1 cup milk
¼ cup vegetable oil

Preheat the oven to 350°F. Lightly grease 12 muffin cups. In a large bowl, combine the flour, cornmeal, sugar, baking powder, and salt. In a separate bowl, combine the cheeses, egg, milk, and oil. Add the cheese mixture to the dry ingredients and stir just until moistened. Fill the muffin cups and bake until a toothpick inserted in the center comes out clean, about 20 minutes. Cool for 5 minutes before turning out of the pan. Serve warm.

Makes 12

Brie and Sausage Casserole

Accompany this rich, sophisticated dish with fresh fruit and assorted muffins.

1 8-ounce round Brie cheese
1 pound ground hot pork sausage
6 slices white bread
1 cup grated Parmesan cheese
7 large eggs
3 cups whipping cream

2 cups fat-free milk
1 tablespoon chopped fresh sage
1 teaspoon seasoned salt
1 teaspoon dry mustard
Chopped green onions

Lightly butter a 9x13-inch baking dish. Trim and discard the rind from the top of the Brie and cut the cheese into cubes.

In a large skillet, cook the sausage over medium-high heat, breaking it up with a spoon, until it is no longer pink. Drain well.

Remove the crusts from the bread and arrange the slices in the baking dish. Top with the cooked sausage, Brie, and grated Parmesan cheese. In a large bowl, lightly beat 5 eggs with a whisk. Whisk in 2 cups of whipping cream, the milk, sage, seasoned salt, and dry mustard. Pour the mixture over the casserole. Cover and chill for at least 8 hours or overnight.

Preheat the oven to 350°F. In a small bowl, whisk together the remaining 2 eggs and 1 cup of whipping cream. Pour over the casserole. Bake for 50 minutes or until set. Garnish with chopped green onions and serve.

Serves 8 to 10

Cheese Grits Soufflé

Originally from a historic bed and breakfast in Natchez, Mississippi, this refined version of a down-home favorite is wonderful with eggs, as a side dish, or as a light main course.

1 cup grits
  (not instant or quick-cooking)
Milk
Water
2 teaspoons salt
4 tablespoons butter
¼ teaspoon garlic powder

¼ teaspoon cayenne pepper
  or Tabasco
1 cup grated mild or sharp
  Cheddar cheese
6 extra large eggs, separated, whites
  at room temperature

Preheat the oven to 350°F. Butter a 2-quart soufflé dish. Cook the grits according to package directions, using half milk and half water for the liquid. When the grits are done, add the salt, butter, garlic powder, cayenne pepper, and cheese. Stir until the cheese is melted and all the ingredients are combined.

Beat the egg yolks with a whisk and slowly add them to the grits, stirring constantly. Beat the whites in the bowl of an electric mixer until stiff. Stir a large spoonful of the whites into the grits. Fold in the remaining whites. Pour the mixture into the prepared dish and bake until puffed, set, and browned, about 40 minutes.

Serves 8

Curried Eggs and Shrimp

Most of this great brunch dish can be prepared in advance.

1 pound raw shrimp
12 hard cooked eggs
¼ teaspoon salt
¼ teaspoon pepper
¼ teaspoon dry mustard
½ teaspoon curry powder

½ cup mayonnaise
1 10¾-ounce can cream
  of shrimp soup
1 cup dry white wine
½ cup crushed seasoned croutons
½ cup grated Parmesan cheese

Boil the shrimp in salted water until barely pink. Plunge them into cold water to cool. Peel and devein. Cut the eggs lengthwise in half, remove the yolks and mash them with a fork. Add the salt, pepper, dry mustard, and curry powder. Add enough mayonnaise to moisten and combine well. Stuff the egg whites. Place the stuffed eggs in a 9x11-inch baking dish. Arrange the shrimp among the eggs. (The dish can be refrigerated overnight.)

Combine the soup and wine in a saucepan and stir over medium heat until blended. Pour the sauce over the shrimp and eggs. Combine the crushed croutons and cheese and sprinkle evenly over the casserole. Bake for 30 minutes or until bubbly and brown.

Serves 8 to 10

Eggs Santa Fe

For a southwestern-style breakfast, serve this piquant casserole with warm flour tortillas and black beans.

2½ cups cubed ham	1¼ cups shredded Monterey Jack cheese
12 eggs	
1 4-ounce can chopped green chilies, drained	1 large Hass avocado, peeled, pitted, and sliced
Salt and freshly ground pepper	2 to 3 ripe tomatoes, sliced
3 tablespoons butter	Sour cream
¾ pound mushrooms, sliced	Tabasco and/or prepared salsa

Preheat the oven to 325°F. Butter a 2½-quart baking dish able to withstand broiler heat. Place the ham in the bottom of the dish. Beat the eggs in a bowl and add the chilies, salt, and pepper. Pour over the ham. Bake until the eggs are just set, about 30 minutes, stirring once or twice with a wooden spoon during the first 15 minutes.

While the eggs cook, heat the butter in a heavy skillet until foaming and add the mushrooms. Sauté until browned and no liquid remains. Set aside.

Remove the baking dish from the oven and turn on the broiler. Scatter half the cheese over the eggs. Top with the mushrooms, sliced avocado, and tomatoes. Sprinkle with the remaining cheese. Run the dish under the broiler just until the cheese is melted. Serve with sour cream, Tabasco, and/or salsa.

Serves 6 to 8

Bloody Maria

Fernand Petiot, a bartender at Harry's New York Bar in Paris, is credited with creating the Bloody Mary in the 1920s. When asked how he came up with the name, Petiot said that one of the boys where he worked suggested it because it reminded him of the "Bucket of Blood" Club in Chicago (the infamous Chopin Club, renovated and reopened in 1920 as Union League Boys' Club One) and a girl who worked there named Mary. This recipe is one of dozens of variations on the original drink.

2 ounces (2 shots) tequila	Dash celery salt
8 ounces tomato juice	Freshly ground black pepper
Juice from ½ lime	2 celery stalks
Dash Worcestershire sauce	Dash Tabasco or other hot sauce

Combine all the ingredients except the celery stalks and Tabasco. Pour into ice-filled glasses and garnish each with a celery stalk. Offer Tabasco.

Serves 2

Elegant Shrimp and Grits

A gourmet version of a low-country favorite that can be served for brunch, lunch, or a light supper.

GRITS

2 cups water
2 tablespoons butter
½ cup grits (not instant or quick-cooking)

½ cup milk
¼ teaspoon salt

SHRIMP

6 slices bacon
⅓ cup chopped green pepper
1 cup sliced fresh mushrooms
1 clove garlic, minced
2 tablespoons all purpose flour
½ cup chicken broth
2 tablespoons lemon juice

1 pound medium shrimp, peeled and deveined
1 cup chopped green onions
¼ teaspoon salt
⅛ teaspoon cayenne pepper
Dash Creole Seasoning
Dash Tabasco
Chopped parsley

Bring the water and butter to a boil in a heavy saucepan. Add the grits in a thin stream, stirring constantly. Return to a boil. Reduce the heat and simmer gently, stirring occasionally, for 10 minutes or until thickened. Stir in ¼ cup of milk and simmer for 10 minutes. Add the salt and the remaining ¼ cup of milk and simmer for an additional 10 minutes. Cover and keep warm.

Meanwhile, cook the bacon until crisp and drain on paper towels. Reserve the drippings. Crumble the bacon and set aside. Reheat the drippings and add the green pepper, mushrooms, and garlic. Sauté until the vegetables begin to soften. Sprinkle the flour into the pan and cook, stirring constantly, for about 2 minutes. Add the broth, lemon juice, shrimp, green onions, salt, cayenne pepper, Creole Seasoning, and Tabasco. Bring to a simmer and cook just until the shrimp are pink and firm. Spoon the grits into soup plates and top with the shrimp. Garnish with the bacon and chopped parsley.

Serves 6 to 8

Heavenly Blueberry-Buttermilk Pancakes

These pancakes practically float off the plate. Serve them with whipped butter and warm maple or blueberry syrup. Sliced bananas or raspberries are good alternatives to the blueberries.

4 tablespoons unsalted butter
2 cups bleached all-purpose flour
2 teaspoons baking powder
1 teaspoon baking soda
½ teaspoon salt

3 tablespoons sugar
2 large eggs, lightly beaten
3 cups buttermilk
1 cup fresh or individually
   frozen blueberries (unthawed)

Melt the butter and cool to tepid. Preheat the oven to 200°F. Preheat a griddle. Place a wire rack on a baking sheet.

In a medium bowl, combine the flour, baking powder, baking soda, salt, and sugar. Whisk lightly to blend. Make a well in the center and add the eggs, buttermilk, and melted butter. Whisk just until moistened. The batter should be somewhat lumpy.

Spray the griddle with cooking spray or grease with oil or butter. Use ½ cup of batter for each pancake. Quickly scatter blueberries over the pancakes. When the tops are covered with bubbles and the edges look dry, flip the pancakes and cook the other side. Place the cooked pancakes on the rack in a single layer. Keep warm in the oven, uncovered, while making additional pancakes.

Makes 9 large (6-inch) pancakes

Hot Curried Fruit

An unusual and delicious addition to a brunch menu, the compote can also be served with ham or pork.

1 29-ounce can pear halves, undrained
1 29-ounce can peach halves, undrained
1 20-ounce can pineapple chunks,
   undrained
1 17-ounce can apricot halves, undrained
1 16½-ounce can pitted Royal Anne
   cherries, undrained

¼ cup sugar
3 tablespoons all-purpose flour
3 tablespoons butter or margarine
¼ cup dry white wine or juice
   from the canned fruit
1 teaspoon curry powder

Preheat the oven to 350°F. Lightly butter a 9x13-inch baking dish. Drain the fruit, reserving all the juices. Combine the fruit in a large bowl. Measure out ¾ cup of juice (1 cup if not using white wine). Discard the remaining juice.

Combine the sugar and flour in a heavy saucepan. Gradually stir in ¾ cup of juice. Add the butter and cook over medium heat, stirring constantly, until the mixture thickens and is bubbly. Remove from the heat and stir in ¼ cup wine or juice and the curry powder.

Pour the sauce over the fruit and stir gently. Spoon the compote into the baking dish. Cover and bake for 30 minutes or until hot.

Serves 10 to 12

Maple-Cinnamon French Toast Casserole

Assemble this divine cinnamon-scented casserole the night before. It needs only a few minutes of attention before it's popped into the oven in the morning.

5 large eggs, lightly beaten
1½ cups milk
1 cup half & half
1 teaspoon vanilla
½ teaspoon cinnamon

8 slices cinnamon swirl or
   white bread, buttered
½ cup butter, softened
1 cup lightly packed light brown sugar
2 tablespoons maple syrup
1 cup chopped pecans

Butter a 9x13-inch glass or ceramic baking dish. In a medium bowl, whisk together the eggs, milk, half & half, vanilla, and cinnamon. Arrange the buttered bread in the prepared dish. Pour the egg mixture evenly over the slices. Cover and refrigerate overnight.

Preheat the oven to 350°F. In a bowl, combine the softened butter, brown sugar, and maple syrup. Stir in the pecans. Spread the topping over the bread. Bake until puffed and golden brown, about 40 minutes. Serve immediately.

Serves 4 to 8

Moroccan Baked Eggs with Vegetables

The vegetables for this flavorful Moroccan-inspired dish improve in flavor if cooked in advance.

3 tablespoons olive oil
2 small zucchini, sliced in half moons
1 medium Spanish onion, thinly sliced
2 red bell peppers, seeded and sliced
3 cloves garlic, finely minced
Salt and freshly ground pepper
1 pound ripe tomatoes, peeled,
   seeded, and sliced ½-inch thick

2 tablespoons coarsely chopped
   parsley
Dash paprika
Pinch dried red chili flakes
4 eggs
Ground cumin
Cilantro sprigs

Heat 1 tablespoon of oil in a large skillet over medium-high heat. Add the zucchini and sauté until lightly browned. Remove to a plate. Add 2 tablespoons of oil to the skillet. Add the onion and peppers and cook until tender. Do not brown. Lower the heat to medium-low and stir in the garlic, salt, and pepper. Lay the tomatoes over the vegetables. Cover and simmer gently until the tomatoes have given up their juice. Uncover the skillet, raise the heat, and cook to evaporate the juice. Be careful not to scorch the vegetables. Lower the heat and add the zucchini, parsley, paprika, and chili flakes. Cover and cook gently for 2 or 3 minutes. Transfer the vegetables to a shallow baking dish or individual gratin dishes. Cool, cover, and refrigerate overnight.

Preheat the oven to 325°F. Reheat the vegetables, covered, if necessary. Make 4 indentations in the vegetables and break an egg into each. Cover the dish and bake just until the whites are set, or cook the eggs to your liking. Sprinkle each egg with a pinch of cumin, garnish with small sprigs of cilantro, and serve.

Serves 4

Orange-Pineapple Compote

Great for breakfast, brunch, or for dessert with a scoop of sorbet, this colorful winter compote takes advantage of sweet navel oranges and pineapple at the height of their season.

6 large navel oranges
½ ripe pineapple, cut into chunks, or
   canned pineapple chunks
   packed in juice

1 pint strawberries, sliced
1 to 2 bananas

Cut off the ends of the oranges and place them on a cutting board, cut side down. With a small, sharp knife, remove all of the rind and bitter white pith. Working over a bowl, cut between the membranes to release the segments. Squeeze the juice from the pulp into another bowl. Add the pineapple and strawberries to the oranges. Add a few spoonfuls of orange juice to the fruit and set aside for 15 minutes. (If using canned pineapple, add a little of the juice to the bowl.)

When ready to serve, slice the banana and add it to the compote. Add more juice if desired.

Serves 8

Ratatouille Tart

Serve this versatile tart as part of a brunch, as a first course, or with a green salad for lunch.

1 9-inch pastry shell, partially baked
   and cooled
4 tablespoons unsalted butter
½ pound small zucchini, sliced thinly
   on the bias
½ pound eggplant, cut in ½-inch dice
1 green onion, sliced
½ cup diced green and/or red bell pepper
Salt and freshly ground pepper

½ cup peeled, seeded, and
   diced tomato
1 clove garlic, minced
1 tablespoon chopped fresh basil
½ teaspoon coarsely chopped
   fresh thyme
½ cup grated Parmesan cheese
3 large eggs
½ cup heavy cream

Preheat the oven to 375°F. In a large skillet, heat the butter over medium heat until foaming. Add the zucchini, eggplant, onion, and bell peppers. Season with salt and pepper and sauté until the vegetables have softened, about 5 minutes. Stir in the tomato, garlic, and herbs. Cook over low heat until any liquid has evaporated. (The vegetables can be cooled and refrigerated overnight.)

Spread the vegetables evenly in the pastry shell and sprinkle with the cheese. In a bowl, beat the eggs lightly and add the cream. Pour over the vegetables. Bake until the filling is set and a knife inserted 1 inch from the edge comes out clean, about 30 to 35 minutes. Cool for 10 minutes before slicing.

Serves 6

Shirred Eggs with Oyster, Leek, and Saffron Sauce

This southern favorite is reminiscent of the elegant brunch specialties served in New Orleans.

3 tablespoons unsalted butter
8 eggs
1 medium leek (white part only),
 thinly sliced
12 shucked oysters, drained, ¼ cup
oyster liquor reserved (add clam juice
 if liquor is insufficient)

1½ cups heavy cream
Large pinch of saffron threads,
 crumbled and soaked in
 1 tablespoon boiling water
Salt
White pepper

Preheat the oven to 350°F. Melt 2 tablespoons of the butter. Brush 4 individual ramekins with some of the butter. Carefully break two eggs into each ramekin. Pour a bit of the melted butter over the yolks. Place the ramekins in a larger pan and add enough hot water to reach halfway up their sides. Bake just until the whites are set, about 6 to 7 minutes.

While the eggs bake, heat the remaining tablespoon of butter in a small skillet over medium heat. Add the leeks and cook until softened. Do not brown. Add the drained oysters. Increase the heat to medium high and cook just until the oysters are curled and heated through.

Meanwhile, in a heavy saucepan, simmer the cream over medium heat until reduced by half. Add the oyster liquor and scald. Remove the pan from the heat and add the oysters and leeks, saffron, salt, and pepper. Keep warm.

Remove the ramekins from the water bath. Sprinkle the eggs with salt and pepper. Spoon the sauce over the eggs and serve immediately.

Serves 4

Mexican Confetti Corn Bread

Serve this colorful corn bread any time of day with almost anything!

2 eggs, slightly beaten
¼ cup milk
⅓ cup corn oil
1 16-ounce can cream-style corn
1 onion, minced or grated
1 2-ounce can chopped pimentos
1 cup yellow cornmeal

1 teaspoon salt
½ teaspoon baking powder
5 teaspoons sugar
1 4-ounce can chopped green
 chilies, drained
¾ cup grated sharp Cheddar cheese

Preheat the oven to 350°F. Butter a 9x13-inch baking pan. Combine all of the ingredients except the cheese in a large bowl and mix well. Pour the batter into the pan and bake for 40 to 45 minutes. Sprinkle with the cheese. Return to the oven and bake for 5 minutes. Cool the corn bread for several minutes before cutting into squares. Serve warm.

Serves 6 to 8

Skillet-Baked Apple Pancake

Rich, glistening, and sinfully good, this is an adaptation of a Chicagoland favorite.

3 medium cooking apples, peeled, cored,
    and sliced ¼-inch thick
1 teaspoon cinnamon
¼ teaspoon ground ginger
¼ teaspoon ground nutmeg
Pinch ground cloves
4 tablespoons butter

1 tablespoon white sugar
2 tablespoons packed brown sugar
¾ cup all-purpose flour
¼ teaspoon salt
4 large eggs
¾ cup whole milk
1 teaspoon vanilla

Preheat the oven to 425°F. In a large bowl, toss the apples with the spices. Melt the butter in a well-seasoned 10-inch cast iron skillet or a heavy, ovenproof, non-stick skillet. Add the white and brown sugars and stir until dissolved. Spread the apples in the skillet. Cook over medium heat, stirring occasionally, until slightly softened, about 4 minutes. Remove the pan from the heat.

In a bowl, whisk together the flour and salt. In another bowl, lightly beat the eggs and add the milk and vanilla. Make a well in the center of the flour and pour in the egg mixture. Whisk until fairly smooth. Pour the batter over the apples. Bake until the pancake is puffed and golden brown, about 20 to 30 minutes.

Place a large plate over the skillet. Holding tightly, flip it over so that the apples are on top. Cut the pancake in half or in quarters and serve immediately.

Serves 2 to 4

Tomato and Swiss Strata

Sweet tomatoes and nutty Swiss cheese set this lovely casserole apart. Serve it hot or at room temperature. It also makes a terrific sandwich on crusty bread or foccacia with lettuce.

2 tablespoons butter, melted
5 ripe tomatoes, seeded and
    thinly sliced
2 slices rustic-style bread, cubed
4 ounces Swiss cheese, thinly sliced
5 eggs

⅔ cup milk
Salt and freshly ground pepper
¼ teaspoon dried oregano
1 teaspoon chopped parsley
Dash Tabasco

Place a 9-inch square cake pan in the oven and preheat to 400°F. Remove the pan from the oven and brush with butter. Arrange the tomatoes in the bottom of the pan and top with the bread cubes and cheese. In a bowl, beat the eggs and add the milk and seasonings. Pour over the bread. Bake until the eggs are set, about 20 minutes. Serve hot or at room temperature.

Serves 4

Spinach Torta

This free-form tart is just the thing to round out a brunch. It also makes a fine appetizer or light entrée. Swiss chard can be substituted for all or part of the spinach.

PASTRY

1¼ cups all-purpose flour
¼ teaspoon salt

8 tablespoons unsalted butter, cut into
   ½ inch cubes and chilled
3 to 5 tablespoons ice water

FILLING

2 pounds fresh spinach, tough stems
   removed, washed and well drained
2 tablespoons butter
1 cup finely chopped onion
2 cloves garlic, finely minced
4 whole green onions, thinly sliced
4 ounces mascarpone cheese, at room
   temperature, or crumbled ricotta
   salata, or feta

¼ cup plus 2 tablespoons freshly grated
   Parmesan cheese
¼ cup chopped flat leaf parsley
¼ cup finely chopped fresh dill
2 tablespoons milk
½ teaspoon ground nutmeg
Salt and freshly ground pepper
1 egg, lightly beaten
1 egg beaten with 1 tablespoon milk
   for egg wash

Combine the flour and salt in a bowl. Cut the butter into the flour with a pastry blender or your fingertips until evenly distributed, but still in chunky pieces. Add 3 tablespoons of ice water and mix with a fork until the dough just comes together. Add more water, 1 tablespoon at a time, if the dough is too dry. Turn the dough out onto a sheet of plastic wrap, gather it together, and press it into a disk. Wrap in the plastic and refrigerate for 1 hour or overnight. (The dough can be frozen. Thaw in the refrigerator.)

Heat a large skillet over high heat. In batches, add the spinach with only the water clinging to the leaves and toss until wilted. Transfer to a sieve to drain and cool. Press the spinach to remove as much excess liquid as possible. Chop it coarsely and place it in a large bowl. Heat the butter in a large skillet. Add the chopped onion and sauté until wilted. Add the garlic and stir briefly. Add to the spinach along with the green onions, mascarpone, ¼ cup of Parmesan, the parsley, dill, milk, nutmeg, salt, and pepper. Combine well.

Preheat the oven to 400°F. Line a rimless cookie sheet with parchment. Roll the dough between two sheets of plastic wrap into a 15-inch circle. Transfer the dough to the cookie sheet. Beat 1 egg, add it to the spinach mixture, and toss to combine. Spread the filling over the dough, leaving a 2-inch border all around. Sprinkle the filling with 2 tablespoons of grated Parmesan. Fold the edge of the dough over the spinach, pleating as necessary to form a rustic tart with an open center. Brush the top of the dough with egg wash. Bake until the crust is golden brown, about 30 to 35 minutes.

Transfer the parchment with the tart to a wire rack and cool for 5 minutes. Slide the tart off the parchment onto the rack and cool for at least 30 minutes before cutting into wedges. Serve warm or at room temperature. The tart can be reheated.

Serves 6 as an appetizer

Summer Fruit Compote with
Yogurt, Honey, and Almonds

Colorful and naturally sweet, the compote is delicious with or without the yogurt topping. Try it for dessert with angel food or pound cake and a dollop of the yogurt or whipped cream.

2 to 3 mangoes, peeled and cut
    into chunks
2 to 3 large peaches, peeled and sliced
2 to 3 large nectarines, sliced
3 to 4 plums, sliced
4 cups melon chunks, such as
    honeydew and/or cantaloupe
    (don't use watermelon)
3 kiwi, peeled, halved, and sliced
2 cups sweet cherries, pitted

2 tablespoons sugar
1 12-ounce container Greek yogurt
    or other unflavored yogurt
Honey
1 pint strawberries, hulled and sliced
½ to 1 pint blueberries and/or
    blackberries
2 to 3 bananas, sliced
½ to 1 pint raspberries
Sliced almonds, lightly toasted

Combine all the fruit, except the bananas and berries, in a large bowl. Add 2 tablespoons of sugar and toss to combine. Refrigerate for 1 to 2 hours. Combine the yogurt with honey to taste and refrigerate.

Thirty minutes before serving, slice the strawberries and add them to the compote along with the blueberries and blackberries. Let stand at room temperature.

When ready to serve, slice the bananas and combine with the compote. Spoon the fruit into stemmed glasses or bowls. Add raspberries to each serving and spoon some of the fruit juices over the top. Top with a large dollop of yogurt and sprinkle with almonds.

Serves 12 or more

Bellini

An authentic Bellini is made with Prosecco and white peach puree. Other fruit purees may not be authentic, but they're very good indeed.

2 ounces fruit puree or nectar (peach, apricot, strawberry, or raspberry)
Chilled Prosecco (Italian sparkling wine)

Spoon the puree into a champagne flute and top off with Prosecco. If desired, add 1 tablespoon Grand Marnier to the peach or apricot puree, 1 teaspoon Framboise to the strawberry puree, or 1 teaspoon Chambord to the raspberry puree.

Serves 1

Very Berry Buttermilk Waffles

Light and crisp, these waffles go together in no time. Serve them with whipped sweet butter and warm maple syrup. Leftover waffles can be frozen and reheated in a toaster oven.

FRUIT TOPPING

1 pint strawberries, hulled and sliced
1 pint blueberries

1 pint raspberries
1 to 2 tablespoons confectioners' sugar

WAFFLES

3 cups unbleached all-purpose flour
1 tablespoon baking powder
¾ teaspoon baking soda
1 teaspoon salt

3 large eggs, separated
3½ cups buttermilk
1½ sticks unsalted butter,
    melted and cooled

Preheat the oven to 200°F. Place a large wire rack on a baking sheet. Place the berries in a bowl and toss with the sugar. Set aside. Preheat a waffle iron.

In a large bowl, whisk together the flour, baking powder, baking soda, and salt. Lightly beat the egg yolks and combine with the buttermilk. Make a well in the center of the flour mixture and add the buttermilk. Whisk just until moistened. Stir in the butter. The batter will be thick and should be somewhat lumpy. Beat the egg whites until fairly stiff, but not dry. Fold them into the batter with a rubber spatula. Pour the batter into the waffle iron using about ½ cup for each Belgian waffle and ¼ cup for each standard waffle. Quickly spread the batter evenly in the iron and bake.

Transfer the waffles to the wire rack in a single layer. Keep warm in the oven, uncovered, while making more waffles. Top the waffles with berries and serve.

Makes about 12 Belgian (4-inch) waffles, or 24 standard (4-inch) waffles

Fruit Smoothie

A nice addition to breakfast or brunch, or a healthy afternoon treat.

1½ cups orange juice
⅔ cup plain yogurt
12 frozen strawberries

12 frozen peach slices
½ cup frozen banana chunks
Honey or sugar to taste

Place all the ingredients in a blender and process until smooth and foamy. Serve in tall, frosted glasses.

Serves 2

Mango Lassi

This frothy creation from Southern India is traditionally made with mangoes, but peaches are a good substitute.

2 cups diced mango
3 cups plain yogurt
½ teaspoon fresh lemon juice

¼ to ½ cup sugar or honey
8 ice cubes
Fresh mint sprigs for garnish

Place all the ingredients except the ice cubes in a blender and blend until smooth. Add more sugar or honey to taste. Add the ice and blend until the ice is finely crushed and the drink is frothy. Add more ice or ice water to thin if necessary. Serve in tall frosted glasses garnished with mint.

Serves 4

Minted Grapefruit Cooler

This non-alcoholic cooler is refreshing any time of day.

3½ cups strained, freshly squeezed
   grapefruit juice
2 tablespoons sugar
6 fresh mint sprigs

6 tablespoons strained, freshly squeezed
   lemon juice
3½ cups ginger ale
Mint sprigs for garnish

Combine the grapefruit juice, sugar, and 6 mint sprigs in a pitcher. Refrigerate for several hours or overnight. Just before serving, add the lemon juice and ginger ale. Strain into tall, ice-filled glasses. Garnish with mint sprigs.

Serves 6

Peach-Ginger Frost

A smooth and creamy summer favorite. To spike it, add a little vodka or peach Schnapps.

3 ripe peaches, peeled and quartered
⅓ cup light corn syrup
¼ teaspoon ground ginger
1 cup pineapple or lemon sherbet

1 cup vanilla ice cream
½ cup ginger ale
Peach slices for garnish

Process the peaches, corn syrup, and ginger in an electric blender until smooth. Add the sherbet and ice cream. Process just until smooth. Add the ginger ale and blend for 30 seconds. Pour into frosted glasses and garnish with peach slices.

Serves 4

Braided Dill and Onion Loaf

The braided loaf is pretty, fun to make, and very, very good.

1 envelope dry yeast
¼ cup warm water (105 to
   115 degrees)
Pinch sugar
1 cup sour cream
1 egg, beaten
2 tablespoons sugar
1½ teaspoons salt

2 tablespoons butter, softened
2½ to 3 cups unbleached
   all-purpose flour
⅓ cup finely chopped onion
1 tablespoon dill seed
1 to 2 teaspoons chopped fresh dill
1 egg yolk beaten with 2 teaspoons
   water for egg wash

Sprinkle the yeast over the warm water and stir to combine. Add a pinch of sugar, cover, and let stand until foamy. Pour the yeast into a bowl and add the sour cream, egg, sugar, salt, butter, and 1 cup of flour. Beat with an electric mixer on medium speed for 2 minutes. Add the onion, dill seed, and fresh dill. Gradually add enough flour to make a stiff dough. Turn the dough out onto a floured board and knead until smooth and elastic, about 5 minutes. Transfer the dough to a deep, greased bowl and turn to grease all sides. Cover the bowl with plastic wrap and a kitchen towel and place in a warm spot until the dough has doubled in bulk.

Punch the dough down and divide it into 3 pieces. Cover and let rest for 10 minutes. With your hands, roll the pieces into 16-inch long ropes, braid them together, and tuck the ends under. Transfer the braid to a baking sheet, cover loosely with plastic wrap and a kitchen towel, and let rise until doubled.

Meanwhile, preheat the oven to 350°F. Brush the loaf with the egg wash and bake for 30 to 40 minutes. When done, the loaf will sound hollow when the bottom is tapped. Transfer to a wire rack and cool completely before storing.

Makes 1 loaf

Grandma Megan's Dinner Rolls

Born in the 1870s, May Megan was one of the first women to sit on a jury in Illinois. Her grand-daughter shared her recipe for classic dinner rolls.

1 cup milk
8 tablespoons butter
¼ cup plus ½ teaspoon of sugar
1 envelope active dry yeast

¼ cup warm water (105 to
   115 degrees)
1 teaspoon salt
1 egg, beaten
4 cups flour

Place the milk in a saucepan and scald. Remove the pan from the heat and add 6 tablespoons of butter and ¼ cup of sugar. Stir until the butter is melted and the sugar is dissolved. Cool to tepid.

Sprinkle the yeast over the warm water and stir to dissolve. Add the ½ teaspoon of sugar, cover, and let it stand until foamy.

Pour the yeast into the bowl of an electric mixer. Add the salt, beaten egg, and cooled milk. On low speed, gradually beat in 2 cups of flour. Continue to beat until the dough is smooth, about 5 minutes. Switch to the dough hook. Add the remaining 2 cups of flour, ½ cup at a time. Knead until the dough is smooth and begins to climb up the hook, about 8 minutes, adding a little more flour if necessary. (If your mixer does not have a dough hook, knead in the remaining flour by hand.) Butter a large, deep bowl. Transfer the dough to the bowl, turning it over to grease all sides. Cover the bowl with plastic wrap and a kitchen towel and let rise in a warm place until doubled, about 1 hour, or refrigerate for 6 to 8 hours.

Turn the dough out onto a lightly floured board and roll it out to a thickness of ¼ inch. Melt the remaining 2 tablespoons of butter and brush the top of the dough. With a biscuit cutter, stamp out 2-inch circles. Fold the circles in half and place them on a baking sheet so that they barely touch. Roll out the scraps and cut more circles. Cover the rolls loosely with plastic wrap and a towel and let rise again until doubled, about 40 minutes or longer if the dough was refrigerated.

Meanwhile, preheat the oven to 375°F. Bake the rolls until they are golden, about 10 to 12 minutes. Serve hot.

Makes 2½ to 3 dozen rolls

Fantastic Popovers

These airy creations can be served with an entrée or a salad, or at breakfast with butter or honey butter. They are best when fresh out of the oven, but they can be reheated.

6 extra large eggs
2½ cups bleached all-purpose flour
¼ teaspoon salt

3¼ cups whole milk
2 tablespoons unsalted butter, melted

Position a rack in the lowest part of the oven and preheat to 425°F. Grease 12 popover cups or spray with cooking spray. In a bowl, beat the eggs well with an electric mixer. Sift the flour and salt over the eggs and add ½ cup of milk. Beat just until moistened. Add the remaining 2¾ cups of milk and the melted butter. Beat on high speed for 1 minute.

Divide the batter among the prepared cups and bake for 35 minutes without opening the oven door. Quickly check the popovers. They should be deep gold in color. If not, continue to bake. With a small, sharp knife, quickly make a slit in the side of each popover to allow steam to escape. Return them to the oven for 2 to 3 minutes. Serve immediately, or cool and rewarm before serving.

Makes 12

Herbed Roquefort Biscuits

These flavorful biscuits are especially good with a green salad, tomato or winter squash soup, or beef.

3 ounces Roquefort cheese, crumbled
2 tablespoons minced green onion tops
1 teaspoon dried basil
½ teaspoon dried thyme
2 cups all-purpose flour
1 tablespoon baking powder

½ teaspoon salt
¼ teaspoon baking soda
½ cup plus 2 tablespoons cold,
   unsalted butter, cut into pieces
¾ cup buttermilk

Preheat the oven to 450°F. Lightly grease a baking sheet. Combine the cheese, green onion tops, basil, and thyme in a small bowl. In a medium bowl, combine the flour, baking powder, salt, and baking soda. Cut the cheese mixture and butter into the dry ingredients with a pastry blender until the mixture resembles coarse meal. Stir in the buttermilk.

Turn the dough out onto a floured surface and knead lightly 7 to 8 times. Roll the dough into a ½-inch thick circle. Stamp out biscuits with a 2½-inch biscuit cutter (do not twist the cutter). Transfer the biscuits to the baking sheet. Press the scraps together and roll lightly. Cut out more biscuits. Bake until the tops are golden brown, about 13 to 15 minutes. Serve hot.

Makes 14 biscuits

Appetizers

Angel Wings

Super easy and finger lickin' good!

25 chicken wings
1 16-ounce jar orange marmalade

1 5-ounce bottle soy sauce
4 teaspoons ground ginger

Cut each wing into 3 pieces. Discard the wing tips or save them for stock. Combine the chicken, marmalade, soy sauce, and ginger in a plastic bag or nonreactive container. Refrigerate overnight, turning occasionally.

Position the oven racks on the lowest and middle levels and preheat the oven to 350°F. Line 2 large, rimmed baking sheets with foil. Add the wings and pour on the marinade. Bake for 45 minutes, turning occasionally. Switch the position of the pans and bake for an additional 45 minutes, turning occasionally. Serve hot.

Makes 50 pieces

Asian Cocktail Skewers

Make plenty of these tasty tidbits and watch them disappear!

Soak bamboo skewers in warm water for 1 hour before using. Thread the shrimp, chicken, or beef lengthwise on the skewers. Cook on a hot charcoal fire or under a preheated broiler. If broiling, cover the exposed wood with foil.

THAI SHRIMP SKEWERS
¼ cup olive oil
¼ cup chopped lemongrass, tender, inner portion of the bulb only
1 large clove garlic, minced
2 tablespoons honey mustard
1 teaspoon honey
Juice from 2 limes

Several large sprigs cilantro, torn into pieces
24 extra large raw shrimp, peeled and deveined
Chopped fresh basil and cilantro for garnish

Combine the marinade and shrimp in a glass bowl. Cover and refrigerate for 1 to 2 hours. Thread the shrimp on skewers and grill or broil for 2 to 3 minutes per side, or until pink and firm, basting with the marinade before turning. Sprinkle with chopped basil and cilantro.

CHINESE CHICKEN SKEWERS

1½ pounds skinless, boneless chicken
  breasts or chicken tenders
2 teaspoons toasted Asian sesame oil
¼ cup pineapple juice
2 tablespoons hoisin sauce

2 tablespoons soy sauce
2 teaspoons fresh lime juice
1 large clove garlic, minced
1 teaspoon minced fresh ginger
Minced scallions for garnish

Cut the chicken into 24 strips about 1x3x½-inch thick. Combine with the marinade in a glass bowl, cover, and refrigerate for 3 or 4 hours. Thread the chicken on skewers and grill or broil for about 2 to 3 minutes per side, basting with the marinade before turning. Sprinkle with minced scallions.

KOREAN BEEF SKEWERS

1 pound beef sirloin or tenderloin
½ cup soy sauce
2 teaspoons toasted Asian sesame oil
3 tablespoons brown sugar
½ teaspoon dried chili flakes
3 to 4 large cloves garlic, minced

4 green onions, white and light
  green parts only, chopped
1 tablespoon finely chopped
  or grated ginger
2 tablespoons ketchup
Toasted white sesame seeds for garnish

Slice the beef into strips about 1x3x½-inch thick. Combine with the marinade in a glass bowl, cover, and refrigerate for 3 to 4 hours. Thread the beef on skewers and grill or broil for about 1 to 2 minutes per side for medium rare, basting with the marinade before turning. Sprinkle with sesame seeds.

Makes 24 of each kind

BLT Dip

If you like BLTs—and who doesn't?—you'll love this easy dip.

1 cup mayonnaise
1 cup sour cream
1 medium tomato, diced
¼ pound bacon, cooked crisp and crumbled

Combine all the ingredients in a bowl and chill overnight. Serve with chips, crackers, or raw vegetables.

Makes 2 cups

Avocado Mousse with Smoked Salmon and Shrimp

Serve this delicate and sophisticated first course in pretty glass bowls or stemmed glasses.

2 large, ripe Hass avocados
6 to 8 tablespoons simple vinaigrette
2 tablespoons mayonnaise
Juice from ½ lemon
2 tablespoons heavy cream
Salt and freshly ground pepper

2 ounces smoked salmon, diced
¼ pound small shrimp, cooked, peeled, and deveined
1 English cucumber, unpeeled, thinly sliced
Lemon wedges

Peel, pit, and slice the avocados. Place them in a bowl and add 6 tablespoons of the vinaigrette. Marinate for 1 hour. Puree the avocado with the marinade in a blender until smooth, adding a little more vinaigrette if necessary. Scrape the puree into a bowl. Fold in the mayonnaise and lemon juice. Lightly whip the cream and fold it into the mousse. Season with salt and pepper. Cover tightly and chill for several hours.

Fold the diced salmon into the mousse. Spoon the mousse into individual ramekins, glass bowls, or small stemmed glasses. Garnish with the shrimp, cucumber slices, and lemon wedges.

Serves 4

Benne Seed Cheddar Crisps

Sesame seeds were brought to the colonies by West African slaves who called them benne seeds. They team up beautifully with the Cheddar cheese in this delightful hors d'oeuvre.

¼ cup plus 1 tablespoon sesame seeds
1¼ cups all-purpose flour
¼ teaspoon salt
¼ teaspoon cayenne pepper

8 ounces sharp Cheddar cheese, grated
1 stick butter, softened
1 tablespoon toasted Asian sesame oil

Place the sesame seeds in a large skillet and stir over medium heat until golden, about 4 minutes. Transfer to a bowl and cool.

Combine the flour, salt, and cayenne pepper in a bowl and set aside. In another bowl, beat the cheese and the butter with an electric mixer until well blended. Beat in the oil. Gradually add the flour mixture. Add 3 tablespoons of the sesame seeds. Turn the dough onto a work surface and knead gently until the dough comes together. Shape it into a 10-inch log, wrap in plastic, and refrigerate until firm, about 45 minutes.

Preheat the oven to 350°F. With a sharp knife, cut the log into ¼-inch thick slices. Transfer the slices to an ungreased baking sheet and bake for 15 minutes.

Remove the pan from the oven and immediately sprinkle the crisps with the remaining sesame seeds. Remove to wire racks and cool. Store in an airtight container for up to 1 day. Rewarm in a 350°F oven for about 5 minutes before serving.

Makes about 3 dozen

Blue Cheese Stuffed Mushrooms

Serve these delicious mushrooms as hors d'oeuvres or nestle one atop mixed greens as part of a stylish salad course.

1 pound large mushrooms
Olive oil
1 bunch green onions, finely chopped
1 clove garlic, minced

1 tablespoon butter
½ cup bread crumbs
4 ounces blue cheese, crumbled
Salt and pepper

Preheat the oven to 400°F. Wipe the mushrooms clean and remove the stems. Brush the caps with olive oil and place them on a baking sheet. Sauté the onions and garlic in the butter until softened. Add the bread crumbs and blue cheese, and season with salt and pepper. Stuff the caps and bake until the cheese is just melted, about 5 to 7 minutes. Serve hot. (The caps can be stuffed in advance and refrigerated.)

Makes about 16

Caviar Torte

An elegant appetizer for a festive occasion. Serve the torte with blinis or crackers and champagne or icy cold vodka.

1 pound cream cheese, softened
Dash Worcestershire sauce
Dash Tabasco sauce
1 cup mayonnaise
¼ teaspoon lemon juice

½ medium onion, grated
4 ounces black caviar
4 hard-boiled eggs, finely chopped
Minced parsley

Place the cream cheese, Worcestershire, Tabasco, mayonnaise, lemon juice, and onion in a blender or food processor and blend just until combined. Do not overblend or the mixture will be soupy. (Alternatively, combine well by hand.) Turn the mixture into a shallow serving bowl or ceramic mold and refrigerate until firm, about 2 hours.

Gently spread the caviar over the cheese. Sprinkle the chopped eggs evenly over the caviar and cover with minced parsley. The torte can be refrigerated overnight.

Serves a crowd

Strawberry Cheese Ring

The combination of ingredients may seem a little unusual, but this is a real crowd pleaser!

1 pound sharp Cheddar cheese, grated
1 cup chopped pecans
1 cup mayonnaise
¼ teaspoon pepper
1 medium onion, grated

1 clove garlic, finely minced
½ teaspoon Tabasco
½ teaspoon salt
1 cup strawberry jam or preserves

Lightly oil a 6-cup ring mold. Combine all the ingredients except the jam and pack into the mold. Refrigerate for several hours or overnight.

When ready to serve, unmold the cheese ring and top with the preserves. Serve with toasted bread rounds or wheat crackers.

Serves 25 to 30

Chicken Liver Pâté

To really put the pâté over the top, serve it with the classic accompaniments—small slices of toasted bread or brioche, cornichons, and tiny pickled onions.

1 pound chicken livers, trimmed
½ pound butter, softened
½ cup chopped onions
2 tablespoons chopped shallots
¼ cup peeled, chopped apple
¼ cup cognac

3 tablespoons heavy cream
1 teaspoon lemon juice
1 teaspoon salt
¼ teaspoon white pepper
½ pound butter, clarified (optional)

Rinse and dry the chicken livers, cut them into quarters, and set aside. In a heavy skillet, heat 3 tablespoons of butter over medium heat. Add the onions and sauté for 5 minutes. Add the shallots and apples and sauté for 2 minutes. Transfer to a food processor and process until smooth. Reserve in the processor bowl.

Add 3 tablespoons of butter to the skillet and place it over medium-high heat. When the butter is foaming, add the chicken livers and sauté for 5 to 6 minutes until browned. Add the cognac and cook for 2 minutes. Add the chicken livers to the onion mixture and process until smooth. Add the cream and process just until incorporated. Transfer the pâté to a bowl and cool to room temperature. (For a silky smooth pâté, force the puree through a sieve before cooling.)

Add the remaining softened butter to the cooled pâté along with the lemon juice, salt, and white pepper. Combine until thoroughly blended and smooth. Scrape the pâté into a ceramic mold or serving dish and smooth the top. Pour the clarified butter over the top to cover completely (or cover tightly with plastic wrap). Chill at least 2 hours or overnight. Bring the pâté to cool room temperature before serving.

Makes 2 cups

Chinese Chicken Rolls

These crisp rolls always garner raves. They are time-consuming to assemble, but they can be made well in advance and frozen. Serve them hot with sweet and sour sauce, plum sauce, or Chinese mustard.

½ cup dried shitake mushrooms,
   soaked in hot water for 30 minutes
1 pound skinless, boneless chicken
   breasts, partially frozen
½ cup bamboo shoots, cut
   into small dice
½ to ¾ cup fresh bean sprouts
2 tablespoons plum sauce
2 teaspoons Chinese brown bean paste
½ cup hoisin sauce
2 tablespoons Chinese dark soy sauce
2 tablespoons dry sherry
2 tablespoons cornstarch

2 tablespoons Asian
   sesame oil
2 garlic cloves, finely minced
¼ cup minced scallions
¼ cup chopped fresh cilantro
¼ teaspoon freshly ground pepper
1 pound phyllo pastry sheets,
   fresh if possible
⅓ cup (approximately) mixed
   canola and peanut oil
Sweet and sour sauce, plum sauce, or
   Chinese mustard for serving

Remove and discard the stems from the shitakes and thinly slice the caps. Trim any fat or gristle from the chicken and slice it into thin slivers. In a bowl, combine the mushrooms and chicken with the remaining filling ingredients. Sauté a spoonful of the filling in a little oil and taste for seasoning.

Place 1 or 2 sheets of plastic wrap on the counter. Working quickly, unroll the phyllo on a cutting board and cut it crosswise into 3- to 4-inch wide strips. Place the strips on the plastic wrap. Immediately cover with more plastic and cover the plastic with dampened kitchen towels.

Remove 2 strips of phyllo at a time and place with the short ends facing you. Brush each lightly with oil, taking care to cover the edges. Bring the bottom up and fold each strip in half. Brush lightly with oil. Place a heaping teaspoonful of filling 1 inch above the bottom edge. Fold the bottom edge of the phyllo over the filling, fold the sides in, and roll into a neat cylinder. Transfer the roll to an ungreased baking sheet, seam side down, and brush the top with oil. Repeat with the remaining phyllo.

Preheat the oven to 350°F. Bake until the rolls are golden brown, about 20 to 30 minutes.

Note: If freezing the rolls, line the baking sheets with waxed paper. Freeze in single layers until firm. Transfer the rolls to a container or freezer bags, keeping sheets of waxed paper between the layers, and store for up to 3 months. Do not thaw before baking.

Makes about 60

Colette's Gougeres

These Gruyère-flavored bites are made from cream puff pastry. They're lovely with Champagne, their classic accompaniment. Abondance, Beufort, or Vigneron cheese can be substituted.

1 cup water	4 eggs
1 stick unsalted butter	1 cup grated Gruyère cheese
1 teaspoon salt	1 teaspoon pepper
1 cup sifted flour	Pinch nutmeg

Preheat the oven to 425°F. Grease a cookie sheet or line it with parchment. In a two-quart saucepan, bring the water, butter, and salt to a simmer. Remove the pan from the heat and add the flour all at once. With a wooden spoon, thoroughly blend in the flour. Stirring constantly, cook over low heat until the dough pulls away from the side of the pot and forms a ball. It will be stiff. Continue to cook and stir for a few moments to dry the dough slightly. Remove the pan from the heat and cool for a minute or two.

Make a well in the center of the dough. Add the eggs one at a time, beating with the spoon after each addition until thoroughly incorporated. The dough will be slippery at first, but will come together again. Add the cheese, pepper, and nutmeg and mix well. Drop by generous teaspoonfuls onto the prepared sheet, 3 to 4 inches apart. If desired, moisten a fingertip in water and smooth the tops. Bake until the puffs are golden brown, about 20 minutes. Pull one of the puffs apart; the interior should be slightly moist, but not doughy. If so, quickly slit the side of each puff with a small knife and pop back into the oven for another minute or two. (If the gougeres are in danger of over-browning, turn off the oven while they finish baking.) Serve warm. The puffs may be prepared a few hours ahead and reheated.

Makes 24

Crab Puffs

The same cream puff pastry used for Colette's Gougeres is the base for these airy crab puffs.

6 ounces canned crabmeat, drained and flaked	1 cup water
½ cup shredded Cheddar cheese	½ cup butter
3 green onions, chopped	¼ teaspoon salt
1 teaspoon dry mustard	1 cup flour
1 teaspoon Worcestershire sauce	4 eggs

Preheat the oven to 400°F. Grease a baking sheet or line it with parchment. Combine the crabmeat, cheese, green onions, dry mustard, and Worcestershire in a bowl and stir well.

In a two-quart saucepan, bring the water, butter, and salt to a simmer. Remove the pan from the heat and add the flour all at once. With a wooden spoon, thoroughly blend in the flour. Stirring constantly, cook over low heat until the dough pulls away from the side of the pot and forms a ball. It will be stiff. Continue to cook and stir for a few moments to dry the dough slightly. Remove the pan from the heat and let cool for a minute or two.

Make a well in the center of the dough. Add the eggs one at a time, beating with the spoon after each addition until thoroughly incorporated. The dough will be slippery at first, but will come together again. Add the crab mixture and mix well. Drop by generous teaspoonfuls onto the prepared sheet, 3 to 4 inches apart. If desired, moisten a fingertip in water and smooth the tops. Bake the puffs for 15 minutes. Reduce the heat to 350°F and bake for an additional 10 minutes. Serve warm.

Makes 24

Endive Spears with Boursin Cheese and Walnuts

Endive spears are wonderful containers for cocktail fare. For a pretty presentation, arrange the spears around a bell pepper "vase" filled with a bouquet of small flowers or flowering herbs.

  5 to 6 heads Belgian endive
  2 5-ounce containers Boursin Garlic and Herb cheese, at room temperature
  ½ cup walnut halves, toasted and chopped

Trim the base from each endive and separate the leaves, discarding any that are damaged or discolored. Use as many heads as necessary to obtain 24 suitably sized spears. Roll the spears in a slightly damp kitchen towel, place the towel in a plastic bag and chill for 2 to 3 hours.

Spoon the cheese into a pastry bag fitted with a plain tip (or use a plastic freezer bag and snip off one end). Pipe the cheese into the lower end of the spears and sprinkle with chopped nuts. The spears can be tented with foil and refrigerated for an hour or so before serving.

Makes 24

Watermelon Wine Cooler

Try this festive cooler at your next summer party or backyard barbecue.

  1 oval watermelon   ⅓ of a fifth of gin
  1 bottle berry wine   Lemon and/or lime slices
  1 quart club soda   1 pint fresh raspberries

With a heavy knife, cut out a large oval from the side of the watermelon. Scoop out the fruit with a melon baller (or use a spoon and cut the fruit into chunks). If necessary, cut off a thin slice from the bottom so that the shell is stable. Chill.

In a large pitcher, combine the wine, club soda, and gin. Stir in several lemon and/or lime slices, watermelon balls, and raspberries. Chill for 4 to 6 hours.

Pour the wine cooler into the watermelon shell and serve.

Serves 8 to 10

Grecian Cocktail Meatballs

Greek cooking abounds with wonderful "meze"—little tidbits to enjoy with a glass of wine or ouzo. These tasty little meatballs are easy on the cook as they need to marinate in the sauce at least overnight.

MEATBALLS

1¼ pounds ground chuck
½ cup dry breadcrumbs
1 tablespoon chopped parsley
3 teaspoons dried Greek oregano, crushed
½ cup grated onion, grated on the large holes of a box grater

Salt and freshly ground pepper
3 teaspoons dried mint, crushed
½ teaspoon cinnamon
Pinch ground cloves
2 teaspoons finely minced garlic
1 egg, lightly beaten

SAUCE

2 cups canned tomato sauce
½ to 1 teaspoon cinnamon
¼ teaspoon allspice

Salt and freshly ground pepper
1 cup water

Preheat the oven to 450°F. Lightly grease a rimmed baking sheet. Combine all the ingredients for the meatballs in a bowl and knead together until well blended. Roll the mixture into small balls, about ¾ inch in diameter. Place them on the prepared pan and bake for 10 minutes. Turn and bake for 10 minutes longer or until the meatballs are cooked through. Drain on paper towels and place them in a casserole dish.

Combine the sauce ingredients and simmer for 5 minutes. Taste and adjust the seasoning. Pour enough sauce over the meatballs to completely cover them. Cool, cover, and refrigerate overnight or up to 3 days. Reheat, covered, and serve warm.

Makes about 50

Lemony Goat Cheese Spread with Herbs

This tangy spread is delicious on toasted baguette slices, or serve it with thinly sliced fresh fennel, celery and carrot sticks, red bell pepper strips, and Belgian endive spears.

5 ounces (about ½ cup) fresh, soft goat cheese at room temperature
Salt and freshly ground pepper
2 teaspoons chopped fresh thyme

2 teaspoons grated lemon zest
1 garlic clove, minced
5 teaspoons olive oil
16 slices French baguette, toasted

Place the goat cheese in a bowl and season with salt and pepper. Combine the thyme, lemon zest, and garlic in another bowl. Add half of the herb mixture to the goat cheese and combine thoroughly. Form the goat cheese into a slightly flattened round, about 2½ inches in diameter. Place the round in the center of a serving plate. Add the olive oil to the remaining herb mixture and spoon it over the cheese. Surround the cheese with the toasts and serve.

Serves 8

Pesto and Sun-Dried Tomato Torte

The torte looks as good as it tastes and comes with a bonus: it gets better with age. Make it two days in advance. Serve it with crackers, baguette slices, or crostini.

3 8-ounce packages cream cheese
¾ cup butter
4 garlic cloves
1½ cups lightly packed fresh basil leaves
¼ cup pine nuts, toasted
2 to 3 tablespoons olive oil
1 teaspoon lemon juice

¼ cup grated Parmesan cheese
1⅓ cups oil packed sun-dried
 tomatoes, drained
⅓ cup tomato paste
Basil sprigs
Grape tomatoes
Toasted pine nuts

Blend two packages of cream cheese with the butter in a food processor and transfer it to a bowl.

Chop the garlic in the processor. Add the basil, pine nuts, olive oil, lemon juice, and Parmesan cheese. Add one-half of the remaining package of cream cheese and blend well. Transfer it to another bowl.

Chop the sun-dried tomatoes in the processor. Add the tomato paste and the remaining cream cheese. Blend well and reserve in the processor bowl.

Spray a 1½-quart soufflé dish with non-stick vegetable spray and line it with plastic wrap, leaving an overhang. Spread a layer of the cream cheese and butter mixture in the bottom of the mold. Top with a pesto layer. Add another layer of the cream cheese and butter mixture. Top with a sun-dried tomato layer. Repeat the layers until all of the ingredients are used. Cover the mold with the plastic wrap and chill for up to three days.

To serve, invert the mold onto a serving platter and peel away the plastic. Garnish the torte with sprigs of basil, grape tomatoes, and toasted pine nuts.

Serves 20

Pesto Bruschetta

Similar to pizza bread, this is an easy appetizer to prepare for a crowd.

1 loaf Italian bread
½ cup basil pesto
4 to 6 ripe plum tomatoes,
 thinly sliced

2 cups shredded mozzarella cheese
½ to 1 cup freshly grated
 Parmesan cheese

Preheat the oven to 400°F. Cut the loaf lengthwise in half. Place the bread on a cookie sheet and toast it in the oven until golden. Spread with pesto, top with tomato slices, and sprinkle with the cheeses. Bake until the cheese is bubbly, about 8 to 10 minutes. Slice and serve hot.

Serves 8 to 16

Pistachio and Walnut Stuffed Mushrooms

These piquant hors d'oeuvres can be prepared in advance and served at room temperature or reheated.

16 large mushrooms, cleaned
  and trimmed
1 cup chutney
¼ pound butter

½ cup shelled pistachio nuts
½ cup walnuts, coarsely chopped
Salt and freshly ground pepper
  (optional)

Remove and chop the mushroom stems. Chop any large pieces of chutney. Heat a skillet over medium-high heat and add the butter. When the butter is foaming, add the mushroom caps and chopped stems. Sauté for 2 minutes. Turn the caps and sauté for 1 minute longer. Remove the caps to a plate. Add the nuts and chutney to the skillet and stir to combine. Sauté for 1 minute. Season with salt and pepper. Remove from the heat.

Fill the mushroom caps with the chutney mixture. Serve hot, or let stand for an hour or two and serve at room temperature. The mushrooms can be reheated under the broiler.

Makes 16

Shrimp in Peppered Bacon

The shrimp make a fine lunch when served with a field greens salad. If peppered bacon is unavailable, use your favorite smoked bacon or pancetta.

12 bamboo skewers
12 raw, extra-large shrimp,
  peeled and deveined
½ cup dry white wine
⅓ cup olive oil

2 cloves garlic, crushed
2 sprigs fresh rosemary
2 sprigs fresh thyme
6 to 12 thick slices smoked,
  peppered bacon, or pancetta

Soak the skewers in warm water for 1 hour before using. Combine the shrimp, wine, olive oil, garlic, and herbs in a zip-top bag or nonreactive bowl. Refrigerate for 30 minutes. Marinate for an additional 30 minutes at room temperature, turning occasionally. Drain the shrimp and wrap the bacon in a spiral around each one, trimming as necessary. The shrimp should not be completely covered. Thread each shrimp lengthwise onto a skewer, catching the bacon to secure.

Preheat the broiler. Place the shrimp on a broiler pan and cover the exposed wood with foil. Broil, turning as necessary and replacing the foil, until the bacon is lightly browned and the shrimp are just cooked through, about 6 minutes. Serve hot.

Makes 12

Shrimp on Corn Bread Rounds with Mustard Sauce

Serve this rich first course alongside a small mesclun or frisee salad tossed with a simple vinaigrette. Uncork a Chardonnay.

CORN BREAD

1 cup whole milk

1 tablespoon white vinegar
  or lemon juice

1 teaspoon baking soda

1 cup all-purpose flour

1 cup yellow cornmeal

1 teaspoon salt

2 eggs

2 tablespoons unsalted butter,
  melted

SHRIMP

½ cup diagonally sliced scallions

2 tablespoons vegetable oil

18 to 24 jumbo shrimp, peeled and
  deveined, with tails left on

2 shallots, minced

½ cup dry white wine

½ cup heavy cream

8 tablespoons unsalted butter, cut
  into small pieces

2 tablespoons whole grain
  Dijon mustard

Salt

White pepper

Freshly squeezed lemon juice

Raw scallions, sliced on the diagonal
  into 3-inch lengths for
  garnish (optional)

Position an oven rack in the lower third of the oven and preheat to 450°F. Generously butter an 11x17-inch rimmed baking sheet. Combine the milk, vinegar, and baking soda in a small bowl. Combine the flour, cornmeal, and salt in a food processor. With the machine running, pour in the milk mixture, eggs, and melted butter. Process just until combined. Pour the batter into the prepared pan, smoothing the top. Bake until the corn bread shrinks from the sides of the pan and springs back when lightly pressed, about 10 to 14 minutes. Cool on a wire rack. Turn the corn bread out of the pan and cut into 4-inch rounds.

Blanch the sliced scallions in a large saucepan of boiling, salted water until crisp-tender, 1 to 2 minutes. Drain and plunge them into ice water. Drain, dry, and set aside.

Heat a large heavy skillet over high heat until very hot and add the oil. Add the shrimp, in batches if necessary, and sauté for 1 to 2 minutes until almost done. Do not crowd the pan. Remove the shrimp with a slotted spoon and set aside.

Reduce the heat to medium. Add more oil to the skillet if necessary and sauté the shallots for 30 seconds. Pour in the wine, scraping up any browned bits. Stir in the cream and cook until the mixture thickens and coats the back of a spoon, about 4 minutes. Reduce the heat to low and gradually whisk in the butter. (To increase the amount of sauce, add up to 1 more stick of butter.) Whisk in the mustard. Do not let the mixture boil. Add salt, pepper, and lemon juice to taste. Keep warm.

To serve, reheat the corn bread in a low oven. Place 1 corn bread round on each heated plate and top with 3 shrimp. Spoon the sauce over the shrimp and sprinkle with the blanched scallions. Garnish with raw scallions and serve.

Serves 6 to 8

Spanish Tortilla

This frittata-like dish is served throughout Spain at all hours of the day and night. Serve it at room temperature with a glass of Rioja or dry, Spanish sherry. Resist the urge to add pepper.

1 medium yellow onion	Salt
4 large potatoes	8 eggs
½ cup plus 2 teaspoons	
Spanish olive oil	

Peel and chop the onion. Peel the potatoes and cut them into ⅛-inch thick slices. Heat ½ cup of olive oil in a 9-inch skillet over medium heat. Add the onions and potatoes and cook until tender. Do not brown. If necessary, cover the skillet to help soften the potatoes. Season with salt.

Beat the eggs in a large bowl until combined, but not foamy. With a slotted spoon, add the cooked potatoes and onions to the bowl and combine thoroughly with the eggs. If the skillet is dry, add the remaining 2 teaspoons of oil. Ladle the egg mixture into the skillet. It should be 2 to 3 inches thick. Cook slowly without stirring until the eggs are set, but still a little runny in the center. Place a large plate over the skillet. Holding firmly, flip the skillet over. Slide the tortilla back into the pan and return to the heat for 2 to 3 minutes to cook the second side. Turn out onto a plate and cool. Cut the tortilla into wedges or squares and serve.

Serves 8 or more

Spiced Pecans

It's hard to stop eating these crunchy, cinnamon-flavored nuts. They make lovely gifts.

1 egg white	½ cup sugar
1 teaspoon cold water	¼ teaspoon salt
1 pound pecan halves	½ teaspoon cinnamon

Preheat the oven to 225°F. In a bowl, beat the egg white and water together until frothy. Add the pecan halves and mix well. Combine the sugar, salt, and cinnamon in a plastic bag. Remove the nuts from the bowl with a fork and add to the bag. Shake to coat with the spice mix. Spread the nuts on a cookie sheet and bake for 1 hour, stirring every 15 minutes. Remove to a large plate and cool. Store in an airtight container.

Makes 1 pound

Steamed Mussels in Rosemary Broth

This aromatic first course also makes a light and satisfying meal for two. Be sure to provide soup spoons and plenty of crusty bread for the delicious broth. Pour a Muscadet or a Pouilly Fuisse.

2½ pounds mussels
¼ cup butter
1 large shallot, minced

1 teaspoon minced fresh rosemary
½ cup dry white wine
Lemon slices

Just before cooking, scrub the mussels under cold water. Discard any that will not close when the shells are pressed together. Debeard if desired. (Do not debeard in advance or the mussels will die and spoil.)

Melt the butter in a large, heavy Dutch oven over moderate heat. Add the shallot and minced rosemary. Sauté until the shallot softens, about 2 minutes. Add the wine and mussels and bring to a boil. Cover the pot and steam until the mussels open, about 3 to 4 minutes. Discard any unopened mussels. Transfer the mussels to soup plates and ladle the broth over them. Garnish with lemon slices and serve.

Serves 4

Chinese Barbecued Pork

Serve this flavorful appetizer hot or chilled with Honey-Dijon mustard. If you wish, offer small rolls for little sandwiches.

2 pounds pork tenderloin
⅔ cup soy sauce
¼ cup dry sherry
2 cloves garlic, minced
2 green onions, chopped

4 slices ginger root
Vegetable oil
1 tablespoon sugar
3 tablespoons honey

Trim the tenderloin of all fat and silverskin. Combine the soy sauce, sherry, garlic, green onions, and ginger in a plastic bag or nonreactive container. Add the pork and refrigerate for 12 hours.

Preheat the oven to 375°F. Place a roasting rack in a shallow pan. Brush the rack with vegetable oil. Drain the pork and rub it with the sugar and honey. Transfer it to the rack and roast for 30 minutes. Reduce the heat to 300°F and roast for 30 minutes longer, turning once. Let the pork rest for 10 minutes. Slice and serve warm, or chill before slicing and serve cold.

Makes about 48 slices

Stuffed Apricots

These simple hors d'oeuvres are downright addictive. Bet you can't eat just one!

¼ cup blue cheese, at room temperature
¼ cup unsalted butter, softened
24 dried apricots

24 pecan halves, lightly toasted
Snipped chives

Beat the cheese and butter until smooth and fluffy. With a teaspoon, drop a dollop of the mixture onto each apricot. Top with a pecan half and sprinkle with chives. The apricots can be filled in advance and refrigerated. Bring to room temperature before serving.
Makes 24

Stuffed Dates in Bacon

The salty feta puts a new twist on this Spanish tapa, which is more commonly stuffed with whole almonds or chorizo sausage.

24 Medjool dates, or large pitted dates
½ pound imported feta cheese, cut into 24 sticks
Thinly sliced bacon

Pit the dates if necessary and stuff each with a piece of feta. Cut the bacon strips in half or thirds, depending on the size of the dates. Wrap the dates in the bacon, over-lapping slightly, and secure each with a toothpick. Refrigerate until needed.

Preheat the oven to 500°F. Place the dates on a foil-lined, rimmed baking sheet. Bake for 6 minutes. Turn and bake until the bacon is browned, about 3 minutes longer. Drain on paper towels and cool for several minutes before serving. (The dates can also be broiled.)
Makes 24

Ezra Cooler

Member Jack Bolling owned The Sign of the Trader, a Chicago landmark located in the Board of Trade building, for over thirty years. Andrew Greeley wrote about the bar/restaurant in one of his books. One night, Jack created this drink and called it an Ezra; he just thought it was a good name for a great drink.

2 ounces VO Canadian Whiskey
1 ounce triple sec
1 ounce fresh lemon juice

6 ounces orange juice
Ginger ale

Stir together the VO, triple sec, and juices. Pour into a 12- to 16-ounce ceramic mug or tall glass which has been half filled with ice. Top off with ginger ale. Do not stir.
Serves 1

Stuffed Vine Leaves

Stuffed with rice and herbs, these mouthwatering Grecian appetizers were the specialty of a great-aunt. She used tender vine leaves from her own garden but preserved California leaves work well.

½ cup olive oil
2 cups minced onion
¾ cup converted rice (such as
   Uncle Ben's)
1½ cups chopped scallions
6 tablespoons fresh lemon juice
½ cup finely chopped parsley
   (reserve stems)

½ cup finely chopped fresh dill
   (reserve stems)
¼ cup currants (optional)
Salt and freshly ground pepper
12-ounce jar California grape leaves
1 cup, more or less, boiling water
Lemon wedges

In a large skillet, heat ¼ cup of olive oil over medium heat. Add the onions and cook until wilted. Add the rice, scallions, and 1½ tablespoons of lemon juice. Cook for 2 minutes. Add the parsley, dill, currants, salt, and pepper, and cook for 1 minute. Set the filling aside to cool.

Drain the grape leaves, unroll, and rinse very well under cold, running water. Bring a large pot of water to a boil. Add the grape leaves and boil for 1 minute. Drain and run cold water over the leaves until cool. Drain well. Select 36 medium-size leaves that are not too thick and set aside. Place a double layer of leaves in the bottom of a wide pot and add a few parsley and dill stems.

Place a leaf on a work surface, shiny side down, with the stem end at the bottom. Trim off the stem. Place 1 tablespoon of filling in the lower center of the leaf. Fold the bottom over the filling, fold the sides in, and roll up in a snug, neat package toward the pointed end. Don't roll the packets too tightly, or they may burst during cooking. Place the rolls seam side down in the bottom of the pot, fitting them snugly together. Make another layer if necessary. Drizzle the remaining ¼ cup of olive oil over the rolls and sprinkle them with 1½ tablespoons of lemon juice. Place more herb stems on top and weight the rolls with a heatproof plate. Add boiling water until it comes up to, but not over, the plate. Bring to a boil over medium high heat. Cover tightly and lower the heat. Simmer until the rice is cooked and the water has been absorbed, about 30 minutes. Add boiling water if necessary to prevent the pot from drying out.

Remove the plate and cut one of the rolls in half. The rice should be cooked, but not mushy, and the vine leaves tender. Remove the pot from the heat and sprinkle the rolls with 2 to 3 tablespoons of lemon juice. Place plastic wrap directly on the surface of the rolls, cover the pot and cool.

Remove the rolls to a storage container and pour over any juices from the pot. Place plastic wrap directly on their surface, cover the container, and refrigerate overnight. Serve the rolls lightly chilled or at room temperature with lemon wedges.

Note: There are enough grape leaves in a 1-pound jar for a double recipe of filling.

Makes 36

Frozen Mango Margarita

A tropical sizzler!

Kosher salt and granulated sugar
Lime wedge
1 large ripe mango, peeled, pitted,
   and diced
8 ounces gold tequila
2 ounces Cointreau

4 ounces freshly squeezed lime juice
2 tablespoons cooled simple syrup
   (2 tablespoons each sugar and
   hot water)
Cracked ice
4 lime wedges for garnish

Mix equal parts of kosher salt and sugar in a flat dish or pie pan. Rub the outside edges (not the rims) of 4 margarita or martini glasses with the lime wedge to moisten. Roll the edges in the salt mixture. Chill the glasses.

Combine the mango, tequila, Cointreau, lime juice, and simple syrup in a blender. Fill the blender jar with cracked ice and blend until the ice is finely crushed. Pour into the chilled glasses and garnish with lime wedges.

Serves 4

Mojito

Muddling the mint and sugar is the key to a great Mojito.

2 to 3 large sprigs fresh mint
2 teaspoons sugar
Club soda
Juice from 1 large lime (about 2 tablespoons)

2 ounces light rum
Ice
Mint sprig for garnish

Place the mint sprigs, sugar, and a splash of soda in a tall glass. With a muddler or the handle of a wooden spoon, lightly crush the mint and sugar together until the sugar is dissolved. Squeeze the lime into the glass and drop in one of the rind halves. Add the rum and stir well. Fill the glass with ice, top with club soda, and stir. Garnish with mint.

Serves 1

Ramos Fizz

A New Orleans creation, this frothy cooler is perfect on a sultry summer evening.

2 ounces gin or vodka
2 teaspoons fresh lime juice
1 teaspoon fresh lemon juice
1 teaspoon fresh orange juice
1 teaspoon confectioners' sugar
2 to 3 tablespoons light cream

1 egg white
¾ cup crushed ice
5 to 6 ounces club soda
Orange slice and maraschino
   cherry for garnish

Place all the ingredients except the club soda in a blender. Blend until frothy. Pour into a tall glass and top with club soda. Garnish with an orange slice and a maraschino cherry.

Serves 1

Rum Stone Sour

The recipe for this popular drink was a closely guarded secret at the legendary South Shore Country Club in Chicago—until a large tip to a bartender unlocked the secret.

9 ounces freshly squeezed lemon juice
9 ounces freshly squeezed orange juice
9 ounces freshly squeezed lime juice
18 ounces rum

Cooled simple syrup (½ cup each, sugar
   and hot water) or sugar
Orange slices
Maraschino cherries

Combine the juices and rum. Add simple syrup or sugar to taste. Serve in sour glasses over ice, or shake with ice until chilled and strain into sour glasses. Garnish each with an orange slice and a maraschino cherry. (Frozen lemonade, orange juice, or limeade may be substituted for freshly squeezed juices.)

Serves 6

The Pink Lemonade

A grown-up version of the childhood favorite.

30 ounces Bacardi Limon rum
Sugar
12 ounces Cointreau

6 ounces freshly squeezed lemon juice
6 ounces cranberry juice
12 lemon slices

Moisten the rims of 12 stemmed glasses with rum and sprinkle lightly with sugar. Fill a large pitcher ⅔ full with ice cubes. Add the remaining rum, the Cointreau, lemon juice, and cranberry juice. Stir until chilled and strain into the glasses. Garnish with lemon slices.

Serves 12

Soups & Sandwiches

Andalusian Gazpacho

A prized memento from a trip, this recipe for Spain's best-known soup is the real thing.

GAZPACHO

2 small, day-old hard rolls, torn
2 to 3 medium-size ripe tomatoes
1 pound cucumbers
2 green bell peppers
½ small Spanish onion

2 cloves garlic
½ cup olive oil
2 tablespoons vinegar
Salt and freshly ground pepper

GARNISH

Tomato, seeded
Cucumber, peeled and seeded
Red, green, and/or yellow
   bell peppers

Red onion
Avocado, peeled and pitted
Sour cream (optional)

Soak the hard rolls in warm water until soft. Squeeze dry. Peel and seed the tomatoes and cucumbers. Cut all the vegetables into pieces. Puree the vegetables, soaked bread, garlic, olive oil, and vinegar in an electric blender. Season with salt and pepper. Refrigerate the soup in the blender for several hours or overnight.

Cut the garnish into dice. Blend the gazpacho briefly if it has separated and pour it into chilled bowls or cups. Garnish with the chopped vegetables or a dollop of sour cream.

Note: 2 to 3 small slices of French bread can be substituted for the hard rolls.

Serves 6 to 8

Black Bean and Sausage Soup

Smoked turkey sausage gives great flavor to this hearty soup. Pair it with a red Zinfandel.

2 pounds dried black beans or
   8 15-ounce cans black beans, drained
½ cup olive oil
2 cups diced yellow onions
6 garlic cloves, peeled and crushed
1½ pounds smoked turkey sausage,
   sliced ¼ inch thick
6 quarts water
2 tablespoons plus 2 teaspoons
   whole cumin seeds

1 tablespoon dried oregano
3 bay leaves
1 tablespoon salt
2 teaspoons freshly ground pepper
Pinch cayenne pepper
6 tablespoons chopped fresh parsley
1 medium red bell pepper, diced
¼ cup dry sherry
1 tablespoon brown sugar
1 tablespoon fresh lemon juice

Check the dried beans for pebbles. Place them in a large bowl or saucepan, cover them with cold water by 2 inches and soak overnight, or boil for 2 minutes, remove from the heat, cover, and soak for 1 hour. Drain.

Heat the oil in a large soup pot over low heat. Add the onions and garlic and cook until softened, about 10 minutes. Add the beans, sausage, and water. Stir in 2 tablespoons of the cumin seeds, the oregano, bay leaves, salt, pepper, cayenne pepper, and 2 tablespoons of parsley. Bring to a boil. Reduce the heat and cook, uncovered, until the liquid is reduced by three-quarters, about 1½ to 2 hours. Stir in the remaining parsley and cumin seeds along with the bell pepper, sherry, brown sugar, and lemon juice. Simmer for 20 minutes, stirring frequently. Check the seasoning. Ladle the soup into heated bowls or cool and refrigerate for 2 to 3 days (or freeze). Serve very hot.

Serves 6 as a main course

Cheddar Cheese Soup

Make this easy soup on a cold winter day when you crave something comforting.

4 tablespoons butter or olive oil
1 medium onion, finely chopped
3 stalks celery, finely chopped
2 carrots, finely chopped
4 tablespoons flour
½ teaspoon dry mustard

1 quart chicken, turkey, or vegetable
   stock, or beer
2 or more cups milk
2 cups shredded sharp Cheddar cheese
Salt and freshly ground pepper

Heat the butter or oil in a large saucepan over medium heat. Add the onions and cook until softened, about 3 minutes. Add the celery and carrots and continue to cook until the vegetables are tender. Stir in the flour and cook until lightly browned, stirring constantly. With a wire whisk, whisk in the dry mustard and add the stock. Stir until smooth and slightly thickened. Stir in the milk and heat through. Do not allow the soup to boil at any point. Add the cheese and stir until it is melted and incorporated. Season with salt and pepper. Ladle the soup into warm bowls, or cool and refrigerate. Reheat gently.

Serves 2 to 4

Butternut Squash Soup with Pancetta

It's hard to believe this creamy soup contains no cream! Roasting the squash brings out its natural sweetness and intensifies the flavor. It's a lovely first course for Thanksgiving dinner. Offer a glass of Chardonnay.

2 to 3 butternut squash, about
    4 pounds total
4 teaspoons unsalted butter
4 teaspoons light brown sugar
2 tablespoons olive oil
1 large Spanish onion, chopped
2 medium carrots, chopped
2 medium celery ribs, chopped
1 medium leek, white and light green
    parts only, halved, well-washed, dried,
    and thinly sliced

2 sprigs fresh thyme
1 bay leaf
6 cups homemade chicken stock or
    canned low-sodium chicken broth
1 pound Yukon Gold or boiling
    potatoes, peeled
1 teaspoon salt
½ teaspoon cayenne pepper
4 thin slices pancetta, diced
Minced fresh chives or parsley

Preheat the oven to 400°F. Cut the squash in half lengthwise, scoop out the seeds, and place in a roasting pan. Add 1 teaspoon of butter and 1 teaspoon of brown sugar to each cavity. Roast for 5 minutes. With a pastry brush, brush the butter over the flesh of the squash. Roast until the squash is tender, about 45 minutes. Cover with foil if the edges appear to be burning. Set aside to cool.

Meanwhile, in a heavy pot, heat the olive oil over medium heat. Add the onions, carrots, celery, and leeks and cook until softened. Do not brown. Add the thyme sprigs, bay leaf, and chicken stock. Cut the potatoes into small dice and add them to the pot. Cover and simmer gently until the vegetables are very tender, 20 to 30 minutes.

When the squash is cool enough to handle, scoop out the flesh and add it to the pot. Add the salt and cayenne pepper and bring the soup to a boil. Reduce the heat, cover, and simmer gently for 15 minutes. Cool for a few minutes and remove the thyme sprigs and bay leaf.

In batches, puree the soup in a blender until smooth and creamy. (Do not fill the jar more than one-third full; hold the lid slightly askew to allow steam to escape.) Pass each batch through a sieve set over a clean pot. Discard any solids. Reheat the soup gently, adding water to thin to the desired consistency. (The soup can be refrigerated for up to 3 days.)

Fry the pancetta until crisp and drain on paper towels. Ladle the soup into warm bowls. Garnish each serving with pancetta and sprinkle with minced chives or parsley.

Serves 8 as a first course

Cheese Fondue

This recipe came from a traveler who removed all doubt that she was a tourist in Switzerland when she ordered this winter dish in August! Her recipe puts an American twist on the Swiss classic.

2 to 4 cloves garlic, halved
1½ cups grated Gruyère cheese
1½ cups grated Swiss cheese
1½ cups grated Monterey Jack cheese
1 cup grated Colby cheese
1 tablespoon cornstarch
1 cup dry white wine
¼ cup apple juice

2 tablespoons lemon juice
Pinch nutmeg
Pinch baking soda
1 or 2 loaves day-old French bread,
    cut into cubes, and/or steamed
    vegetables, such as potatoes
    and broccoli

Rub the bottom and sides of an earthenware fondue pot with the cut sides of the garlic. Leave the garlic in the pot. Add the grated cheeses and sprinkle with the cornstarch. Pour in the wine, apple juice, and lemon juice. On the stovetop, slowly melt the cheese over medium-low heat, stirring constantly with a wooden spoon. When bubbling gently, add the nutmeg and cook for 3 minutes. Add a pinch of baking soda. Remove from the stove when the reaction to the soda has subsided and the fondue is smooth. Place the pot over its warmer and serve accompanied with the bread and/or vegetables.

Serves 4

Cold Beet and Cucumber Soup

Serve this soup in cups with dark bread or rolls. Use disposable gloves or place your hand inside a plastic bag when grating the beets to avoid stains.

2 cups beef broth
2 medium onions, thinly sliced
1 large cucumber, peeled and sliced
½ teaspoon salt
½ teaspoon freshly ground pepper

12 whole, canned beets, drained
½ cup sour cream
Thinly sliced cucumber
Snipped chives

In a heavy saucepan, combine the broth, onions and cucumber. Bring to a boil. Lower the heat and simmer for 5 minutes or until the onion is tender. Cool slightly. Transfer to a blender and process until smooth. (Do not fill the jar more than one-third full; hold the lid slightly askew to allow steam to escape.) Pour the broth into a glass or stainless container and season with salt and pepper. Grate the beets coarsely and add them to the broth. Cover and chill well.

Just before serving, fold in the sour cream. Ladle the soup into chilled cups and garnish with cucumber slices and chives.

Serves 6

Chicken Soup with Escarole and White Beans

Light enough for a first course, this richly flavored soup makes a satisfying meal with a salad and crusty bread. If available, fresh cranberry beans are especially good.

1 cup dried cannellini, navy, or great
    northern beans, or 2 cups fresh
    cranberry beans (2 pounds unshelled),
    or 2 cups canned white
    beans, drained and rinsed
3 slices mild bacon, cut into ½-inch pieces
1 tablespoon unsalted butter
¾ cup finely chopped onion
½ pound sliced cremini mushrooms

1 or 2 cloves garlic, minced
2 quarts chicken stock or canned
    low-sodium chicken broth
1 pound escarole, tough outer leaves
    discarded, coarsely chopped, or
    fresh spinach or green Swiss chard
    leaves, tough rib removed, chopped
Salt and freshly ground pepper

Check the beans for pebbles. Place them in a bowl or saucepan, cover with cold water by 2 inches and soak overnight, or boil for 2 minutes, remove from the heat, cover, and soak for 1 hour. Drain. Cook the bacon in a large, heavy soup pot over medium heat until just beginning to color. Drain on paper towels. Drain the fat from the pot and return it to the heat. Add the butter and heat until foaming. Add the onions and mushrooms. Lower the heat, cover, and cook until the vegetables have wilted, stirring occasionally. Do not brown. Add the garlic and cook briefly. Add the chicken stock, bacon, and dried beans and bring to a boil. Lower the heat, cover, and simmer until the beans are tender, 40 minutes to an hour or more. (Fresh beans will take about 20 minutes.) Add the escarole and season with salt and pepper. Simmer for 10 to 15 minutes. (Refrigerate for 2 days or freeze.) Ladle the soup into heated bowls and serve very hot.

Note: If using canned beans, simmer the cooked vegetables, stock, and bacon for 20 minutes. Add the beans along with the escarole.

Serves 4

Warm Ham and Brie on Pumpernickel

You'll never go back to plain old ham and cheese! If available, use raisin pumpernickel.

6 to 8 ounces Brie cheese
8 slices pumpernickel bread
1 pound sugar cured ham, thinly sliced

Red or green leaf lettuce
Honey mustard

Preheat the oven to 425°F. Slice the Brie fairly thin. (Freeze for 15 minutes if the cheese is too soft to slice.) Lightly pile the ham on the bread and top with Brie. Warm in the oven along with the remaining bread. Do not allow the bread to toast. Transfer to plates, top with lettuce, and close the sandwiches. Serve with honey mustard.

Serves 4

Panini Caprese

Sweet, vine-ripened tomatoes, fresh mozzarella, and good olive oil are musts for this simple sandwich.

1 loaf foccacia, preferably
  with rosemary
Extra-virgin olive oil
6 to 8 ounces fresh, water packed
  mozzarella cheese, drained and sliced

1 large, vine-ripened garden
  tomato, sliced
Coarse salt
Fresh basil leaves

Cut the bread into 2 sandwich-sized pieces, split them in half, and lightly toast. While still warm, drizzle a little olive oil over the bottom pieces of bread and add mozzarella, tomatoes, a sprinkling of coarse salt, and basil leaves. Drizzle a little more olive oil over the sandwich and top with the remaining bread. Press down lightly and serve immediately.

Makes 2 sandwiches

Chilled Broccoli Bisque

A dash of curry powder adds a nice touch of spice to this beautiful, spring green soup. Don't omit the sour cream or lime juice; they are important to the color and texture of the soup.

2 10-ounce packages frozen
  chopped broccoli
2 14-ounce cans chicken broth
2 tablespoons butter
1 medium onion, thinly sliced
1 teaspoon salt

Freshly ground pepper
Dash curry powder
¼ cup sour cream
¼ cup heavy cream
2 tablespoons lime juice

GARNISH
  Sour cream
  8 thin lemon slices
  Snipped fresh chives

Place the broccoli, broth, butter, onion, and seasonings in a heavy saucepan. Simmer, covered, until the vegetables are tender. Cool slightly. Transfer the soup to a blender and puree. (Do not fill the jar more than one-third full; hold the lid slightly askew to allow steam to escape.) For a silky texture, pass the pureed soup through a sieve. Refrigerate for at least 4 hours.

When ready to serve, stir in the sour cream, heavy cream, and lime juice. Ladle the soup into chilled bowls. Garnish with a spoonful of sour cream, a lemon slice, and a sprinkle of chives.

Serves 8 as a first course

Cold Curried Apple Soup

An elegant hot-weather soup to serve in pretty chilled cups with raisin rolls and a glass of dry Reisling.

1 tablespoon unsalted butter
1 small white onion, finely chopped
2 teaspoons curry powder
1 quart chicken stock or
   low-sodium broth
2 teaspoons cornstarch
2 pounds apples

Juice from ½ small lemon
⅔ cup half & half
1 egg yolk
Salt and freshly ground pepper
Watercress leaves
Chopped apple

Melt the butter in a heavy saucepan and add the onion. Sauté until softened. Add the curry powder, stir for 1 minute, and add the stock. Combine the cornstarch with a little water to make a thin paste and whisk it into the pan. Simmer for 8 minutes.

Peel, core, and thinly slice the apples. Add them to the soup along with the lemon juice. Simmer until the apples are soft, about 10 minutes.

In a saucepan, warm the half & half. Remove the pan from the heat. Beat the egg yolk. Stirring constantly, slowly add it to the half & half. Gradually add the half & half to the soup, again stirring constantly, and season with salt and pepper. Do not allow the soup to boil. Remove the pan from the heat and cool slightly. Process the soup in a blender until smooth. (Do not fill the blender more than one-third full; hold the lid slightly askew to allow steam to escape.) Cool to room temperature, cover, and refrigerate overnight.

Ladle the soup into chilled cups and garnish with watercress leaves and chopped apple.

Serves 4 as a first course

Creole Shrimp and Crab Soup

Similar in flavor to a traditional Cajun/Creole gumbo, this soup contains no roux and is a snap to prepare. For best flavor, make it a day or two in advance.

2 pounds small, raw shrimp
1 pound Alaskan King crab leg meat
   (shelled weight)
1 pound fresh okra or a 10-ounce
   package frozen okra, thawed
3 stems flat leaf parsley
2 sprigs thyme
1 bay leaf
4 tablespoons unsalted butter
1 medium Spanish onion, diced
4 stalks celery, chopped

1 medium green bell pepper, diced
2 cloves garlic, minced
3½ cups whole canned tomatoes,
   drained and chopped or well crushed
6 cups low-salt chicken broth
Salt and freshly ground pepper
¼ cup thinly sliced green onions
   (white and light green parts only)
2 tablespoons chopped flat leaf parsley
Tabasco or other hot sauce
2 cups cooked long grain white rice

Peel and devein the shrimp. Refrigerate ½ pound for garnish. Cut the remaining shrimp and the crab into pieces. Refrigerate about ¼ of the crabmeat for garnish. Cut the okra into ½-inch pieces. Tie the parsley, thyme, and bay leaf together with kitchen twine. In a large, heavy soup pot, melt the butter over medium heat until foaming. Add the onions, celery, and green pepper. Cook, stirring occasionally, until softened, about 5 minutes. Add the okra and cook for 2 or 3 minutes. Add the garlic and cook briefly. Add the tomatoes, broth, herb bundle, shrimp, crabmeat, salt and pepper. Cover the pot and simmer slowly for 2 to 2½ hours until the soup is lightly thickened. Remove the herb bundle. Cool and refrigerate.

Reheat the soup. Add the green onions and the reserved shrimp and crabmeat. Simmer until the shrimp are pink and just cooked through, about 1 minute. Add the chopped parsley and Tabasco to taste.

For each serving, pack ¼ cup of rice into a small, lightly oiled ramekin or custard cup. Unmold in the center of a soup plate. Ladle the soup around the rice. Serve with Tabasco.

Serves 8 as a first course

Grilled Veggie Sandwich with Basil Mayo

Healthful and delicious, the sandwich is best when the veggies are still slightly warm from the grill.

Olive oil mixed with 1 or more
  cloves crushed garlic or
  roasted garlic oil
2 zucchini, sliced lengthwise
  ¼-inch thick
2 yellow squash, sliced lengthwise
  ¼-inch thick
4 portabella mushroom caps
1 red onion, sliced ¼-inch thick

1 medium eggplant, peeled and
  sliced in ½-inch thick rounds
Salt and pepper
1 large vine-ripened tomato,
  sliced
1 large roasted red bell pepper,
  quartered
4 whole grain rolls
Basil Mayonnaise

Brush the zucchini, yellow squash, mushroom caps, onion, and eggplant with garlic oil and season with salt and pepper. Grill until tender. Warm the tomato slices on the grill. (The vegetables can be broiled, or roasted in a 400°F oven.) Split the rolls, spread with mayonnaise, and layer on the vegetables. Serve warm or at room temperature.

BASIL MAYONNAISE
1 cup mayonnaise
1 small clove garlic, chopped
2 teaspoons fresh lemon juice

½ cup packed fresh basil leaves
Salt and freshly ground pepper

Process all the ingredients in a blender until smooth. Refrigerate for at least 1 hour.

Serves 4

G. D.'s Cajun Gumbo

G. D. recommends wearing padded slippers (you'll be on your feet a long time) and rewarding your efforts with the rest of the bottle of wine while making this dish. Time-consuming, but well worth the effort, this dish has real Cajun flavor. Make a double batch and freeze one for a future meal.

⅓ cup vegetable oil
⅓ cup flour
½ to ¾ cup chopped onion
¼ to ½ cup sliced green onions
½ cup chopped celery
½ to ¾ cup chopped green bell pepper
6 cups chicken broth, heated
1 cup dry red wine
1 pound boneless, skinless chicken breasts
   or thighs, cut into chunks
½ to 1 pound smoked Polish sausage,
   quartered and sliced
½ to 1 pound andouille (preferred)
   or chorizo sausage, sliced

1 smoked ham steak, cubed
1 to 1½ teaspoons cayenne pepper
½ teaspoon black pepper
¼ teaspoon white pepper
½ teaspoon minced fresh thyme
   or ¼ teaspoon dried thyme
½ to ¾ teaspoon salt
2 bay leaves
2 tablespoons chopped
   flat leaf parsley
1 tablespoon filé powder
1½ cups white rice, cooked
1 bunch green onions, chopped
Tabasco or other hot sauce

Heat the oil over low heat in a large, heavy pot or Dutch oven, preferably cast iron or enameled cast iron. Add the flour all at once. Cook, stirring frequently, until the roux is a rich, deep golden brown, about 45 minutes to 1 hour. Watch it carefully and lower the heat if necessary. (If the roux blackens, discard it and start again or the entire dish will taste burned.) Add the chopped onions, green onions, celery, and green pepper to the roux. Increase the temperature to medium and cook, stirring almost constantly, until the vegetables have softened. Add wine or broth if the mixture gets too thick. Gradually stir in the warm broth and bring to a boil, stirring constantly. Add the wine, chicken, sausage, andouille, ham, pepper, thyme, salt, and bay leaves. Partially cover the pot and simmer for 45 minutes to 1 hour, occasionally skimming off fat.

Taste the gumbo for seasoning. Add the parsley, sprinkle the filé powder over the top, and stir to blend. (The gumbo tastes best if made a day ahead. Add the filé powder and parsley after reheating.)

Spoon mounds of hot rice into individual bowls. Ladle the gumbo around the rice and sprinkle with chopped green onions. Serve with hot sauce.

Note: If using chorizo, remove it from the casing and fry separately until the edges begin to brown. Drain on paper towels.

Serves 6 to 8

Pan Bagnat

More like a Niçoise salad on a roll, this ultimate tuna sandwich is served in Nice where Pan Bagnat (bathed bread) is doused with enough olive oil to drip down your arm!

1 clove garlic
Salt and freshly ground pepper
¼ cup red wine vinegar, plus
   more for the tuna
⅔ to ¾ cup good, extra-virgin
   olive oil
6 ounces light tuna packed in
   olive oil, drained, oil reserved
Juice from ½ lemon
2 kaiser rolls, split
1 or 2 vine-ripened tomatoes, sliced
Red onion, thinly sliced

1 small cucumber, peeled
   and sliced
1 small red or green bell
   pepper, sliced
1 or 2 hard-cooked eggs, sliced
4 or more anchovy fillets
   packed in oil, drained
1 or 2 green onions, chopped
Niçoise olives, pitted and sliced
   or chopped
Whole basil leaves
Red or green leaf lettuce

Put the garlic through a garlic press into a small bowl. Add salt, pepper, and the wine vinegar. Stir to dissolve the salt. Slowly whisk in the olive oil. Taste and adjust the balance and set the vinaigrette aside.

Place the tuna in a bowl and season with salt, pepper, lemon juice, and a little red wine vinegar. Add enough olive oil to moisten well (use the reserved oil from the tuna and/or fresh oil). Mix gently, being careful not to mash the tuna. Split the rolls and pull out some of the soft crumb. Drizzle the bottom halves of the rolls with vinaigrette and top with the tuna and all of the remaining ingredients, except the lettuce. Drizzle the top halves of the rolls with more vinaigrette, add lettuce, and close the sandwiches. The sandwiches may be covered and refrigerated for 1 hour. Add lettuce just before serving.

Serves 2

Iced English Cucumber Soup with Mint and Baby Shrimp

The quintessential English summer soup to serve with brown bread. The garnish is particularly lovely.

1½ seedless English cucumbers,
  unpeeled
⅔ cup heavy cream
⅔ cup whole milk yogurt
⅔ cup sour cream
1½ cloves garlic, crushed
3 cornichons, chopped
2½ tablespoons tarragon vinegar

Salt and freshly ground pepper
2½ tablespoons chopped
  fresh mint leaves
8 tiny cooked shrimp or salmon
  roe for garnish
Brown bread, crusts removed,
  cut into triangles

Scrub the cucumbers and grate them fairly coarsely. Place them in a bowl and stir in the cream, yogurt, sour cream, garlic, cornichons, vinegar, salt, and pepper. Add more cream, yogurt, or sour cream to taste. Chill well.

When ready to serve, stir in the mint. Add a little ice water or cold milk if the soup is too thick. Spoon into chilled goblets, cups, or small bowls. Garnish with the shrimp or a spoonful of salmon roe and serve with the brown bread.

Serves 4 as a first course

Mushroom and Barley Soup

This robust, deeply flavored soup is a meal in itself. It tastes better on the second—or third—day and freezes well. If you make your own beef stock, the boiled beef can be added to the soup.

A generous ¼ cup dried porcini
  mushrooms
1 cup very hot water
3 tablespoons vegetable oil
3 cups finely chopped Spanish onion
1 large leek (white and light green parts
  only) halved, well-washed, and
  thinly sliced
3 carrots, peeled and sliced
2 ribs celery, sliced

¾ pound cremini mushrooms, sliced
3 cloves garlic, minced
2 quarts brown beef or chicken stock
  or 1 quart low-salt beef broth
  combined with 1 quart low-salt
  chicken broth
½ cup pearled barley
Salt and freshly ground pepper
Chopped flat leaf parsley

Place the porcini mushrooms in a sieve and rinse quickly under cold water. Transfer them to a small bowl, cover with the hot water and soak until softened, about 30 minutes. Scoop the mushrooms from the soaking liquid and squeeze them over the bowl. Rinse again under cold water and squeeze dry. Cut them into ½ inch pieces. Strain the soaking liquid through a small sieve lined with several layers of damp cheesecloth or a damp paper towel to remove any grit. Set aside.

In a heavy soup pot, heat the oil over medium heat. Add the onions and leeks and sauté until they begin to wilt, about 3 minutes. Add the carrots and celery and sauté for

2 minutes. Add the cremini mushrooms and sauté until they begin to color. Add the porcini mushrooms and garlic and sauté briefly. Add the stock, reserved soaking liquid, barley, salt, and pepper. Cover and bring the soup to a simmer. Simmer until the barley is tender, but not mushy, about 45 minutes. Check the seasoning. (The soup can be refrigerated for up to 3 days or frozen.) Ladle the soup into heated bowls and sprinkle with chopped parsley.

Serves 4

New England Fish and Corn Chowder

Cod and haddock are native to New England waters, but any firm, white, mild fish will do nicely. The chowder is a satisfying one-dish meal. Serve it with rustic bread and a Chardonnay.

1 tablespoon olive oil
½ pound thick-sliced bacon,
    cut into ¼-inch dice
2 medium onions, chopped
3 cloves garlic, chopped
2 tablespoons minced fresh thyme
    or 1 tablespoon dried thyme
2 bay leaves
2 pounds Yukon Gold potatoes,
    peeled and sliced ¼-inch thick

2 cups fresh corn kernels or
    frozen white shoepeg corn
16 ounces bottled clam juice
3 cups chicken stock or low-salt broth
Kosher salt and freshly ground pepper
2 to 3 pounds skinless, 1-inch thick
    cod or haddock fillets, left whole
1½ cups heavy cream
3 tablespoons chopped chives

Heat a large, heavy pot over medium-high heat. Add the olive oil and bacon. Cook until the bacon is crisp. Transfer to paper towels to drain. Add the onions, garlic, thyme, and bay leaves to the bacon drippings and cook until the onions are softened, stirring occasionally. Add the potatoes, corn, clam juice, and chicken stock. The liquid should cover the potatoes by 1 inch. If not, add water. Turn the heat to high and bring to a boil. Cover and cook until the potatoes are soft on the outside, but still firm in the middle. If the stock has not thickened, mash some of the potatoes against the side of the pot. Reduce the heat to a simmer and add salt and pepper. Add the fish fillets and cook over low heat for 5 minutes without stirring. Remove the pot from the heat. Cover and let the chowder stand for 10 minutes. The fish will finish cooking as it stands. Gently stir in the cream, being careful not to break up the fish. Let the chowder stand for 1 hour to allow the flavors to blend.

Reheat the chowder gently without stirring. Do not allow it to boil. Mound fish chunks, onions, and potatoes in the center of warm bowls. Spoon broth around the fish. Garnish with the reserved bacon and chopped chives.

Serves 8

French Onion Soup Gratinée

Join the Celebration! illustrator Guy Buffet sent us his recipe for French onion soup. Make it the day before and it will taste even better. Bon appetit!

4 medium onions, thinly sliced	Salt and freshly ground pepper
3 tablespoons butter	Freshly grated Parmesan cheese
6 cups beef stock or broth	Day-old French bread or toast

In a soup pot, cook the onions very gently in the butter until light brown. Add the beef stock, salt, and pepper, and bring the soup to a boil. Reduce the heat and simmer for 10 minutes. Set aside, uncovered, for an hour or so (or chill). Reheat the soup to piping hot and sprinkle in some cheese. Ladle into individual crocks. Top with slices of bread and sprinkle with cheese. Bake in a preheated 400°F oven until the cheese browns.

Serves 4

Pumpkin and Shrimp Bisque

This festive soup would be a great first course for a holiday dinner, or offer it in tea cups as a prelude as guests finish pre-dinner drinks and hors d'oeuvres.

6 tablespoons unsalted butter	¼ teaspoon or more freshly
1 large onion, sliced	ground nutmeg
1 cup finely chopped leeks	1 pound raw shrimp, peeled and
(white part only)	deveined
2 16-ounce cans pureed pumpkin	1 tablespoon freshly squeezed
6 to 7 cups chicken stock	lemon juice
½ cup mined fresh parsley	10 medium shrimp, cooked, peeled,
3 cups milk	and deveined, for garnish
Salt and freshly ground pepper	Small parsley sprigs

Melt the butter in a large, heavy soup pot over medium heat. Add the onions and leeks and sauté until they are soft and golden, about 8 to 10 minutes. Stir in the pumpkin. Add 6 cups of chicken stock and the minced parsley. Simmer over low heat for 15 to 20 minutes. Stir in the milk, add salt, pepper, and nutmeg and simmer for 10 minutes. Do not allow the soup to boil.

Coarsely chop half the shrimp and set aside. Add the remaining shrimp to the soup and cook just until they turn pink, about 1 to 2 minutes. With a slotted spoon, transfer the solids to a blender or food processor. Add about ¾ cup of the liquid and puree until smooth. (Hold the lid of the blender jar askew to allow steam to escape.) Return the puree to the pot. Add the lemon juice and stir well. Cook gently for 5 to 10 minutes. Taste for seasoning and add more chicken stock if the soup is too thick. Add the reserved chopped shrimp and cook just until they turn pink. Ladle the soup into heated bowls. Garnish each serving with 1 shrimp and a parsley sprig.

Serves 10

Roasted Carrot Soup with Seared Shrimp
and Curried Crème Fraîche

An elegant and sophisticated soup to serve hot or cold. A glass of chilled Sauvignon Blanc is a perfect accompaniment.

½ cup crème fraîche or sour cream
½ teaspoon curry powder, or to taste
1 pound carrots, peeled, thick ends halved
Unsalted butter
1 tablespoon vegetable oil
3 cups thinly sliced Spanish onion
Salt and freshly ground pepper
Pinch sugar
1 pound sweet potatoes, peeled and
   thinly sliced

1 tablespoon chopped fresh ginger
1 garlic clove, minced
2 quarts homemade chicken stock or
   4 14-ounce cans low-sodium chicken
   broth plus 1 cup water
2 teaspoons grated orange zest
Olive or vegetable oil
3 small shrimp per person, peeled
   and deveined
Chopped cilantro

Combine the crème fraîche and curry powder in a small bowl. If necessary, add water to thin slightly so that it is pourable. Cover and refrigerate for at least 1 hour or overnight.

Preheat the oven to 400°F. Place the carrots in a shallow roasting pan in a single layer and toss them with a little melted butter or oil. Add water to barely film the bottom of the pan. Cover tightly with foil and roast for 15 minutes. Uncover, turn the carrots over and continue to roast, uncovered, until tender, turning occasionally. Add more water if necessary to prevent scorching. Cut the carrots into pieces and set aside.

While the carrots roast, heat 2 tablespoons of butter and 1 tablespoon of vegetable oil in a large, heavy soup pot over low heat. Stir in the onions and sprinkle with salt. Cover and cook until wilted. Uncover and add a pinch of sugar. Cook, stirring and scraping the bottom of the pot frequently, until the onions are very tender and golden in color, about 20 minutes. Add the potatoes and ginger. Cook, stirring often, for 2 or 3 minutes. Stir in the garlic and cook until fragrant. Add the carrots, stock, and 1 teaspoon of grated orange zest. Reduce the heat, cover, and simmer until the carrots and potatoes are very soft, about 30 minutes. Cool slightly and puree the soup in a blender until smooth. (Do not fill the jar more than one-third full; hold the lid slightly askew to allow steam to escape.) Pass the puree through a fine sieve into a clean pot. Discard any solids. Bring the soup to a simmer and season with salt and pepper. If desired, add the remaining teaspoon of grated orange zest. Simmer gently for 5 minutes. Thin with a little water or orange juice if the soup is too thick. Keep warm. (If serving chilled, cool and refrigerate for several hours or overnight.)

Heat a skillet over high heat. Add a little oil to the skillet and sear the shrimp just until pink and firm, turning once. (If serving the soup chilled, boil the shrimp.) Ladle the soup into soup plates or cups. Place 3 shrimp in the center of each serving. Drizzle with curried crème fraîche and sprinkle with a pinch of chopped cilantro.

Serves 8 as a first course

Roasted Tomato and Blue Cheese Soup

Roasting the tomatoes concentrates their sweet flavor. The blue cheese adds a tangy counterpoint.

3 pounds medium-size,
   ripe tomatoes,
   peeled, quartered, and seeded
2 cloves garlic, minced
Salt and freshly ground pepper
2 tablespoons butter
1 leek (white and light green part
   only), chopped

1 carrot, peeled and chopped
5 cups unsalted chicken stock
4 ounces blue cheese, crumbled
3 tablespoons whipping cream
2 tablespoons chopped fresh basil
2 strips bacon, cooked
   and crumbled
Basil sprigs

Preheat the oven to 400°F. Spread the tomatoes in a shallow baking dish. Sprinkle them with the garlic, salt, and pepper. Roast for 35 minutes.

Heat the butter in a large saucepan. Add the leek and carrot and season lightly with salt and pepper. Cook over low heat, stirring often, until the vegetables are tender, about 10 minutes. Do not let them color. Add the stock and roasted tomatoes and bring to a boil. Lower the heat, cover, and simmer for 20 minutes. Add the blue cheese, cream, and chopped basil. Remove the pan from the heat and cool slightly. Transfer the soup to a blender or food processor and process until smooth. (Do not fill the jar more than one-third full; hold the lid slightly askew to allow steam to escape.) If desired, pass the puree through a fine sieve into a large bowl. Adjust the seasoning. Rinse out the pot. Return the soup to the pot and reheat. Do not allow it to boil. Ladle the soup into bowls and garnish with bacon and sprigs of fresh basil. Serve hot.

Serves 6

Hot Roast Beef with Gruyère and Horseradish Sauce

French baguette, split lengthwise, is a good alternative to rye bread for this hearty sandwich.

⅓ cup mayonnaise
2 tablespoons prepared horseradish
2 slices rye bread
8 to 10 ounces thinly sliced roast beef

1 tomato, thinly sliced
Thinly sliced red onion
Thinly sliced Gruyère or Swiss cheese

Preheat the broiler. Combine the mayonnaise and horseradish. Pile the roast beef on the bread and top with horseradish sauce, tomatoes, onions, and Gruyère. Broil until the cheese is melted and the bread is warm. Serve open-faced with additional horseradish sauce.

Serves 2

ULC Navy Bean Soup

It isn't Thursday if this all-time favorite isn't on the Club's menu! Serve it in cups as a first course, or in bowls with salad and crusty rolls as a hearty main course.

1 pound dried navy beans
3 tablespoons butter
4 tablespoons flour
2 tablespoons vegetable oil
1½ cups diced onions
1 cup diced carrots
2 ounces thick-sliced,
    smoked ham, diced
3 large cloves garlic, minced

1½ teaspoons dried thyme
1 bay leaf
½ cup diced tomatoes
2 to 3 heaping tablespoons tomato paste
2 quarts chicken stock
1 teaspoon Worcestershire sauce
½ teaspoon Tabasco
Salt and freshly ground pepper

Check the beans for pebbles. Place them in a bowl or saucepan, cover them with cold water by 2 inches and soak overnight, or boil for 2 minutes, remove from the heat, cover, and soak for 1 hour. Drain. Cover the beans with 3 inches of fresh water and slowly bring to a simmer over moderate heat. Simmer gently until the beans are tender, about 45 minutes to 1 hour, adding more water if necessary. Drain.

While the beans are cooking, melt the butter in a skillet over moderate heat. Add the flour all at once. Whisk until smooth and cook, stirring, for 2 minutes. Do not allow the roux to color. Transfer it to a bowl and set aside.

Heat a large, heavy soup pot over medium heat and add the oil. Add the onions, carrots, ham, garlic, thyme, and bay leaf. Sauté until the onions have softened. Add the tomatoes, tomato paste, and chicken stock. Bring to a simmer. Add the roux and stir well to thoroughly incorporate. Simmer, uncovered, until the vegetables are tender, about 20 minutes, skimming occasionally. Add the drained beans, Worcestershire sauce, Tabasco, salt, and pepper. Simmer for 10 minutes. Taste for seasoning and serve. (The soup can be cooled and refrigerated for 3 days or frozen. The flavor is best if made in advance.)

Note: The Club's recipe makes gallons of soup. In testing the recipe after scaling it down for home use, we found that adding 2 to 3 heaping tablespoons of tomato paste was necessary to achieve the right flavor.

Serves 4 as a main course

Gingered Broth with Shrimp and Rice Stick Noodles

This light soup is addictive. The addition of Scotch sounds a little strange, but it adds a nuance that really works with the Southeast Asian flavors.

1 medium head bok choy
2 tablespoons vegetable oil
2 teaspoons Asian sesame oil
1 large carrot, thinly sliced
½ to ¾ of a red bell pepper, thinly sliced
12 medium shitake mushroom caps, sliced
A 3-inch piece of fresh ginger, peeled and
   cut into fine julienne
2 cloves garlic, minced
1 teaspoon Madras curry powder
¼ cup Scotch whiskey
1 quart low-salt chicken broth

2 teaspoons sugar
6 to 8 green onions, white and 3 inches
   of green stalks, thinly sliced
1 tablespoon Asian fish sauce (nuoc mam)
½ teaspoon crushed red pepper flakes
Salt and freshly ground pepper
6 ounces Asian rice stick noodles
   (rice vermicelli) or angel hair pasta,
   broken in half
12 ounces small shrimp, peeled and
   deveined
Fresh cilantro leaves

Wash and trim the bok choy and separate the leaves from the stalks. Thinly slice the leaves and cut the stalks diagonally into ½-inch pieces. In a large, heavy saucepan, heat the oils over medium-high heat. Add the bok choy stalks, carrots, peppers, mushrooms, and ginger and sauté for 1 minute. Add the garlic and curry powder and sauté briefly. Add the Scotch, chicken broth, and sugar. Cover the pan and simmer for 5 minutes. Add the bok choy leaves, green onions, fish sauce, and red pepper flakes and continue to simmer until the vegetables are tender, about 3 to 4 minutes. Season with salt and pepper and keep warm.

Meanwhile, boil the noodles in plenty of salted water until they are white and tender, but still firm, about 4 minutes (boil angel hair pasta until al dente). Drain. Add the noodles and shrimp to the broth and bring to a simmer. Cover and simmer just until the shrimp are cooked, about 1 minute. Ladle the soup into warm bowls and sprinkle with cilantro leaves. Serve immediately.

Serves 4 as a light main course

Virginia Peanut Soup

One of the first truly "American" dishes, this rich, early American soup was—and is—a great favorite. It's still served in Colonial Williamsburg and has become justly famous.

3 cups chicken broth	½ cup creamy peanut butter
2 tablespoons butter	Dash celery salt
¼ cup finely diced onion	¼ teaspoon salt
1 stalk celery, thinly sliced	1 teaspoon lemon juice
2 tablespoons flour	2 tablespoons chopped peanuts

Heat the chicken broth in a saucepan. Melt the butter over moderate heat in another saucepan. Add the onion and celery and sauté for five minutes without browning. Whisk in the flour until blended. Gradually whisk in the hot chicken broth. Simmer for 30 minutes. Remove the pan from the heat and strain the soup into a bowl. Add the peanut butter, celery salt, salt, and lemon juice. Whisk until smooth. Ladle the soup into warm bowls and sprinkle with chopped peanuts.

Serves 4

Napa Valley Grilled Chicken Sandwich

This great sandwich can also be made with croissants.

3 boneless, skinless chicken breasts	6 slices applewood or hickory smoked bacon, cooked and cut into pieces
⅓ cup olive oil	
2 cloves garlic, chopped	
2 to 3 sprigs each, fresh rosemary and thyme, bruised with the back of a knife	Arugula or watercress, tough stems discarded
Salt and freshly ground pepper	Roasted red bell pepper strips
4 ciabatta rolls or other rustic-style rolls	Vine-ripened tomatoes, sliced
Mayonnaise	1 medium avocado, peeled, pitted, and sliced

Pound the chicken breasts between 2 sheets of plastic wrap to a thickness of ¼-inch. Combine the chicken, olive oil, chopped garlic, and fresh herb sprigs in a zip-top bag. Refrigerate for several hours or overnight.

Drain the chicken and season with salt and pepper. Grill on a hot, outdoor grill, or on a hot, ridged grill pan or in a heavy skillet until just done, about 2 minutes per side. Slice each breast crosswise on the bias. Split the rolls, pull out some of the soft crumb, and spread with mayonnaise. In this order, layer the bottom half of each sandwich with bacon, arugula, roasted pepper, tomatoes, chicken, salt and pepper, more arugula, avocado, and bacon. Top with the remaining bread and serve.

Serves 4

Wild Mushroom and Rice Soup

Wild mushrooms and wild rice give rich, woodsy flavor to this superb soup while homemade stock adds body and depth. It's a great beginning to a special dinner. Serve it with a basket of crisp cheese straws and a white Rhône or a Pinot Noir.

½ cup wild rice
2 cups water
1 ounce dried morel mushrooms
½ cup Madeira
9 cups rich homemade beef stock or
   1 quart each low-salt beef and
   chicken broth and 1 cup water
4 tablespoons unsalted butter
1 medium Spanish onion,
   cut into small dice
2 large leeks (white and pale green
   parts only) halved, well-washed,
   and thinly sliced

¾ pound cremini mushrooms,
   sliced
½ pound mixed exotic mushrooms,
   such as shitakes or chanterelles
   (do not use portabellas), sliced
   (discard shitake stems)
Salt and freshly ground pepper
About 5 handfuls fresh spinach,
   stemmed, washed, well-drained, and
   coarsely chopped
Snipped fresh chives

Place the rice in a fine mesh sieve and rinse well under cold water. Transfer it to a medium saucepan, add 2 cups of water, and bring to a boil. Cover, reduce the heat, and simmer until the rice is tender but still chewy, about 30 to 40 minutes. Add more boiling water if necessary. Drain any unabsorbed water and set aside.

Rinse the morels briefly under cold, running water. Place them in a small saucepan and add the Madeira and ½ cup of stock. Bring to a boil. Remove the pan from the heat and let stand for 30 minutes. Scoop the mushrooms from the liquid and squeeze gently. Cut them in half or quarters, rinse them quickly under cold water, and squeeze gently over the saucepan. Strain the soaking liquid through a small sieve lined with several layers of damp cheesecloth or a damp paper towel to remove any grit. Set aside.

Melt 2 tablespoons of butter in a large, heavy soup pot over medium-low heat. Add the onions and leeks and cook until the onions are translucent. Do not brown. Transfer the mixture to a bowl. Raise the heat to medium and add the remaining 2 tablespoons of butter. When the butter is foaming, add the fresh mushrooms and sauté until they begin to brown around the edges and their liquid has evaporated. Add the morels about 1 minute before the fresh mushrooms are done. Return the onions to the pot. Add the remaining stock, the strained soaking liquid, salt, and freshly ground pepper. Simmer gently, uncovered, for 15 minutes. (The soup can be refrigerated for up to 3 days or frozen up to 2 months. The flavor is best if made in advance.)

Add the rice to the simmering soup. Cover and simmer for 5 minutes or until the rice is tender but has not burst. Add the spinach by handfuls, allowing each to wilt before adding more. Taste for seasoning. Ladle the soup into a heated tureen or individual bowls. Garnish with chives and serve very hot.

Serves 8 as a first course

Italian Pressed Picnic Sandwich

This is a serious sandwich. The weight compresses the layers, blending the flavors and making it easier to slice. Make the olive salad at least one day in advance for best flavor.

1 cup thinly sliced fresh fennel
   and/or celery
1½ cups pitted black and/or green olives
3 tablespoons small capers
1 or 2 cloves garlic, put through a press
1 anchovy, mashed to a paste
2 tablespoons chopped parsley
1 teaspoon dried oregano
Freshly ground pepper
2 tablespoons balsamic or
   red wine vinegar
4 to 6 tablespoons olive oil
1 large, round, rustic-style loaf of bread,
   such as ciabatta or sourdough
1 roasted red pepper cut into strips

1 6-ounce jar marinated artichokes,
   drained and sliced
⅓ pound Genoa or Toscano
   salami, very thinly sliced
⅓ pound ham, very thinly sliced
⅓ pound cappicola,
   very thinly sliced
⅓ pound mortadella,
   very thinly sliced
⅓ pound provolone or Swiss cheese,
   thinly sliced
½ pound mozzarella, thinly sliced
Thinly sliced tomatoes, to taste
Thinly sliced red onion, to taste
Arugula or leaf lettuce

Pulse the fennel and/or celery in a food processor until coarsely chopped and transfer to a bowl. Coarsely chop the olives in the processor and add them to the fennel along with the capers. In a separate bowl, combine the garlic, mashed anchovy, parsley, oregano, black pepper, vinegar, and oils. Add the vinaigrette to the olives and fennel and stir well. Set aside for several hours or refrigerate overnight. (The salad will keep for a week or more.)

Cut the bread in half horizontally and remove most of the soft crumb, leaving a ½-inch-thick shell. (Save the bread to make bread crumbs or croutons.) Drain the olive salad, reserving the oil. Spread some of the olive salad over the bottom half of the loaf. Add the red pepper strips and artichokes. Add alternate layers of meats and cheeses, top with more olive salad, and replace the top crust. Wrap the loaf tightly in plastic wrap. Set a heavy weight, such as a cast iron skillet or a pan filled with canned goods or a bag of sugar, on top of the loaf and refrigerate for at least 1 hour and up to 4 hours. Unwrap the loaf, drizzle vinaigrette over the filling, and rewrap. Pack the loaf into your picnic hamper. (If the sandwich will not be eaten within an hour or so, or if the day is very hot, pack it into an ice chest. Remove the loaf from the ice chest, drizzle with vinaigrette, and let it stand until no longer cold.) When ready to serve, add the tomatoes, onions, and lettuce, cut the loaf into wedges and serve.

Serves 6 to 8

Salads

Crab, Grapefruit, and Avocado Salad

A sparkling first course or luncheon salad. A crisp Sauvignon Blanc will accent the citrus.

2 pink grapefruits
2 Hass avocados
Salt and freshly ground pepper
1 pound cooked, fresh crabmeat

4 ribs celery, diced
⅔ cup mayonnaise
Red and/or green lettuce leaves
Lemon or lime wedges

Cut off the ends of the grapefruits. With a small, sharp knife, cut along the curve of the fruit and remove all of the rind and bitter, white pith. Working over a bowl, cut along the membranes to release the segments. Squeeze the juice from the pulp into the bowl. Peel and pit the avocados and cut them into an even number of slices. Place the slices on a plate, drizzle with some of the grapefruit juice, and season lightly with salt and pepper. Place the crabmeat in a bowl and break it into pieces with a fork. Add the diced celery, salt, pepper, and mayonnaise. Gently fold together. Drain the grapefruit segments and add half of them to the crab. Toss lightly to combine.

Arrange lettuce leaves on 4 chilled plates and top with the salad. Garnish with the remaining grapefruit segments, the avocado slices, and lemon or lime wedges.

Serves 4 as a first course

Ensalada de Camarones

Sweet shrimp, creamy potatoes, and crisp vegetables provide textural interplay in this simple salad. Serve it as a light main course or as part of a buffet.

2 pounds red potatoes
½ cup mayonnaise
½ cup sour cream
3 cups cooked, cut up jumbo shrimp
1 teaspoon cayenne pepper
Salt

1 cup seeded and diced
   cucumber with skin
1 cup chopped celery
3 hard-cooked eggs,
   coarsely chopped
Lettuce leaves

Place the potatoes in a saucepan and cover them with cold water. Bring to a simmer, and simmer until just tender. Drain. When the potatoes are cool enough to handle, remove the skins and cut them into dice.

Combine the mayonnaise and sour cream in a small bowl. In another bowl, combine the potatoes, shrimp, cayenne pepper, salt, cucumber, celery, and eggs. Fold in the mayonnaise and taste for seasoning. Chill the salad well.

Line a large salad bowl with lettuce leaves. Arrange the salad over the lettuce and serve.

Serves 4 to 6 as a main course

Fattoush

This Middle Eastern bread salad offers a refreshing change from green salads. Purslane adds a light, citrus flavor and can often be found at farmers' markets or gourmet grocers. Crushed sumac berries lend an exotic, sour-lemon flavor. Look for it in Middle Eastern markets.

1 cucumber, peeled, seeded, and sliced
2 slightly stale 7- to 8-inch pita
  breads with pockets
2 to 4 ripe tomatoes (about 1 pound),
  cut into wedges
4 to 6 scallions (white and light
  green parts only), sliced
1 green bell pepper, sliced
1 red bell pepper, sliced
1 cup purslane leaves or
  torn young arugula

¼ cup chopped flat leaf parsley
¼ cup chopped fresh mint leaves
¼ cup chopped fresh cilantro
Salt and freshly ground pepper
Juice from 1 large lemon
  (about 1/4 cup)
Pinch sugar
⅓ to ½ cup olive oil
1 clove garlic, put through
  a garlic press or mashed
1 teaspoon crushed sumac (optional)

Sprinkle the cucumber with salt and let stand in a colander for 30 minutes. Rinse and pat dry. Preheat the oven to 375°F. Split the pitas into rounds and tear them into bite-sized pieces. Spread the pieces on a baking sheet and bake until lightly colored and dry, about 10 to 15 minutes. Cool to room temperature.

In a large salad bowl, combine the cucumber, tomatoes, scallions, bell peppers, purslane, parsley, mint, and cilantro. Season with salt and pepper and set aside for 5 to 10 minutes.

In a bowl, whisk together the lemon juice, sugar, olive oil, garlic, sumac, and salt. Add more lemon juice or oil to taste. Toss the vegetables with enough dressing to coat. Add the pita and toss again. Add more dressing as necessary. Grind fresh pepper over the salad and serve.

Serves 4

Field Greens with Mandarin Oranges, Fresh Berries, and Onion-Poppy Seed Dressing

The colors in this first course salad are dazzling. Vary the proportions of the fruit to suit your own taste.

DRESSING

1 bunch green onion tops, thinly sliced

½ cup cider vinegar

½ cup granulated sugar

1 tablespoon Dijon mustard

1 cup canola oil

1 tablespoon poppy seeds

SALAD

1 cup slivered almonds

12 ounces mesclun

3 cups shredded red cabbage

1 15-ounce can mandarin oranges, drained

1½ pints strawberries, sliced, and/or whole raspberries and/or blueberries

Place all of the ingredients for the dressing except the poppy seeds in a blender and process until smooth. Stir in the poppy seeds. Refrigerate until needed. Preheat the oven to 350°F. Place the almonds on a baking sheet and toast for 5 to 7 minutes until lightly colored, stirring occasionally. Remove from the pan immediately and cool.

Combine the greens, cabbage, oranges, and berries in a large salad bowl. Toss with enough dressing to coat. Add the almonds, toss again, and serve.

Serves 8

Frico
(Lacy Cheese Crisps)

Easy to make, the crisps are a delightful salad garnish or cocktail nibble.

½ cup finely shredded Parmesan cheese
(preferably imported Parmigiano-Reggiano)
½ cup finely shredded aged Asiago cheese

Position a rack in the middle of the oven and preheat to 350°F. Line a baking sheet with parchment. Using a ramekin or cup, trace circles, about 3½ inches in diameter, on the parchment about 1 inch apart. Turn the parchment over, pencil side down, onto the baking sheet.

Combine the cheeses in a bowl. Spoon well-rounded tablespoons of cheese onto the parchment and gently spread into circles, using the pencil outlines as guides. Bake until pale gold. Remove the parchment sheet from the pan and let the crisps cool for a minute until they firm up enough to remove to wire racks. Cool completely. Store in an airtight container between layers of waxed paper for up to 2 days. The crisps taste best if allowed to rest for several hours before serving.

Makes 12 to 14

Greek Orzo Salad

This zesty salad can be served as a main course or as a side dish with grilled or simply cooked meat, seafood, or poultry. It holds up well on a buffet.

DRESSING

1 medium clove garlic, minced
¼ cup red wine vinegar
1 cup olive oil

1 teaspoon dried basil
1 teaspoon Greek oregano

SALAD

1 pound orzo pasta
6 plum tomatoes, diced
½ cup diced red onion
2 small zucchini, diced

½ pound Kalamata olives, pitted
    and sliced
1 pound feta cheese, crumbled

In a small bowl, whisk together the garlic, vinegar, olive oil, basil, and oregano. Set aside. Boil the pasta in plenty of salted water until al dente. Drain, rinse in cold water, and drain well.

In a large bowl, combine the orzo with the tomatoes, onions, zucchini, olives, and feta and toss. Add dressing to taste and toss again. Serve immediately or cover and chill.

Serves 4 to 8

Strawberry and Onion Salad with Creamy Poppy Seed Dressing

Strawberries and onions? It may sound like an odd combination at first, but wait until you try this gorgeous salad!

DRESSING

½ cup mayonnaise
2 tablespoons vinegar
⅓ cup sugar

¼ cup whole milk
2 tablespoons poppy seeds

SALAD

1 head romaine lettuce, torn
1 pint fresh strawberries, sliced
1 avocado, cut into chunks

1 small to medium red or sweet white
    onion, thinly sliced

Place all the ingredients for the dressing in a jar. Cover and shake until blended. Add more sugar or vinegar to taste. (The dressing can be refrigerated for several days.)

Place the salad ingredients in a large bowl. Add enough dressing to coat lightly. Toss well and serve.

Serves 4 to 6

Fruited Chicken Salad
with Tarragon Mayonnaise

Raisins, grapes, prunes, and macadamia nuts add lots of taste and texture to this pretty main course salad. The mayonnaise is delicious with cold shrimp or salmon, or on a chicken sandwich.

Mayonnaise

2 large eggs, at room temperature
2 teaspoons freshly squeezed lemon juice
2 teaspoons tarragon vinegar
1 teaspoon dry mustard
1 teaspoon dried tarragon

¾ teaspoon curry powder
1½ to 2 teaspoons salt
Freshly ground pepper
2 cups vegetable oil

Chicken Salad

4 whole chicken breasts, split
2 quarts chicken stock or low-salt broth
2 celery stalks, cut into fine julienne
¾ cup seedless green grapes
½ cup golden raisins
½ cup dried pitted prunes, cut crosswise
1 bunch chives, snipped

½ cup coarsely chopped
   macadamia nuts
Salt and freshly ground pepper
Boston lettuce cups
Thin slices of melon, peaches,
   and/or pears
Lime wedges

Combine all the ingredients for the mayonnaise except the oil in a food processor or blender. With the machine running, dribble in the vegetable oil until the mixture emulsifies. Add the remaining oil in a thin stream. Adjust the seasoning and refrigerate until needed. (Makes about 2 cups.)

Poach the chicken breasts in enough barely simmering stock to cover for 15 to 20 minutes or until just done. Remove the breasts from the stock and cool. Remove the skin and bones and cut the meat into 1-inch cubes. Place the chicken in a bowl and add the celery, grapes, raisins, prunes, chives, nuts, salt, and pepper. Gently toss with enough mayonnaise to moisten well. Adjust the seasoning and chill.

To serve, spoon the salad into the lettuce cups. Garnish with the sliced fruit and lime wedges.

Serves 6 to 8

Grilled Figs with Prosciutto and Arugula Salad

Fresh figs with prosciutto is a classic Italian antipasto. This luscious, first-course salad gives it a whole new dimension.

2 to 3 tablespoons balsamic vinegar
Salt and freshly ground black pepper
6 tablespoons olive oil
8 large, ripe black or green figs

8 to 12 paper thin slices imported
   prosciutto
1 5-ounce bag arugula
Lemon or lime wedges for garnish

In a small bowl, whisk 2 tablespoons of vinegar with a pinch of salt. Whisk in the oil and season with pepper. Add more vinegar to taste. Set the dressing aside.

Cut the figs in half lengthwise and brush them lightly with olive oil. Grill over an outdoor grill, or indoors on a ridged grill pan, until warmed through, about 1 minute on each side. (The figs can also be carefully broiled.)

Ruffle 2 or 3 slices of prosciutto attractively on each plate. In a bowl, toss 4 to 5 handfuls of arugula with enough dressing to coat lightly and mound on the plates. Arrange the figs on the prosciutto and drizzle them with a little dressing. Grind black pepper over the salads, garnish with lemon or lime wedges, and serve immediately.

Serves 4

Potato Salad with Beets and Walnuts

The beets contribute earthy flavor and turn the dressing in this creamy salad a pretty pink.

3 pounds waxy, new potatoes
2 cups mayonnaise
2 cups sour cream
1 to 2 large yellow onions,
   finely minced or grated
2 16-ounce jars beets, drained, cut
   into pieces or julienned

1 16-ounce jar sweet cucumber pickles
   (without garlic), finely chopped
1 cup finely chopped celery
Lemon juice to taste
8 ounces walnuts, finely chopped
Salt and freshly ground pepper

Place the potatoes in a large pot with cold water to cover. Bring to a simmer and cook until the potatoes are tender, about 15 to 20 minutes. Drain and cool.

Combine the remaining ingredients in a large bowl. Peel and slice the potatoes or cut them into dice. Fold them into the dressing. Taste for seasoning. Refrigerate the salad for several hours or overnight.

Serves 8

Lobster and Soba Noodle Salad

Made from buckwheat flour, Japanese soba noodles have a delicious, nutty flavor. The noodles, sweet lobster, crunchy vegetables, and sesame-soy dressing are a winning combination.

1 tablespoon sesame seeds
6 ounces soba noodles
1 tablespoon vegetable oil
12 ounces steamed lobster tail meat, sliced into medallions
1 red bell pepper, julienned

2 scallions, julienned
1 medium cucumber, seeded and julienned
Sesame-Soy Dressing
Leaves from 6 sprigs fresh mint, torn
Leaves from 6 sprigs fresh cilantro

Place the sesame seeds in a small skillet. Toast them over medium heat until fragrant and golden, about 1 minute. Transfer the seeds to a small bowl.

Bring a large pot of water to a boil. Add the noodles and cook until al dente. Meanwhile, fill a large bowl with water and ice. Drain the noodles and plunge them into the ice bath. Drain well and transfer to a bowl. Drizzle the noodles with the vegetable oil and toss gently to coat. Add the lobster, red pepper, scallions, cucumber, dressing, herbs, and sesame seeds. Toss and serve.

SESAME-SOY DRESSING
3 tablespoons sugar
¼ cup soy sauce

¼ cup wine vinegar
6 tablespoons toasted sesame oil

Combine all of the ingredients in a bowl and whisk until the sugar dissolves. Cover tightly and refrigerate for up to 3 days. Makes 1 cup.

Serves 4 as a main course

Antipasto Pasta Salad

This robust pasta salad is always a hit. Vary the proportions to suit your own taste.

1 pound rotini pasta
3 to 4 tablespoons olive oil
1 can small, pitted, black California olives
1 pint cherry tomatoes, halved
5 or 6 green onions, sliced
1 or more thin pepperoni
  sausage sticks, sliced
1 12-ounce jar marinated mushrooms,
  drained and halved

Garlic powder
2 to 3 teaspoons dried
  Greek oregano
Seasoned salt
Freshly ground pepper
2 or more tablespoons
  balsamic vinegar
½ cup grated Parmesan cheese
¼ cup thinly sliced basil leaves

Boil the pasta in plenty of salted water until al dente. Drain, rinse in cold water, and drain well. Transfer to a large bowl and toss with enough olive oil to lightly coat. Add the olives, tomatoes, green onions, pepperoni, and mushrooms. Combine well. Sprinkle with garlic powder, oregano, seasoned salt, and pepper. Add the balsamic vinegar and grated Parmesan cheese, and toss to combine. Adjust the seasoning. Let the salad stand for 30 minutes or refrigerate overnight. (Bring to room temperature before serving.) When ready to serve, sprinkle sliced basil over the salad and toss.

Serves 8 to 12

Corn and Black Bean Salad

For a smoky flavor, grill the corn for this colorful side salad. It's wonderful with grilled shrimp or lobster.

6 to 7 ears sweet corn, husked
  (3 cups kernels)
4 cups cooked black beans
¾ cup diced red bell pepper
¾ cup diced green bell pepper and/or
  poblano chili pepper
¾ cup diced red onion
½ cup thinly sliced scallions
1 pint cherry tomatoes, halved
2 or more jalapeño peppers,
  seeded and minced

1 bunch cilantro, stems
  discarded, chopped
Juice from 2 to 3 large limes,
  or to taste
1 teaspoon ground cumin,
  or to taste
Salt and freshly ground pepper
2 Hass avocados, diced
  (optional)

Boil or steam the corn until crisp-tender, about 3 minutes, or grill until tender and lightly browned. Cool. Cut the kernels from the cobs and place in a large bowl. Add all the remaining ingredients except the avocado and combine. Let stand for at least 1 hour or refrigerate overnight. Gently fold in the avocado before serving.

Serves 12 or more

Stephanie's Romaine Salad

Everyone raves about this simple salad which is reminiscent of a Caesar. You'll make it again and again.

¼ teaspoon salt
1 small clove garlic, put through
  a garlic press
¼ cup freshly squeezed lemon juice
½ to ¾ cup olive oil

2 to 3 romaine lettuce hearts
Wedge of aged Parmesan cheese
Croutons, homemade or packaged
Freshly ground pepper

Whisk the salt, garlic, and lemon juice together in a small bowl. Whisk in ½ cup of olive oil. The dressing should be on the tart side. Add more oil to taste. (The dressing can be refrigerated for 1 week.)

Cut the romaine hearts crosswise into ½-inch thick ribbons and place them in a large salad bowl. Shred or coarsely grate a generous amount of Parmesan over the top of the salad. Add the croutons and freshly ground pepper. Toss with enough dressing to coat and serve.

Serves 4

My Favorite Potato Salad

Chicago television newscaster Mary Ann Childers shared this recipe. She loves it because it's so easy to make and tastes like she did something fancy!

20 small potatoes, brown and
  red skinned
1 10-ounce package frozen
  baby peas
1 medium Vidalia or white onion,
  chopped
¼ cup chopped scallions

2 to 3 large stalks celery,
  chopped fine
Freshly ground pepper
Chopped fresh basil (to taste)
Finely chopped fresh rosemary,
  (to taste)
¼ to ½ cup Viva Italian Salad Dressing

Scrub the potatoes, pierce them with a fork, and microwave until soft. Cool and refrigerate overnight.

Place the peas in a strainer and run hot water over them just until separated. Drain well. Slice the potatoes into rounds and place them in a bowl. Add the remaining ingredients and toss gently. Refrigerate overnight.

Serves 4

Red and Green Christmas Salad
with Warm Champagne Vinaigrette

A festive salad fit for a Christmas celebration! The ruby red pomegranate seeds add jewel-like color and a sweet-tart accent.

Seeds from one pomegranate
10 cups torn spinach leaves
   or baby spinach

1 medium avocado, peeled, pitted,
   and thinly sliced
1 cup Warm Champagne Vinaigrette

With a small, sharp knife, cut the peel around the top crown of the pomegranate. Try not to cut into the fruit (pomegranate juice stains badly). Score the peel lengthwise into quarters. Working in a large bowl filled with water, strip away the peel and break the pomegranate into pieces. Pull the seeds away from the bitter, white membranes. The peel and membranes will float to the top while the seeds sink to the bottom of the bowl. Skim off the membranes and peel and drain the seeds through a sieve. Pick out any bits of membrane and pat the seeds dry. Set aside or refrigerate for up to 1 day.

Place the spinach in a large salad bowl. Arrange the avocado slices around the edge of the salad and place the pomegranate seeds in the center. Prepare the dressing. At the table, pour 1 cup of the warm dressing over the salad. Toss and serve.

WARM CHAMPAGNE VINAIGRETTE

1 cup champagne vinegar
2 tablespoons sugar
1½ tablespoons all-purpose flour
2 teaspoons dry vermouth
1 teaspoon Dijon mustard

1 egg, beaten
3 tablespoons whipping cream
2 cups olive oil
Salt and freshly ground pepper

Combine the vinegar, sugar, flour, vermouth, and mustard in a small saucepan. Bring to a simmer over medium heat. Turn the heat down to low. Whisk in the egg and cream very gradually. Whisk in the oil in a thin, steady stream. Season with salt and pepper. Use warm. Makes 3 cups.

Serves 8

Scallops and Mussels Remoulade

Serve this delectable New Orleans–style salad with marinated asparagus spears and sliced tomatoes. Don't discard the cooking liquid; it's a great addition to a fish soup, a seafood risotto, or a pasta sauce.

1 cup mayonnaise
Juice from one lemon
1 dill pickle, minced
1 tablespoon prepared mustard
1 tablespoon finely chopped parsley
1 tablespoon finely chopped chives
4 dozen mussels
1 pound sea scallops

1 small onion, chopped
1 clove garlic, minced
1 cup dry white wine
1 cup chicken broth
Boston lettuce leaves
Paprika
Minced chives or parsley for garnish

In a small bowl, combine the mayonnaise, lemon juice, dill pickle, mustard, parsley, and chives. Refrigerate until needed.

Just before cooking, scrub the mussels under cold water and debeard. Discard any that will not close when the shells are pressed together. Remove the side muscle from the scallops. Place the mussels and scallops in a large saucepan and add the onion, garlic, wine, and chicken broth. Cover and bring to a simmer. Simmer until the mussels open and the scallops are barely cooked through, about 3 minutes. With a slotted spoon, remove the seafood to a rimmed baking sheet and cool. Place the scallops in a bowl. Remove the mussels from the shells and add them to the scallops. Discard any unopened mussels. Add the dressing and combine. Chill well.

Arrange lettuce leaves on chilled plates and top with the seafood. If desired, sprinkle with paprika and chives or parsley.

Serves 6

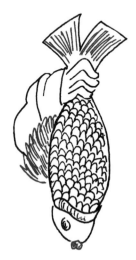

Seafood Pasta Salad with Louis Dressing

The flavorful dressing brings this wonderful salad to center stage. Serve it as part of a buffet or as an entrée.

DRESSING

2 cups mayonnaise
Dash Worcestershire sauce
1 teaspoon prepared mustard

¼ cup chili sauce
4 green onions with tops, chopped
Sweet pickle relish to taste

SALAD

1 pound raw medium-sized shrimp
¾ pound scallops
2 tablespoons olive oil
1 7-ounce box tiny macaroni pasta, such as bows or shells
1 7½-ounce can crabmeat, drained and flaked

1 6½-ounce can white tuna in water, drained and flaked
2 cups chopped celery
1 cup diced cucumber
1 cup diced green pepper
Romaine lettuce leaves

Combine all the ingredients for the dressing in a small bowl, cover, and refrigerate until needed.

Drop the shrimp into 4 quarts of boiling, salted water. Cook just until they are pink and firm (the water may not come back to the boil). Drain and plunge the shrimp into cold water. Peel, devein, and set them aside.

Remove the side muscle from the scallops. Heat a large skillet (non-stick is fine) over medium-high heat until very hot and add the oil. Add as many scallops as will fit in one layer without touching. Cook until they are golden brown and just done, turning once, about 2 minutes per side, depending on thickness. Do not move them around in the pan. Remove the scallops to a plate. Cook any remaining scallops, add them to the plate, and let them cool.

Boil the pasta in plenty of salted water until al dente. Drain, rinse under cold water and drain well. Place all of the salad ingredients, except the lettuce, in a large bowl. Add the dressing and toss lightly. Chill.

Line a serving bowl with lettuce leaves. Spoon the salad into the bowl and serve.

Serves 10 to 12 as part of a buffet

Sesame Beef and Snow Pea Salad

Keep this quick main course salad in mind when you have leftover roast beef or steak.

DRESSING

5 tablespoons vegetable oil

3 to 4 tablespoons rice wine vinegar

5 teaspoons Asian sesame oil

5 teaspoons soy sauce

1 to 2 cloves garlic, minced

¼ to ½ teaspoon crushed
red pepper flakes

Salt and pepper

SALAD

4 ounces snow peas

¾ to 1 pound rare roast beef or
steak, cut into strips

4 ounces white mushrooms,
thinly sliced

1 large yellow or red bell pepper,
cut into strips

4 tablespoons toasted
sesame seeds

3 bunches young arugula,
stems removed

1 small head radicchio, torn into
bite-sized pieces (optional)

Tomato wedges

Whisk the dressing ingredients together in a small bowl. Add more vinegar or oil to taste. Set aside. Place the snow peas in a microwavable container with ¼ inch water. Cover and microwave on high for about 1 minute (or blanch in boiling, salted water until crisp-tender, about 1 to 2 minutes). Drain the peas and plunge them into cold water. Drain, dry, and remove the strings.

Place the salad ingredients in a large bowl. Add dressing to taste and toss.

Serves 6

Southwestern Coleslaw

Colorful, tangy, and spicy, this slaw adds a nice kick to grilled meats, fish, and poultry.

1 large head green cabbage, thinly sliced

1 green bell pepper, thinly sliced

1 red bell pepper, thinly sliced

½ to 1 cup chopped fresh cilantro

2 small jalapeño chilies, halved,
seeded, and minced

3 tablespoons olive oil

3 tablespoons canola oil

2 tablespoons fresh lime juice

½ to 1 tablespoon ground cumin

Salt and freshly ground pepper

Toss the cabbage, peppers, cilantro, and chilies together in a large bowl. In a small bowl, whisk together the oils, lime juice and cumin. Pour the dressing over the cabbage, season with salt and pepper, and toss. The slaw can be refrigerated for 2 hours.

Serves 16 to 24

Spinach Salad with Pineapple, Spiced Almonds, and Raspberry Vinaigrette

Vivid colors and fresh, lively flavor set this salad apart. The dressing is lovely on steamed asparagus.

VINAIGRETTE

1 pint fresh or frozen whole raspberries
½ cup water
1 tablespoon Dijon mustard
¼ cup balsamic vinegar
¼ cup raspberry vinegar

¼ cup olive oil
⅛ teaspoon kosher salt
Freshly ground pepper
⅛ teaspoon dried or fresh thyme
5 to 6 packets sweetener or sugar

SALAD

1 cup slivered almonds
Cooking spray
Old Bay or Emeril's
   Essence seasoning
10 cups baby spinach, well
   washed, spun dry

6 mushrooms, sliced
1½ cups fresh, diced pineapple
½ medium red onion, sliced
½ cup sweetened, dried cranberries

Puree the raspberries with the water in a blender. Force the puree through a fine sieve into a bowl. Rinse the blender and return the strained puree. Add all the remaining ingredients for the dressing and blend. Add more sweetener if needed. (The dressing can be refrigerated for 2 weeks.)

Place the almonds in a skillet. Spray them with cooking spray and season with Old Bay or Emeril's Essence seasoning. Sauté over medium heat, stirring constantly, until lightly browned. Remove them from the pan immediately and set aside to cool.

In a large salad bowl, combine the spinach, mushrooms, pineapple, red onion, and dried cranberries. Add enough dressing to coat and toss. Sprinkle the almonds over the salad and serve.

Serves 4 to 6

Spring Vegetable Salad with Mint and Parmesan Cheese Curls

Bright green and fresh as springtime, this vegetable salad is a superb first course. The key to success is not to overcook the vegetables. Everything but the final assembly is done in advance.

1 pound fresh whole fava beans
Salt and freshly ground pepper
16 slim asparagus stalks, trimmed
½ pound sugar snap peas, strings removed
¼ pound haricots verts, trimmed
¼ cup extra-virgin olive oil

2 tablespoons balsamic vinegar
2 thin slices red onion, quartered
4 medium-size fresh mint leaves
2 to 3 medium-size fresh basil leaves
Wedge of Parmesan cheese
 (preferably imported)

Several hours prior to serving, shell the fava beans. Bring 4 quarts of water and 1 tablespoon of salt to a boil. Blanch the asparagus until crisp-tender, about 1 to 2 minutes. Remove with tongs and plunge them into a bowl of ice water to stop the cooking and set their color. Drain on kitchen towels. Repeat with the snap peas (cook for about 1 minute) and haricots verts (cook about 2 to 3 minutes). Boil the fava beans for 1 minute, drain, and plunge them into the ice water. Discard the blanching water. Remove the outer skin from the favas by pulling it away at the indented end and squeezing gently to pop the bean out. Discard the skins. Pat the vegetables dry and refrigerate until needed.

In a small bowl, whisk together the olive oil and vinegar, and season with salt and pepper. Place the asparagus in a bowl and toss with a little dressing. Arrange the spears on 4 plates. Add the remaining vegetables to the bowl. Cut the mint and basil into fine julienne and scatter over the vegetables. Gently toss the vegetables with enough dressing to lightly coat and spoon them over the asparagus. With a vegetable peeler, shave several Parmesan cheese curls over each salad.

Serves 4

Tomato Salad with Basil Vinaigrette

Make this summery salad when garden tomatoes are at their peak.

½ cup lightly packed fresh basil leaves
2 to 4 fresh arugula leaves
¼ cup wine vinegar
1 teaspoon honey

½ cup olive oil
Dash Tabasco or other hot sauce
Salt and freshly ground pepper
4 ripe tomatoes

Process the basil, arugula, vinegar, honey, and oil in a blender. Season with Tabasco, salt, and pepper. Adjust the balance. (The vinaigrette can be refrigerated for 2 or 3 days.) Slice the tomatoes and arrange them on a platter. Drizzle with vinaigrette and serve.

Serves 4

Fennel, Orange, and Arugula Salad

The crisp, licorice-flavored fennel, tart-sweet oranges, and peppery arugula in this salad really wake up the palate. It's especially nice in the winter months before or after a hearty entrée.

3 tablespoons freshly squeezed lemon juice
¼ teaspoon salt
3 to 4 tablespoons olive oil
5 or 6 blood oranges, or 3 large
  navel oranges
2 medium bulbs fresh fennel

Thinly sliced red onion, to taste
1 bunch young arugula, or 2
  bunches watercress
Freshly ground black pepper
Imported black olives
Wedge of aged Parmesan cheese

In a small bowl, whisk together the lemon juice, salt, and olive oil. Set aside. Cut off the ends of the oranges and place them on a cutting board, cut side down. With a small, sharp knife, remove the peel and all of the bitter, white pith. Working over a bowl, cut between the membranes to release the segments. Squeeze the juice from the pulp over the segments. Cut off and discard the fennel stalks. With a vegetable peeler, peel a thin layer from the outside of each bulb. Trim the root ends and cut the bulbs in half lengthwise. Cut out the core and thinly slice the fennel crosswise. If not using immediately, place the slices in a bowl of cold water. (The dressing, oranges, and fennel can be refrigerated for several hours.)

Drain the oranges, reserving the juice, and place them in a large bowl. Add 2 tablespoons of the juice to the dressing. Drain the fennel, pat dry, and add it to the bowl along with the onions and arugula. Grind fresh pepper over the salad and toss with enough dressing to lightly coat. Arrange the salad on the plates and add a few olives. With a vegetable peeler, shave a few curls of Parmesan over each salad and serve.

Serves 6

Vietnamese Noodle Salad with Seared Shrimp

Despite the lengthy list of ingredients, this main course summer salad goes together quickly. Don't omit the fish sauce; it adds a distinctive flavor that is not at all fishy.

DRESSING (NUOC CHAM)
1 clove garlic
1 or more Thai bird chilies (very hot),
   or small jalapeño or serrano chilies,
   seeded and thinly sliced, or ½ teaspoon
   ground chili paste
⅔ cup water

¼ cup or more sugar
6 tablespoons or more Vietnamese
   fish sauce (available at Asian markets)
3 tablespoons or more fresh lime juice
1 green onion (white part only),
   thinly sliced

NOODLES AND SALAD
8 ounces dried Asian rice
   vermicelli noodles
2 cups shredded romaine or
   leaf lettuce
1½ cups fresh, crisp bean sprouts
2 cups peeled, seeded,
   thinly sliced cucumber

⅓ cup finely julienned or
   shredded carrot
⅓ cup or more small, whole mint
   leaves, or torn larger leaves
⅓ cup or more small, whole basil
   leaves, or torn larger leaves

SHRIMP TOPPING
2 tablespoons vegetable oil
2 large shallots, thinly sliced
1 clove garlic, minced
1 pound large shrimp, peeled
   and deveined
⅓ cup julienned red bell pepper

6 dried shitake or black mushroom
   caps soaked in hot water for
   30 minutes and thinly sliced
1 tablespoon Vietnamese fish sauce
1 teaspoon sugar

GARNISH
½ cup chopped, unsalted, roasted peanuts
Small sprigs of cilantro

For the dressing, pound the garlic and chili together with a mortar and pestle or finely mince them together. (If using chili paste, crush or mince the garlic and combine with the paste.) Combine the remaining ingredients in a bowl and adjust the balance. Add the chili-garlic mixture a little at a time to taste. Let the dressing stand for at least 30 minutes. (Nuoc cham can be refrigerated for 2 weeks.)

Drop the noodles into plenty of boiling water. Cook, stirring and testing frequently, until the noodles are tender but still firm, about 3 to 4 minutes. Drain and rinse under cold water until cool. Let them stand in the colander for 30 minutes. Transfer them to a bowl and set aside for up to 2 hours.

Combine the salad ingredients in a bowl, cover with a damp paper towel, and refrigerate for up to 2 hours. Remove the dressing and salad from the refrigerator 15 minutes prior to serving.

When ready to serve, heat a large skillet over high heat until hot and add the oil. Add the shallots and stir-fry for 30 seconds. Add the garlic and shrimp and stir-fry for 1 minute. Add the bell peppers, mushrooms, fish sauce, and sugar. Stir-fry until the shrimp are pink and just cooked through, 1 to 2 minutes. Remove the topping to a bowl.

Portion the salad into 4 bowls. Loosen the noodles with your fingers and mound them over the salads. Top with the warm shrimp and vegetables and sprinkle with peanuts. Tear the cilantro sprigs over the salads and serve. Each diner should add nuoc cham to taste and toss the salad in the bowl.

Serves 4

Zucchini and Carrot Slaw with Papaya Vinaigrette

With its fruity, slightly sweet dressing, this slaw is terrific with barbecued ribs, pork, and chicken.

VINAIGRETTE

1 medium papaya, peeled, seeded, and diced (about 1 cup)
1 large shallot, chopped (about 2 tablespoons)
8 to 10 medium basil leaves, torn
¼ cup white wine vinegar

3 teaspoons honey
¼ cup safflower or vegetable oil
¼ cup plus 2 tablespoons olive oil
Fresh lemon juice (optional)
Salt and freshly ground pepper to taste
A few drops Tabasco or other hot sauce

SLAW

2 pounds green zucchini
2 pounds yellow zucchini or summer squash
1 pound carrots

Process the papaya, shallot, basil, vinegar, and honey in a blender until smooth. With the machine running, slowly add the oils. Taste and add more oil if necessary. If the vinaigrette needs more acid, add lemon juice instead of vinegar. Add salt, pepper, and a few drops of Tabasco. Set aside.

Slice the vegetables into matchsticks with a mandolin or the julienne blade of a food processor. Place them in a bowl and toss with enough dressing to coat. Cover and chill for several hours or overnight. The slaw will keep for a day or two longer.

Serves 12

Warm Asian Quail Salad
with Bitter Greens and Mango Salsa

These small gamebirds pack lots of rich flavor. The Asian seasoning, slightly bitter greens, and fruity salsa are an inspired combination. The salsa is also delicious with grilled seafood, chicken, and pork.

MARINADE AND QUAIL

¾ cup soy sauce
½ cup water
¼ cup dry sherry
2 tablespoons Asian sesame oil
2 tablespoons light brown sugar
2 whole star anise pods

1 tablespoon chopped fresh ginger
3 cloves garlic, chopped
6 scallions, chopped

6 boneless quail, 3 to 4 ounces each
Freshly ground black pepper

DRESSING AND SALAD

1 tablespoon fresh lime or lemon juice
2 tablespoons rice wine vinegar
¼ teaspoon sugar
Salt and freshly ground pepper

3 to 6 tablespoons canola
   or vegetable oil
6 to 8 ounces mixed baby Asian salad
   greens or mesclun

MANGO SALSA

1½ cups ripe mango in small dice
¾ cup seeded, ripe tomato
   in small dice
⅓ cup red bell pepper in small dice
1 to 2 jalapeño peppers, seeded
   and minced

Juice from 1 to 2 large limes
⅓ cup chopped cilantro
½ teaspoon or more ground cumin
Salt and freshly ground pepper

In a non-reactive saucepan, bring all of the marinade ingredients to a boil. Stir to dissolve the sugar and cool. Butterfly the quail, rinse, and pat them dry. Place them in a non-reactive bowl and pour on the marinade. Cover and refrigerate for 4 hours.

For the dressing, whisk together the lime juice, vinegar, sugar, salt, and pepper in a bowl. Whisk in 3 tablespoons of oil. Add more oil as necessary. Set aside.

Combine the ingredients for the salsa in a bowl and let stand for 30 minutes before serving, or refrigerate for several hours. Bring to room temperature before serving.

Drain the quail and season with pepper. Grill them over ash-covered coals, skin side down, for about 3 to 4 minutes. Turn and grill about 2 to 3 minutes longer. The meat should be juicy and tinged with pink. (The quail can also be broiled.)

In a large bowl, toss the greens with enough dressing to coat lightly and mound on 6 plates. Arrange 1 quail on each salad and top with some of the salsa. Pass the remaining salsa.

Serves 6 as a first course

Warm Scallop Salad with Beets, Oranges, and Citrus Vinaigrette

The color alone is worth making this beautiful salad! If available, use dry-pack scallops. With no water or chemicals added, they keep their sweet, delicate flavor and brown beautifully.

SALAD

4 medium beets, mixed colors if possible
2 large navel oranges
8 cups loosely packed baby greens
1 pound sea scallops (dry-pack preferred)

Salt and freshly ground pepper
2 tablespoons olive oil
1 tablespoon unsalted butter

CITRUS VINAIGRETTE

2 tablespoons fresh orange juice
1 teaspoon grated orange zest
2 tablespoons sherry vinegar

Salt and freshly ground pepper
3 to 6 tablespoons olive oil

Preheat the oven to 450°F. Rinse the beets and trim off all but 1 inch of the tops. Wrap each in foil and place them in a small roasting pan. Roast until the beets are tender when pierced through the foil with a skewer, about 45 minutes to 1 hour. Open the foil and cool. Peel the beets and cut them into wedges. Refrigerate them, covered, until needed. (If using mixed colors, keep red beets separate.)

Cut off the ends of the oranges and place them on a cutting board, cut side down. With a small, sharp knife, remove all of the rind and bitter, white pith. Working over a bowl, cut between the membranes to release the segments. Squeeze the juice from the pulp over the segments. Measure out 2 tablespoons of the juice and place it in a small bowl. Add the grated zest, vinegar, salt, and pepper. Whisk in 3 tablespoons of oil. Taste and add more oil if necessary. Refrigerate the oranges and dressing until needed.

Drain the oranges and place them in a large salad bowl. Add golden or candy striped beets and the salad greens. Set aside.

Remove the side muscle from each scallop and season with salt and pepper. Heat a large skillet over medium-high heat until hot. Add the oil and butter. Add as many scallops as will fit comfortably in the pan without touching and sear until golden, about 2 minutes. Do not move them around in the pan. Turn and cook the second side, about 1 to 2 minutes longer, depending on thickness. Add a little more butter if necessary. When done, the scallops should be golden brown and slightly opaque in the center. Remove them to a plate and keep warm while cooking any remaining scallops.

Toss the salad with enough dressing to lightly coat and mound on 4 plates. Gently toss red beets with a little dressing and tuck them into the salads. Arrange the scallops around the salads and serve.

Serves 4 as a first course

Pasta & Grains

Bucatini Frutti di Mare
(Hollow Spaghetti with Seafood Sauce)

When it comes to pasta, timing is everything! The only trick to this perennial favorite is not to over-cook the seafood or the pasta. Garlic bread and a crisp Pinot Grigio are good accompaniments.

16 littleneck or manila clams
16 cultivated black mussels
½ pound sea scallops
¾ pound medium shrimp
½ pound cleaned squid
3 tablespoons olive oil
1 tablespoon minced garlic
2 tablespoons finely chopped
   flat leaf parsley

½ cup dry white wine or dry
   white vermouth
3 cups canned plum tomatoes in
   juice, drained and well crushed,
   plus ½ cup of the juice
Salt and freshly ground pepper
⅓ cup chopped fresh basil
Crushed red pepper flakes
1 pound bucatini, perciatelli, or spaghetti

Place the clams and mussels in a bowl and refrigerate, uncovered. Remove the side muscle from the scallops and cut them in half crosswise. Peel and devein the shrimp. Cover and refrigerate the scallops and shrimp. Rinse the squid. Cut any large tentacle clusters in half and cut the sacs in ¼-inch thick rings. In a large skillet, heat the olive oil and garlic over medium-high heat. When the garlic starts to sizzle, stir in the parsley and squid. Cook, stirring, for about 1 minute. Do not brown the garlic. Add the wine and reduce it by half. Add the tomatoes, tomato juice, and pepper. Bring to a simmer. Cover and simmer for 15 minutes. Adjust the lid to allow a small opening and simmer until the squid is very tender and the sauce has thickened, about 30 minutes longer. Add salt. (The squid will toughen if salt is added before it is tender.) Set the sauce aside.

Boil the pasta in 5 quarts of salted water until it is about 1 minute from being al dente.

Meanwhile, scrub the clams and mussels under cold water discarding any that will not close. Debeard the mussels. Bring the sauce to a simmer and stir in the basil. Add the clams and mussels. Cover and cook until they open, 2 to 5 minutes. Remove them to a bowl as they open. Discard any that remain closed. Cover and keep warm.

When the pasta is almost ready, add the shrimp and scallops to the sauce and cook, uncovered, until they are barely done, about 2 to 3 minutes. The sauce should be a little loose, but not soupy. Add some of the pasta cooking water if necessary. Drain the pasta and add it to the skillet. Turn it over in the sauce with tongs until it is al dente, about 1 minute longer. Sprinkle with crushed red pepper flakes and transfer to heated pasta bowls. Top with the clams and mussels and serve immediately.

Serves 4

Cavatappi with Turkey Sausage and Peppers

Cavatappi is a short, curly pasta that holds the bits of sausage and peppers very well. Substitute fusilli or penne in this satisfying, rustic-style dish. Serve it with a crunchy green salad, crusty bread, and a Chianti or Dolcetto d'Alba.

¾ pound turkey Italian sausage,
  hot or mild
2 tablespoons olive oil
½ cup minced onion
1 red bell pepper, quartered,
  peeled with a vegetable peeler, and
  cut into thin strips
3 cloves garlic, minced
1 28-ounce can Italian plum tomatoes
  in juice, drained and well crushed,
  juice reserved

2 tablespoons chopped parsley
Salt and freshly ground pepper
1 pound cavatappi or penne
¼ cup cream or milk (optional)
¼ cup chopped fresh basil
Freshly grated Pecorino Romano
  cheese

Place the sausage in the freezer for 30 minutes. Remove the casing and chop the sausage finely. In a large skillet, heat the olive oil over medium-high heat. Add the onion and sauté until wilted. Add the peppers and cook until they begin to soften. Add the sausage and cook until there are no traces of pink, breaking it up well with a wooden spoon. Make an opening in the center of the pan and add the garlic (add a spoonful of oil if the skillet is dry). Sauté briefly and add the tomatoes, reserved juice, and parsley. Season with salt. Add pepper depending on the spiciness of the sausage. Simmer until the sauce thickens, about 25 minutes. Remove from the heat and set aside. (The sauce can be refrigerated at this point or frozen.)

Boil the pasta in 5 quarts of salted water until al dente. Bring the sauce to a simmer and add the basil and cream. The sauce should be a little loose. Add some of the pasta cooking water if necessary. Drain the pasta, add it to the skillet, and combine well with the sauce. Serve with grated cheese.

Serves 4

Creamy Parmesan Polenta

Polenta is a perfect foundation for almost any hearty braise or stew. While instant polenta will do in a pinch, polenta cooked long and slow is a revelation. This method is amazingly simple.

Butter or olive oil
9 cups water
½ chicken bouillon cube
1 cup medium or coarse polenta
(not instant)

2 tablespoons butter, softened
⅓ cup freshly grated Parmesan
cheese
¼ to ⅓ cup freshly grated Pecorino
Romano cheese

Position a rack in the middle of the oven and preheat to 350°F. Grease a wide, heavy saucepan with butter or olive oil. Add the water, bouillon cube, and polenta. Stir well. Bake, uncovered, for 1¼ to 1½ hours or until the water is absorbed and the individual grains are no longer gritty. Stir the polenta with a whisk. If necessary, continue to bake until the polenta is creamy and mounds softly in a spoon. Remove the pan from the oven and let the polenta rest, partly covered, for a few minutes. Add the softened butter and cheese and stir vigorously. Taste for seasoning and serve.

Serves 4

Curried Couscous

This easy side dish is a real winner! It can be prepared a day or two in advance and served hot, at room temperature, or lightly chilled. Try it with pork tenderloin, chicken, or fish, along with a fruit salsa.

1 tablespoon unsalted butter
¼ cup minced shallots
¼ cup finely diced or finely
chopped carrots
1½ cups unflavored couscous
1 cup golden raisins
1 teaspoon salt

Freshly ground pepper
1 teaspoon Madras curry powder
¼ teaspoon ground turmeric
1½ cups boiling water
¼ cup chopped parsley
½ cup sliced almonds, lightly toasted
3 whole green onions, thinly sliced

Heat the butter in a saucepan over medium heat. Add the shallots and carrots and sauté until softened. Stir in the couscous and remove the pan from the heat. Stir in the raisins, salt, and pepper. Combine the curry powder, turmeric, and boiling water and quickly stir it into the couscous. Cover the pan and let stand for 10 to 15 minutes. Fluff the couscous with a fork and stir in the chopped parsley, almonds, and green onions.

Serves 6

Fettuccine Primavera with Salmon

In Italy, adding cheese to a seafood sauce is heresy, but it's very good in this delicate preparation. Pour an Italian Chardonnay or a Sauvignon Blanc.

6 thin asparagus spears
3 tablespoons unsalted butter
½ cup finely chopped onion
1½ cups sliced white or cremini
  mushrooms
¾ cup diced yellow bell pepper
¾ cup diced zucchini
¾ cup diced yellow squash
¾ cup baby peas, unthawed if frozen
2 cloves garlic, finely minced

1¼ cups heavy cream
½ pound fresh salmon, cut in
  ½-inch dice
¼ cup freshly grated Parmesan cheese
Salt and freshly ground pepper
1 pound fettuccine or spaghetti
1½ cups halved cherry tomatoes
¼ cup low-salt chicken broth
¼ to ⅓ cup thinly sliced basil leaves

Snap off the woody ends from the asparagus and steam or boil the spears in salted water until crisp-tender. Drain and run cold water over them until cool. Pat them dry and cut them into pieces on the bias. Set aside. (If only thick asparagus are available, peel the stalks with a vegetable peeler before cooking.)

Melt the butter in a large skillet over medium-high heat. Add the onions and cook until wilted. Add the mushrooms and cook until they begin to color and are tender. Add the yellow pepper, zucchini, and squash. Sauté until they begin to color. Stir in the asparagus, peas, and garlic. Sauté for a moment or two and remove the vegetables to a bowl.

Add 1 cup of cream to the skillet and bring to a simmer. Simmer until it begins to thicken. Add the salmon and continue to simmer until the cream has thickened lightly. Add 2 tablespoons of grated cheese and season with salt and pepper. If necessary, remove the pan from the heat until the pasta is almost ready and reheat.

Meanwhile, boil the pasta in 5 quarts of salted water until not quite al dente. Drain and add it to the simmering sauce. Add the cherry tomatoes, broth, and the remaining ¼ cup of cream. Toss until the pasta is well coated. Add the cooked vegetables, basil, and the remaining grated cheese and toss to combine. If necessary, toss over the heat until most of the sauce has been absorbed, but the pasta is still creamy. Transfer to warm pasta bowls and serve immediately. Pass grated cheese.

Serves 4

Fettuccine with Asparagus and Lemon Cream Sauce

This bright, lemony-flavored dish is elegant in its simplicity. Pair it with an Orvieto.

12 fresh, slender asparagus
4 tablespoons butter
2 shallots, minced
Grated zest (no white pith) and
  juice from 2 large lemons
1 cup heavy cream

1 pound fresh fettuccine, or imported
  dried egg fettuccine
1 tablespoon chopped chives
3 tablespoons minced flat leaf parsley
⅓ cup freshly grated
  Parmesan cheese

Snap off the woody ends of the asparagus and steam or boil the spears in salted water until just tender. Drain, run cold water over them, and pat dry. Cut them into pieces on the bias and set aside. (If only thick asparagus are available, peel the stalks with a vegetable peeler before cooking).

Melt the butter in a large skillet over medium-high heat and sauté the shallots until softened. Add the lemon juice and cream, and season with salt and pepper. Simmer gently until the cream reduces slightly, about 3 minutes. Add the asparagus.

Meanwhile, boil the pasta in 5 quarts of salted water until very al dente. Drain and add to the skillet. Combine the pasta with the sauce and remove the pan from the heat. Add the grated zest, chives, parsley, and cheese and toss again. If necessary, toss it over the heat until most of the sauce has been absorbed, but the pasta is still creamy. Divide the pasta among warm bowls and serve with additional grated cheese.

Serves 4

Fragrant Indian Rice

The name says it all. Serve the rice with a curry or with simply cooked meats, fish, or poultry.

2 cups imported basmati rice
1 tablespoon vegetable oil
¾ teaspoon whole cumin seeds
2 whole, green cardamom pods
2 whole cloves
1 small cinnamon stick, broken
  into 3 pieces

1 small Turkish bay leaf
½ cup finely chopped onions
3 cups water
1 10-ounce package frozen
  baby peas, thawed

Wash the rice according to package directions. Cover with 1 inch of water and soak for 30 minutes. Drain and set aside.

Preheat the oven to 325°F. Heat the oil in a saucepan over medium-high heat. Add the cumin seeds, cardamom pods, cloves, cinnamon, and bay leaf. Stir constantly until the cumin seeds have darkened in color. Add the onions and cook until they begin to brown. Add the rice and water. Cover the pan with foil, then add the lid. Transfer to the oven and bake for 25 minutes. Remove the pan from the oven and quickly scatter the peas over the top of the rice. Replace the lid immediately and let the rice stand for 5 minutes. Remove the bay leaf and cinnamon stick. Fluff the rice with a fork and serve.

Note: Long-grain rice can be substituted. Add water according to package directions.

Serves 6

Linguini Alio e Olio with Soft Shell Crabs

Pasta with garlic and olive oil is a trattorria favorite that's even better when topped with sweet soft shell crabs. Have the fishmonger clean the crabs and cook them on the same day. Shrimp are an excellent substitute and, unlike the seasonal crabs, are available all year. Pour a Pinot Bianco.

5 large cloves garlic
½ cup olive oil
8 small to medium soft shell crabs, cleaned, or 1 pound large shrimp, peeled and deveined
Olive oil
1 pound spaghetti
Salt and pepper

2 tablespoons chopped flat leaf parsley
2 cups seeded, diced tomatoes, or halved or quartered cherry tomatoes
⅓ cup chopped fresh basil
1 teaspoon crushed red pepper flakes

Slice 3 cloves of garlic and place in a small saucepan with ¼ cup of the oil. Heat over very low heat until the garlic just begins to sizzle. Do not let it color. Remove the pan from the heat and set aside.

Heat a large, heavy skillet over medium-high heat. Dry the crabs well with paper towels—they will spatter fiercely if wet—and season them with salt and pepper. Film the bottom of the skillet with olive oil and add the crabs. Cook, pressing the small legs into the oil, until red, crisp, and just done, about 2 to 3 minutes per side.

Meanwhile, boil the pasta in 5 quarts of salted water until very al dente. When the pasta is almost done, pour the garlic oil into a large skillet. Add the remaining ¼ cup of oil. Put all of the garlic, stewed and raw, through a garlic press into the skillet. Place the skillet over medium-high heat. Scoop a ladleful of the pasta cooking water into a measuring cup and drain the pasta. When the garlic begins to sizzle, add salt, the parsley, and ½ cup of the pasta cooking water. Add the pasta to the skillet and toss until the liquid has been absorbed and the pasta has finished cooking, about 1 minute. Add a little more water if necessary. Add the diced tomatoes, basil, red pepper flakes, and toss. Transfer to warm pasta bowls, leaving some of the tomatoes in the pan. Top the pasta with the crabs. Spoon the remaining tomatoes over the crabs and serve.

Serves 4

Vegetable Lasagna with No-Boil Noodles

Despite the long list of ingredients, this delicious lasagna goes together quickly and benefits from being made ahead. The no-boil noodles taste just like freshly made pasta.

TOMATO SAUCE

3 tablespoons olive oil
1 large Spanish onion, finely chopped
8 cloves garlic, finely minced
2 28-ounce cans Italian plum tomatoes in juice, drained and chopped, juice reserved

1 28-ounce can Italian crushed tomatoes
⅓ cup chopped flat leaf parsley
Salt and pepper
¼ cup chopped fresh basil

VEGETABLES

3 zucchini
2 yellow summer squash
1½ to 2 pounds eggplant, peeled

1 large red onion, thinly sliced
1 pound mushrooms, sliced
3 roasted red peppers, cut into strips

FOR ASSEMBLY

1 large egg, lightly beaten
1 pound whole milk ricotta cheese
¼ cup chopped fresh basil

2 cups grated Parmesan cheese
1 box instant (no-boil) lasagna noodles
¾ pound mozzarella, coarsely grated

Heat the olive oil in a large, heavy saucepan. Add the onions and sauté until golden. Add the garlic and cook briefly. Add the tomatoes, tomato juice, parsley, salt, pepper, and basil. Simmer until the sauce thickens. Set aside.

Preheat the oven to 450°F. Slice the eggplant, zucchini, and yellow squash lengthwise ¼- to ½-inch thick. Line a large baking sheet with foil or parchment. Brush the eggplant, zucchini, and summer squash with olive oil, sprinkle with salt, and roast until just tender, about 10 to 15 minutes. Cut the slices crosswise into 2 or 3 pieces.

In a large skillet, sauté the sliced onions in a little olive oil until softened. Remove them to a bowl. Add 2 tablespoons of oil to the skillet and sauté the mushrooms until lightly browned. Add them to the bowl along with the roasted peppers.

Preheat the oven to 350°F. In a bowl, combine the beaten egg with the ricotta, chopped basil, and ½ cup of grated Parmesan. Cover the botton of a 9x13x2-inch pan with a thin layer of sauce and add a layer of noodles. Spread with ⅓ of the ricotta and ⅓ of the vegetables. Top with a layer of sauce, being careful to moisten the edges of the noodles. Add ⅓ of the mozzarella and sprinkle with ¼ of the Parmesan. Repeat until there are 3 layers of filling. Add a final layer of noodles, cover with a layer of sauce, and dust with the remaining Parmesan. Cover the pan with foil and bake for 45 minutes. Uncover and continue to bake until the lasagna is bubbling and a knife inserted in the center comes out hot, about 15 to 20 minutes longer. Let the lasagna rest for at least 30 minutes before cutting.

Note: It's best to let the baked lasagna stand for 3 to 4 hours, or refrigerate overnight. Reheat, loosely covered, in a 325°F oven.

Serves 8

Quadrettini Casserole

Baked pasta dishes are ideal for casual entertaining since almost all of the preparation can be done in advance. Double the recipe for the rich sauce and freeze half to serve with spaghetti or penne.

¼ cup olive oil
¼ cup butter or margarine
½ cup finely chopped carrots
½ cup finely chopped onions
1 cup finely chopped celery
2 cloves garlic, crushed and
    finely minced
1 pound ground beef chuck
3 cups peeled, seeded, chopped
    fresh or canned tomatoes

1 6-ounce can tomato paste
2 teaspoons salt
1½ teaspoons dried oregano
1 teaspoon dried basil
½ teaspoon dried thyme
½ teaspoon Tabasco or other hot sauce
1 10-ounce package frozen chopped
    spinach
2 cups dried spinach noodles
½ cup grated Parmesan cheese

Heat the oil over medium-high heat in a large, heavy saucepan. Add the butter. Add the carrots, onions, celery, and garlic and cook until softened. Add the ground meat and cook until browned, breaking the meat up with a wooden spoon. Add the tomatoes, tomato paste, salt, dried herbs, and hot sauce. Simmer, uncovered, for 1½ hours, stirring occasionally.

Preheat the oven to 350°F. Cook the spinach, drain well, and squeeze to remove excess water. Boil the noodles in plenty of salted water until al dente and drain well. Combine the noodles with the spinach and sauce and transfer to a 2-quart baking dish. Sprinkle the grated cheese over the top of the casserole and bake for 20 minutes or until heated through.

Serves 4

Risotto with Forest Mushrooms, Truffle Oil, and Shaved Parmesan

Truffle oil adds fabulous aroma and highlights the earthy flavor of the mushrooms in this risotto. If you are fortunate enough to find fresh porcini mushrooms, use them in lieu of the dried and fresh mushrooms called for. Pour a Chianti or a Rosso di Montepulciano.

½ ounce dried porcini mushrooms
Olive oil
¾ pound cremini or white
  mushrooms, sliced
2 cloves garlic, minced
7 to 8 cups chicken stock, or canned
  low-salt broth
1 cup minced onions
2 tablespoons minced shallots
2 cups imported Italian Carnaroli or
  Arborio rice

⅔ cup dry white wine or dry
  white vermouth
4 tablespoons freshly grated Pecorino
  Romano cheese
4 tablespoons freshly grated
  Parmesan cheese
2 tablespoons unsalted butter,
  softened
Salt and freshly ground pepper
White truffle oil
A wedge of Parmesan cheese

Rinse the dried porcini quickly in cold water. Place them in a small bowl, cover with 1 cup very hot (not boiling) water, and soak until softened, about 20 to 30 minutes. Scoop out the mushrooms, squeeze them over the bowl, and coarsely chop. Strain the soaking liquid through a fine sieve lined with a double layer of damp cheesecloth or a paper towel and reserve. In a large, heavy skillet, heat 2 tablespoons of olive oil over medium-high heat. Add the fresh mushrooms and sauté until browned. Add the porcini and half of the garlic and cook for a few seconds until fragrant. Transfer the mushrooms to a bowl. Deglaze the pan with ¼ cup hot stock, add the soaking liquid, and set aside. Heat the remaining stock and maintain it just below a simmer.

In a wide, heavy saucepan or Dutch oven (about 10 inches across the top), heat 3 tablespoons of olive oil over medium heat. Add the onions and cook until softened. Add the shallots. Cook until the onions are golden. Add the rice. Stir and toss for 1 minute. Stir in the remaining garlic and cook for a few seconds. Add the wine and stir until it evaporates. Add the deglazing liquid and enough hot stock to barely cover the rice. Bring to a simmer. Stirring almost constantly, cook until the stock is almost absorbed. Continue adding stock in this manner until the rice is creamy and tender, but al dente, about 15 to 18 minutes from the time the wine was added. Remove the pan from the heat. The risotto should be somewhat loose. Add the cheeses and the softened butter. Stir vigorously until thoroughly incorporated. Season with salt and pepper and fold in the mushrooms. Add more stock if necessary to loosen the risotto. It should be moist and creamy, but not soupy. Spoon the risotto into heated soup plates. Drizzle each serving with about 1 teaspoon of truffle oil and shave a few curls of Parmesan cheese over the top with a vegetable peeler. Serve immediately.

Serves 4 as a main course

Risotto with Shrimp and Spinach

Risotto waits for no one! Call everyone to the table before this flavorful risotto is finished, or better yet, draft them to help stir. Offer a glass of Pinot Grigio.

Olive oil
¾ to 1 pound small shrimp,
   peeled and deveined
2 large cloves garlic, minced
5 plum tomatoes, peeled, seeded,
   and diced
7 to 8 cups shrimp stock or 6 cups
   clam juice and 2 cups water
¾ cup minced onions
1 large shallot, minced
2 cups imported Italian Vialone Nano,
   Carnaroli, or Arborio rice
⅔ cup dry white wine or dry
   white vermouth

¼ cup tomato sauce, more or less
2 good handfuls baby spinach, or
   larger leaves, stemmed and torn
4 tablespoons freshly grated Pecorino
   Romano cheese
4 tablespoons freshly grated
   Parmesan cheese
3 tablespoons unsalted butter,
   softened
Salt and freshly ground pepper
2 tablespoons chopped fresh basil
   or flat leaf parsley

In a heavy skillet, heat 2 tablespoons of olive oil over medium-high heat. Add the shrimp and sauté until barely cooked. Stir in half the garlic and the tomatoes and cook for 30 seconds. Transfer to a bowl. Deglaze the skillet with ½ cup of stock and set aside. Heat the remaining stock in a 2-quart saucepan and maintain it just below a simmer.

In a wide, heavy saucepan or Dutch oven (about 10 inches across the top), heat 3 tablespoons of olive oil over medium heat. Add the onions and cook until softened. Add the shallot. Continue to cook until the onions are golden. Add the rice. Stir and toss the rice for 1 minute. Stir in the remaining garlic and cook for a few seconds. Add the wine and stir until it evaporates. Add the reserved deglazing liquid and enough hot stock to just cover the rice. Bring to a simmer. Stirring almost constantly, cook until the stock is almost absorbed. Continue adding stock in this manner until the rice is creamy and tender, but the grains are still a little firm in the center, about 15 to 18 minutes from the time the wine was added. Stir in enough tomato sauce to lightly color the risotto. Remove the pan from the heat and stir in the spinach. The risotto should be fairly loose. Add more stock as necessary. Combine the cheeses and add two-thirds along with all of the softened butter. Stir vigorously until well incorporated. Add more cheese and salt and pepper to taste. Fold in the shrimp. Add more stock to loosen the risotto to a porridge-like consistency. Spoon into heated soup plates and sprinkle with chopped basil or parsley. Serve immediately.

Serves 4 as a main course

Saffron Rice Pilaf with Apricots, Currants, and Pistachios

Serve this aromatic pilaf with fowl, pork, lamb, or fish. It's sensational with Lamb Chops with Pomegranate Sauce.

1 medium bay leaf
2 green cardamom pods
1 small cinnamon stick, broken
   into 3 pieces
1 teaspoon cumin seeds
2 tablespoons unsalted butter or olive oil
1 medium onion, finely chopped
2 cups long grain rice
1¾ cups low-salt chicken broth

Large pinch saffron threads, crumbled
   and steeped in ¼ cup hot water
⅓ cup currants or dark or
   golden raisins
¼ cup chopped dried apricots
Salt and freshly ground pepper
½ cup unsalted pistachios or
   pine nuts

Toast the bay leaf and spices in a small, dry skillet over medium heat. Shake the pan and toss the spices until they are fragrant and the cumin seeds darken somewhat, about 2 minutes. Transfer to a bowl.

Heat the butter or oil in a saucepan and add the onions. Sauté until pale gold. Add the rice and stir to coat with the butter and oil. Add the toasted spices, broth, saffron, currants, apricots, salt, and pepper. Bring to a boil. Lower the heat, cover, and simmer until the broth has been absorbed and the rice is tender. Remove the pan from the heat. Remove the lid and quickly cover the pan with a folded kitchen towel. Let the rice rest for 5 minutes. Fluff with a fork and stir in the nuts.

Serves 6 to 8

Spaghetti with Summer Sauce

Sweet, juicy tomatoes are a must for the uncooked sauce in this sublime dish. Serve it with garlic bread (be sure to save some to mop up the delicious juices); a salad of arugula, radicchio, and Belgian endive tossed with balsamic vinaigrette; and a Pinot Grigio or a light red table wine.

3 to 4 medium-size, ripe, garden
   tomatoes, seeded and cut into
   small dice
Coarse salt
1 to 2 cloves garlic, put through
   a garlic press
¼ cup extra-virgin olive oil

¼ cup torn or chopped
   fresh basil leaves
⅓ pound fresh mozzarella cheese,
   drained and diced (optional)
1 pound spaghetti or thin spaghetti
Crushed red pepper flakes
Grated Parmesan cheese

Combine the tomatoes, salt, garlic, olive oil, and basil in a large bowl. Add the mozzarella. Boil the pasta in 5 quarts of salted water until al dente. Drain well, add it to the bowl, and toss. Sprinkle the pasta with pepper flakes and transfer to pasta bowls. Spoon some of the juices over each portion. Serve with grated cheese and more pepper flakes.

Serves 4

Barley Pilaf

This hearty side dish is delicious with braised lamb shanks, pot roast, roast beef, or roast chicken.

2 tablespoons unsalted butter
½ cup minced carrots
¼ cup minced shallots
½ cup minced leeks (white part only)
5 cups chicken stock or broth
½ cup minced onions

1 cup dry white wine
1½ cups pearled barley
½ cup grated Parmesan cheese
2 tablespoons softened butter
¼ cup chopped parsley
Salt and freshly ground pepper

Heat 1 tablespoon of butter in a small skillet. Sauté the minced carrots, shallots, and leeks until softened. Set aside. In a saucepan, bring the stock to a bare simmer, cover, and keep warm.

Meanwhile, heat 1 tablespoon of butter in a wide, heavy, non-aluminum pan over medium heat. Add the minced onions and sauté until golden. Add the wine and reduce by half. Add the barley and stir for 2 minutes. Add enough hot stock to just cover the barley. Cover and simmer until the barley is tender and creamy, about 20 minutes. Stir frequently and add hot stock, ½ cup at a time, as necessary. Remove the pan from the heat and fold in the sautéed vegetables and grated cheese. Stir in the softened butter, one tablespoon at a time. Add the parsley and season with salt and pepper. The pilaf should be slightly loose. Add a little more broth if necessary. Serve immediately.

Serves 4

Spicy Pasta with Chicken

Asparagus or zucchini are good additions to this quick and easy dish.

½ pound boneless, skinless
    chicken breast
¼ cup herbed or plain olive oil
1 cup sliced mushrooms
½ each red, yellow, and green pepper, sliced
½ small onion, thinly sliced
2 teaspoons minced garlic
Salt

1 teaspoon crushed red
    pepper flakes
½ cup dry white wine
1½ cups tomato sauce
½ cup fresh tomato chunks
6 ounces penne pasta
Grated Parmesan cheese

Cut the chicken into pieces. In a large skillet, heat the oil, add the chicken and brown. Add the mushrooms and sauté for 2 or 3 minutes. Add the peppers and onions and sauté until tender. Add the garlic, salt, pepper flakes, wine, and tomato sauce. Bring to a simmer. Add the tomato chunks and heat through. Meanwhile, boil the pasta in 4 quarts of salted water until al dente and drain. Combine the sauce with the pasta and serve with grated cheese.

Serves 2

Strozzapreti with Porcini Mushroom Sauce

Strozzapreti (priest chokers) originated in Italy's Romagna region where, as one tale goes, the village priest ate for free at the local trattorias. The resourceful owners devised this hearty pasta shape to fill him up before the next—and expensive—meat course was served! With its deep, woodsy flavor, this robust pasta is a satisfying dish on a wintry night. Pair it with a Barbera d'Alba.

1 ounce dried porcini mushrooms
4 tablespoons olive oil
½ cup minced onions
¾ pound cremini or white
    mushrooms, sliced
3 large cloves garlic, minced
1 tablespoon finely chopped flat leaf parsley
1 28-ounce can Italian plum tomatoes
    in juice, drained and well crushed,
    juice reserved

Salt and freshly ground pepper
¼ to ⅓ cup chopped fresh basil
1 pound strozzapreti, penne,
    or ziti
2 tablespoons unsalted butter
Crushed red pepper flakes
Freshly grated Parmesan cheese

Place the porcini in a sieve and rinse quickly under cold water. Transfer them to a small bowl, cover with 1 cup very hot water and soak until softened, about 30 minutes. Scoop the mushrooms from the soaking liquid and squeeze them over the bowl. Rinse again under cold water and squeeze dry. Chop them coarsely. Strain the soaking liquid through a small sieve lined with several layers of damp cheesecloth or a damp paper towel to remove any grit and set aside.

Heat the oil in a large skillet over medium-high heat. Add the onions and sauté until beginning to color. Add the sliced mushrooms and sauté until they begin to color and are tender. Add the porcini and sauté briefly. Stir in the garlic and cook for a few seconds. Add the soaking liquid and reduce it by half. Add the parsley, tomatoes, reserved juice, salt, and pepper. Simmer, uncovered, until the sauce thickens. Add the basil. (The sauce can be refrigerated or frozen.)

Boil the pasta in 5 quarts of salted water until al dente. Meanwhile, bring the sauce to a simmer. Thin with some of the pasta cooking water if necessary. Drain the pasta and add it to the sauce along with the butter. Toss until the butter is melted and the sauce and pasta are combined. Transfer to a heated serving bowl and sprinkle with red pepper flakes. Serve with grated cheese and more pepper flakes.

Serves 4

Toasted Israeli Couscous with Vegetables

Israeli couscous look like small pearls and are especially good with fish, chicken, or lamb.

1 cup Israeli couscous
Olive oil
½ cup minced yellow onion
2 cups vegetable or chicken stock, or
    canned low-salt broth
½ teaspoon salt
¼ cup red onion in small dice
¼ cup carrot in small dice
¼ cup celery in small dice
¼ cup red bell pepper in small dice

¼ cup zucchini in small dice,
    each piece with some green skin
¼ cup yellow squash in small
    dice, each piece with some
    yellow skin
1 small clove garlic, finely minced
¼ cup finely chopped flat leaf parsley
½ cup seeded, ripe tomato in
    small dice
Salt and freshly ground pepper

Toast the couscous in a dry skillet over medium-high heat until lightly colored, rolling them around in the pan frequently. Remove them to a bowl.

In a heavy saucepan, heat 2 tablespoons of olive oil over medium-high heat. Add the yellow onions and sauté until golden. Add the couscous and stir to coat with the oil. Add the stock and salt and bring to a boil. Lower the heat, cover, and simmer until the couscous are tender, about 12 minutes. Pour off any unabsorbed stock.

Meanwhile, heat 1 tablespoon of olive oil in a large skillet over medium heat. Add the red onions, carrots, celery, and bell pepper. Cook until softened. Add the zucchini and yellow squash and cook until just tender. Add the garlic, cook for a few seconds, and stir in the parsley. Remove the pan from the heat and scatter the tomatoes over the top. Set aside until the couscous are done. Fold the vegetables into the couscous and season to taste with salt and pepper.

Serves 4

Seafood

Blackened Redfish

Former First Lady Barbara Bush graciously shared one of her favorite recipes. This preparation creates a great deal of smoke and is best done on an outdoor grill. Serve the fish with rice or couscous.

1 tablespoon paprika	1 teaspoon cayenne pepper
2½ teaspoons salt	½ teaspoon dried thyme
1 teaspoon garlic powder	½ teaspoon oregano
1 teaspoon onion powder	3 pounds redfish fillets
¾ teaspoon white pepper	(6 8-ounce fillets)
¾ teaspoon black pepper	Melted butter

Combine the seasonings in a small bowl. Preheat a cast-iron skillet until very hot. If cooking outdoors, place the skillet on a preheated gas grill or over hot coals. Dip the fillets in melted butter and sprinkle generously with the seasoning mixture. Place them in the skillet and cook for 2 minutes. Turn and cook for 1 minute longer. Serve immediately.

Serves 6

Braised Orange Roughy with Tomatoes and Capers

Any mild fish can be substituted for the orange roughy in this light and healthful dish. Accompany it with sautéed chard, seasoned rice, and a crisp white wine.

2 tablespoons olive oil	1 tablespoon chopped fresh basil
1 medium onion, chopped	2 tablespoons dry sherry
2 cloves garlic, minced	2 tablespoons capers
4 medium tomatoes, peeled,	Salt and freshly ground pepper
seeded, and chopped	1¾ pounds orange roughy fillets
1 teaspoon dried oregano	

Heat the oil in a large skillet over medium heat. Add the onion and sauté until softened. Add the garlic and stir briefly. Add the tomatoes and herbs and simmer for 5 minutes. Add the sherry, capers, salt, and pepper and simmer for 1 minute. Remove the vegetables from the skillet with a slotted spoon. Add the fish to the skillet and spoon the vegetables over them. Cover and cook gently for about 6 to 7 minutes, or until the fish is just cooked through.

Serves 6

Chilled Trout with Mustard Sauce

This is a great make-ahead dish for a summer meal or as part of a buffet.

6 fresh, whole, boneless trout
1 cup chicken broth
Juice from one lemon
½ teaspoon salt
2 hard-cooked eggs, finely chopped
2 tablespoons finely chopped parsley

2 tablespoons finely chopped
  green onions
1 cup yogurt
½ cup mayonnaise
1 tablespoon prepared mustard
Salt and freshly ground pepper

GARNISH
3 hard-cooked egg yolks
Minced fresh parsley and dill
Thinly sliced lemon

Preheat the oven to 350°F. Place the trout in a single layer in a shallow baking dish. Add the chicken broth, lemon juice, and salt. Cover with foil and bake for 30 minutes. Cool and chill for several hours.

Combine the remaining ingredients in a bowl and stir until well blended. Season to taste with salt and pepper. Refrigerate until needed.

Remove the trout from the cooking liquid and drain on paper towels. Strip off the skin and neatly remove the heads and tails. Place the trout on a serving platter and spoon the sauce evenly over them. Cover and chill.

When ready to serve, sieve the egg yolks over the fish, sprinkle with chopped parsley and dill, and garnish the platter with lemon slices.

Serves 6

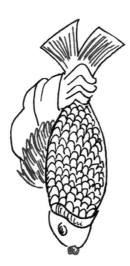

Cold Poached Salmon with Caper Sauce and Fresh Fruit

Cool, pretty, and very appealing on a hot summer day, this lovely dish is prepared completely in advance. Offer a chilled Sauvignon Blanc or an Oregon Pinot Gris.

1½ cups chicken stock or low-salt broth
A generous ½ cup dry white wine
2 cloves garlic, put through a press
1 tablespoon herb mix (such as
    Lawry's 17 Seasoning Mix)
1 tablespoon butter
6 thick salmon fillets, with skin
½ cup mayonnaise

½ cup sour cream
¼ cup capers, drained
Salt and freshly ground pepper
    or white pepper
Red and/or green leaf lettuce
Sliced fresh fruit
Lemon or lime wedges

Combine the stock, wine, garlic, herb mix, and butter in a skillet just large enough to hold the salmon in one layer. Bring the liquid almost to a simmer and add the salmon. Regulate the heat so that the surface of the poaching liquid "shimmers," but does not actually simmer. Poach until the fish is cooked, but still slightly opaque in the center, turning once, about 8 minutes. Remove the fillets and cool. Refrigerate overnight.

Simmer the poaching liquid until reduced by half and cool. Combine the mayonnaise and sour cream in a bowl. Whisk in the reduced poaching liquid until a sauce-like consistency is attained. Stir in the capers and season with salt and pepper. Cover and refrigerate overnight.

Peel away the skin from the chilled salmon fillets and scrape off the gray fat with the back of a knife. Wrap well and refrigerate until serving time. Arrange lettuce leaves on 6 plates. Add the salmon and garnish with fresh fruit and lemon or lime wedges. Place a dollop of sauce on each fillet. Pass the remaining sauce.

Serves 6

Garlic Prawns

Nothing beats the aroma of shrimp sizzling in oil, garlic, and white wine. Be sure to provide crusty bread to mop up the garlicky juices, and plenty of napkins. Pour a Pinot Grigio.

5 or 6 jumbo shrimp per person
    (about 12 to the pound)
¼ cup olive oil
3 large cloves garlic, minced
1 tablespoon minced parsley
½ cup dry white wine or dry
    white vermouth

2 tablespoons freshly squeezed
    lemon juice
1 teaspoon minced rosemary leaves
    (optional)
Salt and freshly ground pepper
Crushed red pepper flakes
Lemon wedges

Devein the shrimp by cutting through the shells along the back with scissors. Make a shallow cut into the flesh, remove the black vein, and rinse under cold water. Pat dry. Do not remove the shells.

Preheat the broiler. Place the shrimp in a shallow pan just large enough to hold them in one layer. Heat the olive oil and garlic in a small skillet. When the garlic begins to sizzle, add the parsley and wine and boil briefly. Add the lemon juice, rosemary, salt and pepper, and pour over the shrimp. Broil until the shrimp are pink and firm, about 2 to 3 minutes per side. Transfer them to a serving dish or individual soup plates and pour the cooking juices back into the skillet. Boil to reduce the juices slightly and pour over the shrimp. Sprinkle with red pepper flakes and serve with lemon wedges.

Serves 4

Grilled Swordfish Agrodolce

Fish in sweet and sour sauce is a great favorite in Italy where it is also prepared with tuna. Grilled or fried polenta triangles are an excellent accompaniment to this delicious dish.

2 tablespoons fruity olive oil
6 anchovy fillets, rinsed and chopped
1 cup sliced onion
2 garlic cloves, finely minced
1 tablespoon finely chopped
   rosemary leaves
2 cups peeled, seeded, chopped
   fresh or canned tomatoes
2 tablespoons balsamic vinegar

1 tablespoon light brown sugar
1 tablespoon chopped, black,
   oil cured olives
1 tablespoon capers
1 tablespoon minced parsley
Salt and freshly ground pepper
1 or 2 swordfish steaks, about
   12 ounces total

Heat the olive oil in a large, heavy skillet over medium heat. Add the anchovies, onions, garlic, and rosemary and cook until the onions are golden. Add the tomatoes and cook for 10 minutes, stirring occasionally. Combine the vinegar and sugar and add to the skillet. Simmer for 10 minutes. Stir in the olives, capers, parsley, salt, and pepper. Remove the pan from the heat and set aside.

Prepare a grill or preheat a grill pan. Rub the fish with olive oil and season with salt and pepper. Grill for 3 to 4 minutes per side or until just done. Serve with the sauce.

Serves 2

Halibut in Smoked Ham with
Warm Tomato Vinaigrette and Lentil Stew

French lentils du Puy are firmer and hold their shape better than other types. Their earthy flavor is a good foil for the mild fish as are the smoky ham and bright vinaigrette. Uncork a Pinot Noir.

LENTIL STEW

1½ cups lentils du Puy
1 14-ounce can low-sodium chicken broth
2 shallots, 1 halved, 1 minced
3 cloves garlic, 1 left whole,
　2 finely minced
2 large sprigs parsley
1 sprig fresh thyme
1 Turkish bay leaf
1 tablespoon olive oil

⅔ cup red onion in ¼-inch dice
1 carrot, cut in ¼-inch dice
　(about 1 cup)
1 parsnip, cut in ¼-inch dice
　(about 1 cup)
2 teaspoons finely chopped
　fresh rosemary
2 tablespoons finely chopped parsley
Salt and freshly ground pepper

VINAIGRETTE

½ clove garlic, put through a
　garlic press, or more to taste
12 to 16 cherry tomatoes,
　halved or quartered
3 tablespoons extra-virgin olive oil

Splash of balsamic or sherry vinegar
Salt and freshly ground pepper
6 to 8 medium basil leaves,
　thinly sliced

FISH

8 very thin slices hickory smoked ham
4 skinless halibut fillets,
　about 6 ounces each
Salt and freshly ground pepper

2 tablespoons unsalted butter
1 tablespoon canola or vegetable oil
Snipped chives for garnish

Place the lentils in a saucepan and add the chicken broth and enough water to cover them by 2 inches. Add the halved shallot, whole garlic clove, parsley, thyme, and bay leaf. Bring to a boil. Cover, reduce the heat and simmer gently until the lentils are tender, about 30 minutes. Drain, reserving 1 cup of liquid (add water if there is less). Discard the vegetables and herbs and turn the lentils into a bowl to cool. In a small skillet, heat 1 tablespoon of olive oil and add the minced shallot, onions and carrots. Cook until the carrots are almost tender. Add the parsnip, minced garlic, rosemary, and chopped parsley, and cook until the vegetables have softened. Fold them into the lentils and set aside or refrigerate up to 1 day. Reheat the lentils in a skillet with ½ cup of the reserved cooking liquid. Add more liquid if necessary. Season with salt and pepper, and keep warm. Do not overcook.

Combine all the ingredients for the vinaigrette except the basil in a bowl, and refrigerate for up to 4 hours. Overlap 2 ham slices, folding the long edges inward to form a rectangle slightly narrower than the width of the fish (the short ends of the fish should be exposed). Season the fish with salt and pepper and place on the ham, skinned side up. Wrap each fillet snuggly, overlapping the ends. Trim as necessary.

(The fish can be refrigerated for up to 4 hours. Let stand at room temperature for 15 minutes before cooking.)

Preheat the oven to 425°F. Heat the butter and oil in an ovenproof skillet over medium-high heat. When the butter is foaming, add the fish, seam side down, and cook until lightly browned, about 1 minute. Turn the fish over and place the skillet in the oven until the fish is just done, about 6 to 8 minutes.

Heat the vinaigrette in a small pan until barely warmed through. Do not allow it to simmer. Remove from the heat and add the basil. Spoon the lentils onto plates and top with the halibut. Spoon the vinaigrette over the fish and garnish with snipped chives.

Serves 4

Annie's Scalloped Oysters

Serve this rich and delicious dish as an appetizer, first course, or part of a buffet.

½ cup (1 stick) butter
¼ cup chopped celery hearts and leaves
¼ cup minced green onions
2 pints select raw oysters, drained
Salt and freshly ground pepper

Freshly ground nutmeg
Saltine cracker crumbs
1 cup half & half
Shredded Swiss or sharp
   Cheddar cheese

Preheat the oven to 400°F. Butter a 2-quart baking dish. In a skillet, melt the butter and sauté the celery and green onions until tender. Layer half the oysters and half of the green onion mixture in the prepared dish. Season with salt, pepper, and nutmeg, and sprinkle with a light layer of cracker crumbs. Repeat. Insert a knife blade in the center of the oysters and around the edges of the dish, pouring the half & half around the blade. Cover the dish and bake for 30 minutes. Uncover and sprinkle with cheese. Return to the oven for an additional 10 minutes. Serve hot.

Serves 6 to 8

Salmon with Asparagus and Orange-Basil Vinaigrette

Serve this vibrant dish with saffron rice or curried couscous and a chilled Vouvray or a crisp, non-oaky Chardonnay.

8 center cut salmon fillets, with skin,
 about 6 ounces each, pin bones removed
1 cup olive oil
4 cloves garlic, coarsely chopped
Several sprigs fresh thyme and rosemary,
 lightly bruised with the back of a knife
5 navel oranges
1 cup fresh orange juice
2 tablespoons chopped shallots or
 red onion

2 tablespoons fresh lime juice
6 small basil leaves, chopped
1 teaspoon Dijon mustard
1 tablespoon red wine or
 balsamic vinegar
1 teaspoon grated orange zest
Coarse salt and freshly ground
 black pepper
2 pounds asparagus spears
Thinly sliced basil leaves

Place the salmon in a glass baking dish, skin side up. Add ½ cup of olive oil, the garlic, and the herbs. Cover and refrigerate for several hours.

With a small, sharp knife, cut off the ends of the oranges, remove the peel and all of the bitter, white pith. Working over a bowl, cut between the membranes to release the segments. Squeeze the juice from the pulp into a measuring cup and add additional juice to measure 1 cup. Boil the juice until reduced to ¼ cup. Let cool for a few minutes and pour it into the jar of an electric blender. Add the shallots, lime juice, chopped basil, mustard, and vinegar, and process until smooth. With the machine running, slowly add the remaining ½ cup of olive oil. Pour the vinaigrette into a container, add the grated zest, and season with salt and pepper. (The oranges and vinaigrette can be prepared up to 1 day in advance. Bring to room temperature before using.)

Snap off the tough stems from the asparagus. If the stalks are thick, peel them with a vegetable peeler. Blanch the spears in a large pot of boiling, salted water until crisp-tender and drain. (If not using immediately, drop the spears into a bowl of ice water to stop the cooking and set the color. Pat dry, wrap in paper towels, and refrigerate in a plastic bag until needed. Toss the spears in a skillet with a little hot butter to reheat.) Season with salt and pepper.

Drain the salmon and season with salt and pepper. Grill the fillets over medium-hot coals until done, but still slightly opaque in the center, about 3 to 4 minutes per side. (Alternatively, broil the salmon or sear it, skin side up, in a hot, cast iron or oven-proof, non-stick skillet for 30 seconds. Turn the fish over, transfer the skillet to a preheated 400°F oven and roast to medium, about 8 minutes.) Divide the asparagus among 4 plates and top with the salmon. Spoon the oranges and vinaigrette over the fish and garnish with sliced basil. Pass the remaining vinaigrette.

Serves 8

Shrimp Curry with Cucumber-Tomato Relish

Indian cooks fry or toast spices to release all of their flavor. The relish provides a cooling counterpoint to this complex red curry. Rice or warm Indian bread is virtually a requirement.

RELISH

1 cup seeded, diced tomato
1 cup seeded, diced cucumber
½ cup diced or shredded radish or
 ¼ cup thinly sliced red onion

Pinch salt
½ cup chopped fresh cilantro
1 tablespoon lemon or lime juice

CURRY

2 cloves garlic, finely minced
2 teaspoons finely grated fresh ginger
1 small jalapeño or serrano pepper,
 seeded and minced
Salt and freshly ground pepper
2 tablespoons vegetable oil
1 medium onion, finely chopped
⅛ teaspoon turmeric
2 teaspoons ground cumin

1 teaspoon ground coriander
⅛ teaspoon ground cloves
2 medium tomatoes, peeled, seeded,
 and chopped
1 tablespoon tomato paste
1 pound medium shrimp, peeled
 and deveined
2 tablespoons chopped cilantro

Combine the relish ingredients in a bowl and let stand while preparing the curry. With a mortar and pestle, pound the garlic, ginger, and hot pepper to a paste with a little salt (or grind as finely as possible in a blender or mini-food processor with a splash of water). In a large skillet, heat 2 tablespoons of oil over moderate heat. Add the onions and cook until softened. Add the paste and fry for 2 minutes, stirring almost constantly. Add the spices and cook, stirring, for 1 minute longer, adding up to ¼ cup of water to prevent sticking. Add the tomatoes and tomato paste and cook until the sauce thickens lightly, 2 to 3 minutes. Add the shrimp and cook until they are firm and just done, about 3 minutes. Transfer the curry to a serving bowl, sprinkle with chopped cilantro, and serve with the relish.

Serves 4

Shrimp Veracruz

Serve this zesty stew with rice, garlic bread, and a crunchy green salad. Any leftover sauce can be frozen and served over broiled or sautéed fish. Try it with a Sauvignon Blanc or an Albariño.

3 tablespoons olive oil
1 large Spanish onion, chopped
  (about 3 cups)
1 large green pepper, cut into 1-inch dice
3 ribs celery, sliced
1 pound white mushrooms, sliced
½ teaspoon cayenne pepper
1½ teaspoons paprika
2 bay leaves
4 large cloves garlic, minced
2 28-ounce cans whole tomatoes in juice,
  drained and crushed, juices reserved

1 cup water
2 or more large jalapeño peppers,
  split half way from tip to stem
Salt and freshly ground pepper
2 to 3 tablespoons tomato paste
A generous ¼ cup chopped flat
  leaf parsley
2½ pounds large raw shrimp,
  peeled and deveined
Cooked white rice
Tabasco or other hot sauce

In a wide, heavy saucepan or Dutch oven, heat the olive oil over medium high heat. Add the onions and sauté for about 2 minutes. Add the green peppers and celery and sauté until they begin to soften, about 2 minutes longer. Add the mushrooms and sauté until their liquid has evaporated. Add the cayenne pepper, paprika, bay leaves, and garlic, and sauté briefly. Add the tomatoes along with the juice, the water, jalapeños, and salt and pepper to taste. Simmer, uncovered, for 15 minutes. Add the tomato paste and parsley, and continue to simmer until the sauce holds its shape fairly solidly in a spoon. Remove the bay leaves and jalapeños and set aside, or cool and refrigerate overnight. When ready to serve, reheat the sauce. Add the shrimp and cook until they are pink and firm, about 2 to 3 minutes. Do not overcook. Taste for seasoning. Serve over hot, white rice. Pass hot sauce.

Serves 6

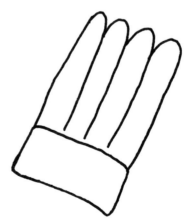

Snapper Rangoon

This Caribbean-inspired entrée is popular in the Florida Keys where it is frequently made with fiery Scotch bonnet peppers. Curried rice is a good side dish. Pour a Viognier.

4 yellowtail or red snapper fillets, about
  6 ounces each
Salt and freshly ground pepper
All-purpose flour
5 tablespoons unsalted butter
1 jalapeño or serrano chili
  pepper, seeded and minced
3 to 4 tablespoons fresh lime juice
1 cup sliced bananas
½ cup mango in ¾-inch dice

½ cup green fleshed melon in
  ¾-inch dice
½ cup yellow fleshed melon in
  ¾-inch dice
½ cup pineapple in ¾-inch dice
1 kiwi, quartered and sliced
½ cup sliced strawberries
Chopped cilantro
Lime wedges

Season the fish with salt and pepper and dust with flour. Heat 2 tablespoons of butter in a large nonstick skillet over medium-high heat until foaming (or use 2 skillets, dividing the butter). Add the fillets, skin side up, and sauté until lightly browned. Turn and sauté the other side, adding a little more butter if necessary. Remove and keep warm. (If the butter has scorched, wipe out the pan.)

Add 2 tablespoons of fresh butter to the skillet and heat until foamy. Add the chili pepper, lime juice, and fruit. Cook until the fruit is just heated through and the sauce thickens. Arrange the fish and fruit on plates, garnish with chopped cilantro and lime wedges, and serve.

Serves 4

Salmon with Pecan Crust

The mustard-honey-pecan crust adds great flavor and crunch to the rich salmon. It's also excellent on skinless chicken breasts. Accompany the salmon with a rice blend, steamed broccoli, and a Pinot Noir.

4 skinless salmon fillets, about
  6 ounces each
Salt and freshly ground pepper
2 tablespoons Dijon mustard
2 tablespoons butter, melted
1½ tablespoons honey

¼ cup soft, fresh bread crumbs
¼ cup finely chopped pecans
2 teaspoons chopped parsley
Parsley sprigs
Lemon wedges

Preheat the oven to 450°F. Season the fillets with salt and pepper and place them skinned side down in a lightly greased 9x13-inch pan. Combine the mustard, butter, and honey in a bowl, and brush it onto the salmon. Combine the bread crumbs, pecans, and chopped parsley, and spoon the mixture evenly over the fillets. Bake for 8 to 10 minutes or until the fish is done but still slightly translucent in the center. Garnish with parsley sprigs and lemon wedges.

Serves 4

Slow-Roasted Cod on Tomato Rosettes

Slow-roasted fish is incredibly moist and silky. Salmon, halibut, and Chilean sea bass are good substitutes for the cod. Serve the fish with a rice or orzo pilaf and a green vegetable. Pour a buttery Chardonnay.

⅓ cup extra-virgin olive oil
1 clove garlic, put through a garlic press
4 skinless cod fillets, about
   6 ounces each
1 tablespoon balsamic vinegar
6 to 8 red plum tomatoes, or
   half red, half yellow

Thinly sliced basil leaves
Salt and freshly ground pepper
3 tablespoons chopped mixed herbs,
   such as rosemary, thyme, parsley,
   or chives

Preheat the oven to 225°F. Cut 4 squares of kitchen parchment, each large enough to hold a rosette. Combine the olive oil and garlic, drizzle a little over each fillet, and rub it all over. Add the vinegar to the remaining oil and garlic. Set the dressing aside.

Peel the tomatoes with a vegetable peeler, slice them crosswise in half, and remove the seeds. Slice the tomatoes into ¼-inch thick rounds, discarding the ends. Place the parchment squares on a baking sheet and brush lightly with olive oil. Overlap slices of tomato on the parchment to form four rosettes. Drizzle a little of the dressing over each and add a few shreds of basil. Top with a cod fillet and season with salt and pepper. Press the herb mixture onto the fish. Roast for 20 to 25 minutes, or until the fish is just done. Slide a spatula under each piece of parchment and transfer to plates. With the help of the spatula, carefully slide the rosettes off the parchment. Top each fillet with a spoonful of the dressing and serve.

Serves 4

Soft Shell Crabs with Asian Slaw and
Mandarin Black Bean Salad

The crabs can be dusted with flour before cooking, but they are much lighter when the flour is omitted.
They can also be grilled over hot coals. Cook them on the same day they are purchased.

SALAD

4 cups cooked black beans
1 15-ounce can mandarin oranges,
 drained, juice reserved
½ cup diced red bell pepper
½ cup diced yellow pepper
¾ cup diced red onion

2 or more jalapeño peppers,
 seeded and minced
1 bunch cilantro, leaves only,
 chopped
Juice from 2 large limes
Salt and freshly ground pepper

SLAW

3 tablespoons rice wine vinegar
2 tablespoons soy sauce or tamari
1 tablespoon toasted sesame oil
1 cup finely shredded red cabbage
1 cup finely shredded napa cabbage
1 cup finely shredded or
 julienned carrots

1 cup finely shredded or
 julienned daikon radish
½ cup julienned zucchini
½ cup julienned jicama
½ cup thinly sliced scallions

SOFT SHELL CRABS

2 tablespoons vegetable oil
8 small to medium soft shell crabs, cleaned

Salt and freshly ground pepper
Lime wedges

P lace the black beans in a bowl and add the juice from the mandarin oranges. Refrigerate for several hours or overnight, stirring occasionally. Pour off the juice and add the remaining ingredients to the beans. Let stand for at least 30 minutes or refrigerate for several hours.

For the slaw, combine the vinegar, soy sauce, and sesame oil in a small bowl. Place the vegetables in a large bowl, add the dressing, and toss. Refrigerate for several hours.

Heat 2 tablespoons of oil in a heavy skillet large enough to hold the crabs in one layer (cook them in batches if necessary). Dry the crabs well with paper towels to prevent spattering and season them with salt and pepper. Pan cook the crabs, lightly pressing the small legs into the oil, until red and crisp, about 2 to 3 minutes per side. Transfer to plates and garnish with wedges of lime. Serve hot with the black bean salad and slaw.

Serves 4

Stir-Fried Shrimp and Crab with Water Chestnuts

This easy Cantonese-style stir-fry goes together in minutes when all of the ingredients are measured out and within reach. Serve it with steamed rice and follow with tropical fruit and fortune cookies.

6 ounces crabmeat
1 (8-ounce) can whole water chestnuts, drained and quartered
1 tablespoon minced fresh ginger
2 tablespoons chopped green onions
2 tablespoons cornstarch
2 cups small shrimp, peeled and deveined
3 tablespoons cold water

½ cup chicken broth
½ teaspoon sugar
2 tablespoons soy sauce
2 cups peanut or vegetable oil
4 cloves garlic, crushed
2 tablespoons dry sherry
Salt and pepper
Minced ginger
Sliced green onions

Combine the crabmeat, water chestnuts, minced ginger, and chopped green onions in a bowl. Place the shrimp in another bowl, add one tablespoon of cornstarch, and toss to coat. Blend the remaining tablespoon of cornstarch with the cold water. Combine the chicken broth, sugar, and soy sauce.

Heat the oil in a large wok or skillet. When hot, add the shrimp and stir-fry, stirring to separate, for about 30 seconds. Remove them with a skimmer or slotted spoon and drain on paper towels. Pour off all but 3 tablespoons of the oil. Add the garlic to the wok and brown. Discard the garlic. Add the crab and stir-fry for about 30 seconds. Add the sherry and stir-fry for 30 seconds. Add the broth and soy mixture and stir-fry for 1 minute. Recombine the cornstarch, add it to the wok and cook, stirring, until thickened. Return the shrimp to the wok and stir-fry for about 30 seconds, or just until the shrimp are heated through. Season with salt and pepper. If desired, sprinkle the dish with additional minced ginger and sliced green onions.

Serves 4

Spicy Stir-Fried Lobster

Spicy hot and finger-lickin' good, this dish is meant for sharing. Steamed jasmine rice, beer or tea, and lots of napkins will be welcome accompaniments.

2 1½-pound lobsters
¼ cup chili sauce (such as Heinz)
1 tablespoon dry sherry
1 tablespoon soy sauce
3 teaspoons Asian fish sauce (nuoc mam)
1 teaspoon Chinese chili-garlic paste
3 tablespoons hoisin sauce

1 teaspoon light brown or white sugar
1 teaspoon sesame oil
½ teaspoon chili oil
1½ tablespoons minced ginger
⅔ cup thinly sliced scallions
1½ tablespoons minced garlic
Peanut oil

Purchase the lobsters on the same day they will be cooked. Have the fishmonger split them lengthwise, remove and crack the knuckles and claws, twist off the tails and cut them crosswise in half, and remove the dark vein, antennae, and head sacs. (Alternatively, plunge the lobsters into a large pot of boiling water, cover, and cook for 2 minutes. Drain, cool, and cut them into pieces.)

Combine the chili sauce, sherry, soy, fish sauce, chili-garlic paste, hoisin, sugar, sesame oil, and chili oil. In a separate bowl, combine the ginger, scallions, and garlic.

Heat a large wok or skillet with a cover over high heat. Add 2 tablespoons of peanut oil and stir fry the lobster for 2 to 3 minutes, or until bright red and partly cooked. Remove the lobster to a bowl. Add more oil if necessary and stir fry the ginger, garlic, and scallions for 15 seconds. Add the sauce, the lobster, and any juices from the bowl. Turn the lobster in the sauce to coat. Lower the heat to medium, cover the wok, and cook for 3 to 4 minutes. The tail and chest pieces should be done. If so, remove them to a serving bowl. Cover the wok and continue to cook the claws for 1 to 2 minutes. Transfer the claws to the bowl. If necessary, boil the sauce until thickened. Pour the sauce over the lobster and serve.

Serves 2

Whole Roasted Snapper

Whole roasted fish is prepared all along the Mediterranean coast, often in wood-fired ovens. Freshness is key in its simple preparation. Sautéed spinach or chard, roasted potatoes, and a dry white wine, such as a Sardinian Vermentino, are perfect partners to the clean, delicate flavor of the fish.

1 whole, very fresh, red snapper, black bass, or stripped bass, 1½ to 1¾ pounds	Several sprigs of fresh thyme, oregano, marjoram, or sage, or a combination
Coarse sea salt or kosher salt	Several thin lemon slices
Freshly ground pepper	Olive oil
	Lemon wedges
	Good extra-virgin olive oil

Have the fishmonger clean, remove the gills, and thoroughly scale the fish. Preheat the oven to 400°F. Line a rimmed baking sheet with kitchen parchment. Rinse the fish inside and out in cold water, place it on the parchment, and measure it at the thickest portion. Slit the belly opening if necessary so that it is about 3 to 4 inches long. Lightly season the cavity with salt and pepper and add several sprigs of herbs and lemon slices. Rub the outside of the fish with olive oil and sprinkle with salt and pepper. Loosely crumple a sheet of aluminum foil and stuff it partly into the cavity to form a "stand." Stand the fish on its belly, curving the tail to fit inside the pan if necessary.

Place the pan in the oven and roast the fish for approximately 13 minutes per inch of thickness. Test for doneness by carefully cutting alongside the backbone and pulling the flesh away from the bone. It should come away fairly easily, but still be moist and slightly translucent near the bone. The fish will continue to cook after it is removed from the oven.

Remove the parchment with the fish to a cutting board and discard the foil and herbs. Fillet the fish and transfer to plates. Sprinkle the fillets with coarse salt and a grind of black pepper. Serve with lemon wedges and a cruet of a fruity, good quality, extra-virgin olive oil for drizzling over the fillets.

Serves 2

Poultry

Arroz Con Pollo a la Chorrera
(Chicken and Rice)

Chicken and rice "a la Chorrera" is a Cuban specialty. The addition of lime juice and beer sets it apart from the Spanish classic as does its very moist consistency. Pour a lighter style Rioja or beer.

1 chicken, cut into serving pieces,
   skin removed
Juice from 1 large lime
Salt and freshly ground pepper
½ cup Spanish olive oil
1 medium onion, finely chopped
1 medium green pepper, seeded
   and finely chopped
2 to 3 cloves garlic, minced
1 cup crushed tomatoes
¼ cup finely chopped Spanish pimientos
   (or substitute roasted red peppers)
2 to 3 bay leaves

½ cup dry white wine
3 cups chicken stock
1 cup water
2 cups Valencia rice, or other
   short-grain rice
¼ teaspoon powdered saffron, or
   4 or 5 saffron threads, crushed
12 ounces beer
1 cup sweet peas, thawed if frozen
2 Spanish pimientos, sliced into
   strips, for garnish (or substitute
roasted red pepper)

Rinse and dry the chicken. Season it with lime juice, salt, and pepper. Heat ¼ cup of oil in a large, heavy pot or Dutch oven over medium heat. Add the chicken, in batches if necessary, and brown slowly. Do not crowd the pan. Remove the chicken from the pan and set aside.

Make the sofrito: Add the remaining oil to the pan. Add the onion, green pepper, and garlic and cook until the onion is very soft. Add the tomatoes, pimientos, and bay leaves. Cook for 5 minutes, stirring frequently. Return the chicken to the pan and combine with the sofrito. Add the wine and simmer for 3 to 4 minutes. Add the chicken stock and water and bring to a boil. Adjust the seasonings (it should be a little salty since the rice will absorb salt later on). Add the rice and saffron and combine well. Bring to a boil over high heat and simmer, uncovered, for 5 minutes. Lower the heat to medium-low, cover, and simmer for 20 minutes. Add the beer and ¾ cup of peas. Cover and continue to simmer for 15 to 20 minutes or until the chicken is done and the rice is tender, but still loose. Garnish with the reserved peas and the pimientos.

Serves 4 to 6

Chicken Breasts with Pears and Stilton

Port, Stilton, pears, and cream combine to give this unusual dish outstanding flavor. Serve it with rice.

6 boneless, skinless chicken breast halves
Flour
6 tablespoons unsalted butter
Salt and pepper
¾ cup unsalted chicken stock or broth
¾ cup tawny port

1½ cups heavy cream
2 to 3 tablespoons Stilton cheese
3 pears, peeled, cored, each cut into
  six slices
2 tablespoons minced flat
  leaf parsley

Preheat the oven to 200°F. Pound the chicken breasts to flatten slightly and sprinkle lightly with flour. In a heavy skillet, heat 4 tablespoons of butter over medium heat until foaming. Add the chicken and cook, turning once, until just done, about 5 to 6 minutes per side. Remove to a shallow pan and sprinkle lightly with salt and pepper. Tent the chicken with foil and keep warm in the oven. Add the stock and port to the skillet and boil until reduced by half, scraping up all of the browned bits. Add the cream and boil until reduced and lightly thickened. Add 2 tablespoons of Stilton to the sauce and heat until melted. Add more to taste.

Meanwhile, heat the remaining 2 tablespoons of butter in a small skillet and sauté the pears for 5 minutes, turning occasionally. Transfer the chicken to plates and top with the pears and sauce. Garnish with chopped parsley.

Serves 6

Oven-Baked Parmesan Chicken Breasts

Crisp, delicious, and so easy! Serve the chicken with lemon wedges and your favorite sides.

1 cup fresh bread crumbs
¾ cup grated Parmesan cheese
1 teaspoon garlic salt
¼ cup chopped parsley

Freshly ground pepper
1 stick butter, melted
4 boneless, skinless, chicken
  breast halves

Preheat the oven to 350°F. Combine the bread crumbs, cheese, garlic salt, parsley, and pepper. Dip the chicken in the melted butter and roll in the crumb mixture, patting to adhere. (Leftover crumbs can be frozen.) Place the breasts in a shallow pan and drizzle evenly with butter. Bake for about 1 hour, or until golden and cooked through.

Serves 4

Chicken Breasts with Tart Cherry Sauce

The tart-sweet, garnet-colored sauce elevates simple chicken breasts to new heights. Wild rice pilaf, steamed broccoli or green beans, and a red Zinfandel or Merlot are good accompaniments.

¼ cup all-purpose flour
¼ teaspoon salt
4 skinless, boneless chicken breast halves
Vegetable cooking spray
1 tablespoon butter
½ cup cranberry juice cocktail
½ cup ruby port

3 tablespoons brown sugar
½ teaspoon dried whole tarragon
¼ cup dried tart cherries
1 tablespoon balsamic vinegar
1 tablespoon cornstarch
2 tablespoons water

Place the flour, salt, and chicken in a large zip-top bag and shake until the chicken is coated. Spray a large skillet with cooking spray and place it over medium heat. Add the butter and heat until foaming. Add the chicken breasts and cook until just done, turning once, about 5 to 6 minutes per side. Remove the chicken from the skillet and keep warm. Add the cranberry juice, port, brown sugar, tarragon, dried cherries, and vinegar to the skillet. Bring to a boil and simmer, covered, for 5 minutes. Combine the cornstarch and water and add it to the skillet. Simmer for 1 minute, stirring constantly, or until the sauce thickens. Transfer the chicken to plates and add any juices to the sauce. Spoon the sauce over the chicken and serve.

Serves 4

Chicken Neapolitan

Share this rustic, southern Italian-style dish with friends on a chilly evening. Serve it with pasta, a green salad, garlic bread, and a bottle of Sangiovese. Offer a choice of sorbets for dessert.

1 frying chicken, about 3½ pounds
Salt and freshly ground pepper
Olive oil
1½ pounds Italian sausage, hot or mild,
   or turkey Italian sausage
1 medium Spanish onion, chopped
3 cloves garlic, finely minced
½ cup dry white wine or dry
   white vermouth

1 28-ounce can Italian plum tomatoes
   in juice, well crushed, including the juice
1 teaspoon dried Greek oregano
3 tablespoons chopped flat leaf parsley
¾ pound cremini mushrooms, sliced
1 or 2 red bell peppers, cut in
   wide strips
1 or 2 green bell peppers, cut in
   wide strips

Cut the chicken into serving-size pieces and season with salt and pepper. In a heavy Dutch oven, heat the oil over medium heat and brown the chicken slowly on all sides. Do not crowd the pan. Remove the pieces to a plate as they brown. Cut the sausage into pieces, add it to the pan, and brown. Remove it to the plate. Pour off the fat and heat 2 tablespoons of fresh oil. Sauté the onions until softened. Stir in the garlic and cook for a few seconds. Pour in the wine and simmer until it reduces by half. Add the tomatoes, tomato juice, oregano, 1 tablespoon of the chopped parsley, salt, and pepper. Bring to a boil. Return the chicken and sausage to the pan, lower the heat, and simmer, partially covered, for 20 minutes.

Meanwhile, heat 2 tablespoons of olive oil in a large skillet. Add the mushrooms and sauté until lightly browned and tender. Remove them to a bowl. Sauté the peppers in 1 tablespoon oil until softened, but still a little crunchy. Add the peppers and mushrooms to the chicken and continue to cook until the chicken is fork tender and the sauce has thickened, about 10 minutes longer. (Add water if the sauce thickens before the chicken is done.) Remove the chicken, sausage, and peppers to a serving platter. Skim the fat from the sauce. Spoon some of the sauce over the chicken and sausage and garnish with the remaining chopped parsley. Serve additional sauce on the side.

Serves 6

Hot Curried Chicken Salad

This family favorite is real comfort food!

2 cups mayonnaise
1 tablespoon finely minced onion
1 to 2 teaspoons lemon juice
1 teaspoon curry powder
Salt and freshly ground pepper
½ cup grated Parmesan cheese
2 cups diced cooked chicken or turkey
2 cups diced celery

¼ cup toasted slivered almonds or
   coarsely chopped walnuts
5 ounce can water chestnuts,
   drained and rinsed
½ cup fresh, soft bread crumbs
Chopped parsley
Butter

Preheat the oven to 375°F. Grease a 1½-quart baking dish. In a large bowl, combine the mayonnaise with the onion, lemon juice, curry powder, salt, pepper, and Parmesan cheese. Fold in the chicken, celery, nuts, and water chestnuts. Transfer the mixture to the baking dish. Top the casserole with the bread crumbs, sprinkle with chopped parsley, and dot with butter. Bake for 25 minutes, or until bubbly.

Serves 4 to 6 generously

Chicken Roulades with Mushroom Sauce

Much of this sophisticated dish can be prepared in advance. Orzo, Israeli couscous, or a simple rice pilaf will compliment the Mediterranean-inspired flavors. Uncork a Pinot Noir or Côtes du Rhône.

CHICKEN

- 2 tablespoons olive oil
- 2 cloves garlic, minced
- 2 pounds fresh spinach, stemmed, washed, and dried, or two 10-ounce packages frozen chopped spinach, thawed and drained well
- 10 ounces feta cheese, crumbled
- 1 egg

- ⅓ cup milk
- 8 boneless, skinless chicken breast halves, or chicken cutlets
- Salt and freshly ground pepper
- 1 cup flour, spread on a plate
- 2 cups bread crumbs, spread on a plate
- 6 tablespoons unsalted butter

MUSHROOM SAUCE

- 3 tablespoons olive oil
- 1 large red bell pepper, sliced
- 2 tablespoons butter
- 1 pound mushrooms, trimmed and sliced
- 2 cloves garlic, minced
- 1½ tablespoons flour

- ¾ cup dry white wine
- 2 cups chicken stock or low-salt broth
- 1 to 2 tablespoons balsamic vinegar
- ¼ cup capers, drained
- Salt and freshly ground pepper
- Chopped parsley

Heat a large skillet over medium-high heat. Add 1 tablespoon of oil, half the minced garlic, and half the fresh spinach. Sauté until the spinach is wilted and any liquid evaporates. (If using frozen spinach, add all of the garlic and all of the spinach.) Repeat with the remaining spinach. Cool, chop coarsely, and combine with the feta.

Preheat the oven to 325°F. Beat the egg and add the milk. Set the egg wash aside. Pound the chicken breasts between sheets of plastic wrap to a thickness of ¼ inch. Season with salt and pepper and top each breast with some of the spinach mixture. Roll up the breasts from the narrow end and secure with toothpicks. (The roulades can be prepared to this point a few hours in advance.) One at a time, dredge the rolls in flour and shake off the excess. Coat them with the egg wash, allowing the excess to drip off, and roll them in the bread crumbs to coat evenly. Press gently to help the crumbs adhere. In a large ovenproof skillet, heat 3 tablespoons of butter over medium-high heat until foaming. Add the chicken and brown on all sides, adding more butter as necessary. Transfer the skillet to the oven and bake until the chicken is cooked through, about 15 to 20 minutes.

For the sauce, heat 1 tablespoon of olive oil in a large skillet. Add the sliced peppers and sauté until softened. Remove them to a bowl. Add 2 tablespoons of oil and 2 tablespoons of butter to the pan and sauté the mushrooms until browned. Add the garlic and sauté briefly. Add a tablespoon of oil or butter if the pan is dry and sprinkle on the flour. Cook, stirring constantly, for less than a minute. Deglaze the pan with the wine, stirring until smooth. Simmer until the liquid reduces by ¾. Add the stock and 1 tablespoon of balsamic vinegar and reduce again by about half or until thickened and flavorful. Remove the pan from the heat and stir in the peppers and capers. Add more vinegar to taste and season with salt and pepper. (The sauce can be prepared several hours in advance.)

Transfer the chicken to a cutting board and remove the toothpicks. Slice the roulades in half on the bias. Spoon the sauce onto plates and top with the chicken. Sprinkle with chopped parsley and serve.

Serves 8

Chicken Vesuvio with Vesuvio Potatoes

This dish is a Chicago original, virtually unknown in other parts of the country. The name supposedly refers to the Vesuvio-like cloud produced when the wine is added to the skillet. The potatoes are divine! Pour a dry Italian white or lighter red wine.

1 chicken, 3 to 3½ pounds
Salt and freshly ground pepper
2 tablespoons olive oil
2 to 3 baking potatoes, peeled
3 to 4 large cloves garlic, finely minced
Pinch crushed red pepper flakes
½ cup dry Marsala wine
½ cup dry white wine or dry white vermouth

½ cup chicken stock or low-sodium broth
2 tablespoons tomato sauce
2 teaspoons finely chopped fresh sage
2 teaspoons finely chopped fresh rosemary
1 teaspoon dried oregano
12 large cremini mushrooms, halved
1 tablespoon chopped parsley

Preheat the oven to 400°F. Cut the chicken into 12 pieces, cutting the breasts cross-wise in half. Season with salt and pepper. In a large, heavy skillet (preferably cast iron), heat the oil over medium-high heat. In batches, add the chicken and brown slowly on all sides, adding more oil as necessary. Do not crowd the pan. Remove the pieces to a shallow roasting pan just large enough to hold the chicken comfortably.

Cut each potato lengthwise into thick wedges. Pat dry and add as many as will fit without touching to the drippings in the pan. Brown well on all sides and drain on paper towels. Sauté the remaining potatoes, adding oil if necessary. Pour out the fat and heat a spoonful of oil in the same skillet. Add the garlic and pepper flakes. When the garlic begins to sizzle, pour in the wines and reduce by one-third, scraping up all of the browned bits. Add the stock, remove the pan from the heat, and stir in the tomato sauce and herbs. Pour the liquid over the chicken. Add the potatoes to the roasting pan. Bake, uncovered, for about 20 minutes or until the chicken is cooked through and the potatoes are tender.

Meanwhile, heat 2 tablespoons of oil in the skillet and add the mushrooms. Sauté until lightly browned and tender. Transfer the chicken and potatoes to a serving platter and add the mushrooms. Pour the wine sauce over the chicken and garnish with chopped parsley.

Serves 4

Chili Verde

Green chilies, corn, tomatillos, and cilantro give this chili real New Mexico flavor.

3 pounds skinless, boneless chicken thighs, cut into ½-inch dice
Salt and freshly ground pepper
5 tablespoons flour
7 tablespoons olive oil
3 cups chopped onions
3 tablespoons chopped garlic
1½ cups chopped Anaheim chilies (about 4)
2 green bell peppers, sliced
5 cups corn kernels, thawed if frozen

6 cups chicken broth
12 tomatillos, husked, coarsely chopped
1 tablespoon oregano
2 tablespoons chili powder
1 tablespoon ground cumin
1 teaspoon paprika
2 cinnamon sticks
1 cup chopped cilantro
Tortilla chips

Season the chicken with salt and pepper. Toss half the chicken with flour, place it in a sieve and shake off the excess. Heat 1 tablespoon of olive oil in a large, heavy skillet over medium heat. Add the floured chicken and brown. Transfer to a heavy Dutch oven. Repeat with the remaining chicken. In the same skillet, heat 2 tablespoons of oil over medium-high heat. Add the onions and garlic and sauté until the onions have softened, about 5 minutes. Add them to the chicken. Heat 1 tablespoon of oil in the skillet and sauté the chilies and green peppers until tender, about 4 minutes. Add them to the chicken. Heat 1 tablespoon of oil in the skillet and sauté half the corn until tender, about 2 minutes. Add it to the chicken and repeat with the remaining corn. Add all the remaining ingredients to the pan except the cilantro and tortilla chips. Bring to a boil, reduce the heat and simmer, uncovered, until the chili thickens, about 2 hours. Stir in the cilantro just before serving. Garnish each portion with tortilla chips.

Serves 6 to 8

Chutney Chicken Breasts

Piquant and complex in flavor, this dish is a snap to prepare. Serve the chicken over rice.

2 tablespoons unsalted butter
6 boneless, skinless chicken breasts
1 medium yellow onion, sliced
½ cup dry white wine or dry white vermouth

½ cup sour cream
1 can artichoke hearts, drained and sliced
Salt and freshly ground pepper
1 bottle mango chutney

In a large, heavy skillet, heat the butter over moderate heat until foaming. Add the chicken and sauté, turning often, until it begins to brown. Add the onion and continue to cook until the chicken is golden and the onion has softened. Combine the wine and sour cream and pour it over the chicken. Add the artichokes to the pan and season with salt and pepper. Pour the chutney over the top. Cover and cook over medium-low heat for 20 to 25 minutes, or until the chicken is very tender.

Serves 6

Deviled Turkey Casserole

Keep this flavorful recipe in mind when you have lots of leftover Thanksgiving turkey.

4 tablespoons butter
1 onion, chopped
6 tablespoons flour
1 tablespoon mustard
2 teaspoons salt
2½ cups milk
1 cup sliced celery

1 cup cooked turkey
1 cup sliced ripe olives
1 2-ounce jar pimentos, drained and chopped
½ cup raisins
½ cup dark rum
1 cup seasoned bread crumbs

Preheat the oven to 350°F. In a saucepan, heat the butter over medium-high heat until foaming. Add the onions and sauté until golden. Whisk in the flour, mustard, and salt. Stirring constantly, add the milk and cook until the mixture thickens. Add the celery, turkey, olives, pimentos, and raisins and cook until heated through. Add the rum. Spoon the mixture into a 2-quart baking dish. Top with the bread crumbs and bake for 30 minutes.

Serves 8 to 10

Duck with Soy-Orange Glaze

The orange sauce adds a Western touch to the duck which is "red cooked" in a traditional Chinese master sauce. Star anise can be added to the braising liquid. Serve the duck with rice and bok choy or broccoli.

3 tablespoons vegetable oil
3 ducks (about 5 pounds each), quartered
9 green onions, thinly sliced
4 slices fresh ginger
2 cups soy sauce
¼ cup dry sherry

¼ cup dark brown sugar
4 cups water
1 12- to 14-ounce jar orange marmalade
3 tablespoons orange Curaçao

Preheat the oven to 325°F. Heat the oil in a large, heavy skillet over medium-high heat. In batches, add the duck to the pan and brown well. Do not crowd the pan. Remove the browned pieces to a large roasting pan and pour off excess fat before adding another batch to the skillet. When all of the duck is browned, pour off all but 2 tablespoons of the fat. Add the green onions and ginger and sauté for a few seconds. Stir in the soy sauce, sherry, brown sugar, and water. Pour the liquid over the duck. Cover the pan tightly with foil and braise for 1½ hours. Uncover and roast for 30 minutes to crisp the skin. Remove the duck to a large platter.

Pour 1 cup of the braising liquid into a saucepan. Discard the remaining liquid or strain and freeze it for braising fowl, poultry, or meats. Skim off any fat. Add the marmalade and Curaçao and bring the sauce to a simmer. Stir until the marmalade is fully melted. Top each duck quarter with a generous spoonful of sauce. Serve the remaining sauce in a sauceboat.

Serves 6 to 12

Herb-Roasted Cornish Game Hens

Richer in flavor than chicken, these tasty little game hens are perfect dinner party fare. Round out the meal with sautéed mushrooms, roasted root vegetables, and a good bottle of Pinot Noir.

4 Cornish game hens, about 1 pound each
4 cloves garlic, minced
1 tablespoon chopped fresh thyme leaves
1 tablespoon minced fresh rosemary leaves
1 tablespoon chopped fresh oregano or marjoram
4 large sprigs fresh sage
Coarse salt and freshly ground pepper
Olive oil

1 lemon, cut into 8 wedges
1 carrot, peeled and cut into chunks
1 stalk celery, cut into chunks
1 medium yellow onion, cut into wedges
½ cup dry white wine or dry white vermouth
1 cup chicken stock, veal stock, or canned low-salt chicken broth
2 tablespoons cornstarch combined with 3 tablespoons cold water (optional)
Chopped parsley

Preheat the oven to 450°F. Rinse and dry the hens inside and out and loosen the skin over the breasts, thighs, and legs. Combine the garlic, thyme, rosemary, and oregano and push some under the skin of each hen. Insert 1 sage leaf on each side of the breasts. Rub the cavities with the remaining herb-garlic mixture and sprinkle with salt and pepper. Rub the hens with olive oil and season with salt and pepper. Stuff a sage sprig and 2 pieces of lemon into each cavity. Tuck the wing tips under but do not truss. Place the hens, breast side up, on a rack in a shallow roasting pan. Scatter the carrot, celery, and onions around the pan and roast for 20 minutes. Turn the heat down to 400°F and roast until a meat thermometer inserted in the thigh registers 155 to 160 degrees, about 20 to 25 minutes longer. Drain the juices from the hens into the roasting pan and transfer them to a carving board. Let them rest while finishing the sauce.

Discard the vegetables from the roasting pan and pour off the fat. Over medium-high heat, add the wine to the roasting pan and reduce it by half, scraping up all of the browned bits. Add the stock or broth and simmer until slightly reduced. Strain into a saucepan and simmer until reduced, thickened, and full flavored. Season with salt and pepper. If necessary, thicken the sauce lightly with the cornstarch slurry, adding it to the simmering sauce a little at a time. Cut the hens in half and arrange on plates. Spoon a little sauce around the hens and sprinkle with chopped parsley. Pass the remaining sauce.

Serves 4

Moroccan Chicken with Chickpeas

Chickpeas are widely used in Moroccan cooking as is turmeric which lends a distinctive, golden yellow color. Zucchini or okra sautéed with chopped tomatoes would compliment the flavors in the dish.

1 pound dried chickpeas
1 quart cold water
4½ teaspoons salt
1 onion, peeled and quartered
1 bay leaf
1 chicken, about 4 pounds
2 cloves garlic, crushed
1 teaspoon ground ginger
¼ teaspoon freshly ground pepper

1 tablespoon water
½ cup chopped onion
2 tablespoons chopped parsley
1 teaspoon turmeric
2-inch piece cinnamon stick
2 tablespoons butter
1 14-ounce can low-salt chicken broth
1 cup sliced onion
½ cup raisins

Pick over the chickpeas to check for stones, cover with cold water, and refrigerate overnight. Drain and place them in a large kettle. Add 1 quart of cold water, 2 teaspoons of salt, the quartered onion, and the bay leaf. Cover and simmer for 1½ hours or until tender. Drain, discard the onion and bay leaf, and set the chickpeas aside.

Meanwhile, rinse and dry the chicken. Sprinkle the cavity with 1 teaspoon of salt. Tuck the wings under the body and tie the legs together. Combine the garlic, ginger, 1½ teaspoons of salt, pepper, and 1 tablespoon water. Rub the chicken with the mixture. Place it in a bowl, cover, and refrigerate for 1 hour.

Combine the chopped onion, parsley, turmeric, cinnamon stick, butter, and chicken broth in a large Dutch oven. Bring to a boil over medium heat, stirring constantly. Lower the heat and add the chicken, breast side down, along with any juices from the bowl. Cover and simmer, turning frequently with 2 wooden spoons, for about 1 hour, or until the chicken is tender. Remove to a platter and discard the cinnamon stick. Add the chickpeas, sliced onion, and raisins to the sauce. Bring to a boil and cook, stirring frequently, until the onion is soft and the flavors have blended, about 15 minutes. Remove the twine from the chicken and return it to the pan. Simmer gently for 5 minutes. Cut the chicken into pieces and serve with the chickpeas and sauce.

Note: Two cups canned, drained chickpeas can be substituted. Simmer for a few minutes with the quartered onion and bay leaf and proceed with the recipe.

Serves 4 to 6

Roast Chicken Stuffed with Potatoes and Olives

The piquant stuffing turns an ordinary roast chicken into an extraordinary dish.

3 or 4 medium red potatoes, unpeeled,
  cooked, and cut into cubes
8 or 10 stuffed green olives, chopped
2 tablespoons minced fresh rosemary leaves,
  or 1 tablespoon dried rosemary
2 tablespoons chopped flat leaf parsley

2 cloves garlic, crushed
3 canned flat anchovies, mashed
1 tablespoon capers
3 tablespoons olive oil
3-pound chicken, rinsed and dried
Salt and pepper to taste

Preheat the oven to 375°F. Place the potatoes, olives, rosemary, parsley, garlic, anchovies, and capers in a bowl. Drizzle with the olive oil and toss to coat. Season the chicken inside and out with salt and pepper. Stuff the chicken loosely with the potato mixture and place it on a rack in a shallow pan. Roast until a meat thermometer registers 160 degrees in the thickest part of the thigh, about 70 to 80 minutes. Let the chicken rest, loosely covered, for 10 minutes. Remove the stuffing to a serving bowl. Cut the chicken into quarters and serve with the stuffing.

Serves 4

Slow-Roasted Duck with Green Peppercorn Sauce

If you love moist, crispy duck, you will love this recipe. Not only is the duck delicious—with or without the sauce—the oven stays clean! Serve it with wild rice, haricots verts, and a good Rhône red.

1 Long Island Duckling (about 5 to
  5½ pounds), rinsed and dried
1 large clove garlic, minced
Salt and freshly ground pepper
Several sprigs fresh thyme
1 wedge of onion
1 large shallot, minced

¼ cup port
¼ cup dry red wine
¾ cup duck, veal, or chicken stock
¼ cup demi-glace
1 tablespoon green peppercorns packed
  in brine, drained and lightly crushed
2 teaspoons butter, softened

Preheat the oven to 300°F. Remove the wing tips and any large pieces of fat from the duck. Rub the cavity with the garlic, salt, and pepper. Insert the thyme and onion. With a small, sharp knife, make tiny slits all over the duck, inserting the knife sideways to pierce the skin but not the flesh. Place the duck breast side up on a rack in a shallow pan and roast for 30 minutes. Using wads of paper towels, turn the duck over and roast for 1 hour. Drain the fat into a bowl, pierce the skin again, turn the duck over, and roast for 1 hour. Repeat the procedure and roast for 1 more hour. Remove the pan from the oven and increase the heat to 375°F. Drain the fat, sprinkle the duck with salt, and roast for 15 minutes. Turn breast side up, sprinkle with salt, and roast until the skin is nicely browned, 15 to 20 minutes. Drain the juices from the cavity into the roasting pan and set the duck on a carving board while preparing the sauce.

Pour off the accumulated fat in the bowl. (Strain and refrigerate the fat for several months. It makes fabulous sautéed potatoes.) Add any brown juices in the bowl to the stock. Drain all but 1 tablespoon of the fat from the roasting pan and place it over medium-high heat. Add the shallots and stir until softened. Deglaze the pan with the port and red wine and boil until reduced by half. Add the stock and demi-glace. Boil, scraping up all of the browned drippings. Simmer until the sauce reduces by half and is lightly thickened. Strain it into a saucepan, add the peppercorns, and keep warm. Quarter the duck. Swirl the softened butter into the sauce and serve with the duck.

Note: ¼ cup dried cherries, plumped in hot water and drained, can be substituted for the peppercorns.

Serves 2 to 3

Braised Rabbit

Farm-raised rabbit is mild, but richly flavored. If unavailable, skinless, bone-in chicken thighs can be substituted. Serve the rabbit with Creamy Parmesan Polenta and a Côtes du Rhône or Chianti Classico.

1 3-pound dressed rabbit, cut
　into 8 pieces
Salt and freshly ground pepper
3 tablespoons olive oil
1 medium Spanish onion,
　coarsely chopped
1 medium carrot, coarsely chopped
1 medium rib celery, coarsely chopped
1 large sprig fresh sage

1 sprig fresh thyme
3 large cloves garlic, smashed
1 cup dry white wine
1 cup chicken stock or canned,
　low-salt broth
1 cup peeled, seeded, and diced
　fresh tomatoes, or canned plum
　tomatoes, well crushed
1 tablespoon chopped parsley

Preheat the oven to 350°F. Rinse the rabbit under cold water and pat dry. Season with salt and pepper. In a nonreactive sauté pan or a Dutch oven, heat 3 tablespoons of olive oil over medium heat. Add the rabbit and sauté slowly, turning frequently, until golden brown all over. Remove the pieces to a plate. Add the onions, carrots, and celery to the pan and sauté until lightly colored. Add the sage, thyme, and garlic and stir briefly. Pour in the wine and simmer until it reduces by half. Return the rabbit to the pan. Cover and simmer very gently for 15 minutes, turning once. Add the stock and tomatoes. Cover the pan tightly and transfer to the oven. Braise until the meat is fork tender, about 1 to 1½ hours.

Remove the rabbit and strain the sauce. Discard the herbs and vegetables. Skim off any fat. If necessary, boil the braising liquid until it thickens lightly. Taste for seasoning and return the rabbit to the pan. Simmer just until heated through. Transfer the rabbit to a serving platter, moisten with some of the sauce, and sprinkle with chopped parsley. Serve the remaining sauce on the side.

Serves 4

Meats

Barbecued Dry Rubbed Ribs

These Memphis-style ribs are so good you may not want to glaze them with barbecue sauce. The rub keeps for two to three months and is excellent on beef, chicken, and pork.

4 slabs St. Louis-style or baby back pork ribs, about 2–2½ pounds each
Barbeque sauce

DRY RUB

½ cup kosher salt
¼ cup packed light brown sugar
¼ cup Hungarian sweet paprika
¼ cup chili powder
¼ cup garlic powder
1 tablespoon onion powder
2 tablespoons dry mustard
1½ tablespoons ground cumin

1 teaspoon cinnamon
1 teaspoon ground coriander
1 teaspoon rubbed sage
1 tablespoon dried Greek oregano
2 teaspoons dried thyme
3 teaspoons freshly ground
   black pepper
1 teaspoon cayenne pepper

Have the butcher remove the thin membrane from the bone side of the slabs. Place the slabs on a rack in a shallow roasting pan. If possible, do not overlap. Combine the ingredients for the dry rub and rub a liberal amount all over the ribs.

Place a pan of water on the lowest rack or on the oven floor and preheat the oven to 300°F. Roast the ribs, turning occasionally, for about 2 to 3 hours (or up to 4 hours if the ribs are very meaty), or until they are very tender and the meat has shrunk away from the ends of the bones. Replenish the water as necessary. (The ribs can be cooled, wrapped well, and refrigerated overnight. Let stand at room temperature for 30 minutes before proceeding.) Prepare a barbecue grill, adding hickory chips if desired. Place the ribs over medium-hot coals. Cover and smoke, turning once or twice, just until they are heated through and browned. If desired, brush with barbecue sauce during the last few minutes to glaze. (The ribs can also be finished under the broiler.) Serve with barbecue sauce on the side.

Note: If placing a separate pan of water in the oven is not possible, add ¼ inch of water to the roasting pan and replenish as necessary.

Serves 8 or more

Cassoulet

The ingredients for this famous dish from southwest France vary from town to town, each of which claims to make the "true" version. Most agree that duck and garlic sausage should be included, but additions, such as veal, lamb, pork, preserved goose, tomatoes, or a bread crumb topping are hotly debated. Serve it on a wintry evening with a green salad and crusty bread followed by a simple fruit dessert. Look for a red wine from the region, such as a Cahors, or try a Gigondas or Zinfandel.

1 pound dried cannellini or other white beans
1 quart chicken broth
¼ cup olive oil
4 strips slab bacon, chopped
1 large yellow onion, peeled and chopped
1 small head garlic, peeled and chopped
1 pound sausage, such as a garlic pork sausage, or smoked chicken or turkey sausage, cut in serving-size pieces

1 pound veal chops (or substitute veal shank)
1 pound duck legs
1 cup dry white wine
2 cups stewed tomatoes, chopped
Salt and freshly ground pepper
1 to 2 teaspoons Herbes de Provence

Pick over the beans to check for stones. Place them in a bowl or saucepan, cover with cold water by 2 inches, and soak overnight, or boil for 2 minutes, cover, and soak for 1 hour. Drain.

Preheat the oven to 325°F. Warm the broth. Heat the olive oil in a large, enameled cast-iron French oven or a heavy Dutch oven. Add the bacon and brown lightly. Remove and drain on paper towels. Add the onions and garlic to the pan and cook until the onions are golden. Remove to a bowl. Add the meats and duck legs in batches and brown well. Do not crowd the pan. Remove the browned pieces to a platter. Drain the fat from the pan and add the beans, bacon, onions, and garlic. Add all of the browned meats. Add the warm broth, wine, tomatoes, salt, pepper, and Herbes de Provence. Add hot water if necessary to cover the ingredients by 1 inch. Bring to a simmer and transfer the casserole to the oven. Bake, uncovered, until the beans are tender and almost all of the liquid is absorbed, 2 to 3 hours (add more hot water if the pan begins to dry out before the beans are done).

Serves 6

Donnie's Ribs

These delicious country-style ribs soak up the sauce and are fall-off-the-bone good!

Vegetable oil
2 to 4 pounds country-style pork ribs
1 cup ketchup
1 cup sugar
4 tablespoons soy sauce
2 cloves garlic, crushed

2 tablespoons Worcestershire sauce
2 tablespoons white vinegar
2 tablespoons flour
1 teaspoon ginger
1 teaspoon salt

Preheat the oven to 350°F. Heat a heavy roasting pan on 2 stovetop burners over medium-high heat. Add enough oil to film the bottom. Add the ribs and brown well. Combine all of the remaining ingredients. Drain the fat from the roasting pan and pour the sauce over the ribs. Roast, uncovered, for 1½ to 2 hours or until the ribs are tender. Add water as needed to keep the pan from drying out.

Serves 2 to 4

Marinated Baked Ham

Fabulous hot or cold, this ham will make your reputation as a cook to be reckoned with. Try it with Virginia Spoonbread Soufflé and Baked Butternut Squash and Apples. Uncork a Riesling or Gewürztraminer.

1 7- to 8-pound fully cooked,
   bone-in or semi-boneless ham
2 cups orange juice
2 cups ginger ale

⅓ cup firmly packed brown sugar
¼ cup orange marmalade
1 teaspoon dry mustard

Place the ham in a large, heavy duty zip-top plastic bag and add the orange juice and ginger ale. Refrigerate for 8 hours, turning the bag occasionally.

Preheat the oven to 325°F. Drain the ham, reserving the marinade. Place it, fat side up, in a shallow roasting pan lined with heavy duty foil. Bake, uncovered, for 1½ hours, basting often with the marinade. Remove the ham from the oven and reduce the temperature to 300°F. Cut the skin away from the ham and score the fat in a diamond pattern. Combine the brown sugar, marmalade, and mustard. Spread the glaze over the ham and bake, uncovered, for 30 minutes. Let stand for 10 minutes before carving.

Serves 16

Pork Chops with Orange and Gin

The gin tenderizes the chops and adds a pleasant juniper flavor which compliments the orange.

4 pork loin chops
Salt and freshly ground pepper
Flour
1 tablespoon olive oil
1 clove garlic, crushed

Grated zest from 1 large orange
½ cup strained, freshly squeezed
 orange juice
½ cup gin
¼ cup finely chopped parsley

Season the chops with salt and pepper. Dredge them in flour and shake off the excess. Heat a large skillet over moderate heat. Add the olive oil. Add the chops and cook until nicely browned, about 3 minutes per side. Sprinkle the chops with the garlic and orange zest. Add the orange juice and gin. Cover the pan and cook over low heat, turning occasionally, until tender, about half an hour. The sauce will have reduced and thickened. Plate the chops, sprinkle with chopped parsley, and serve with rice or potatoes.

Serves 4

Pork Chops with Mustard-Cream Sauce

Serve this zesty cold-weather dish with buttered noodles or spaeztle, a green vegetable, and a Chardonnay.

4 center cut pork chops, 1 to
 1½ inches thick
Salt and freshly ground pepper
2 tablespoons olive oil
1 large shallot, minced
½ cup dry white wine or dry
 white vermouth

½ cup chicken or veal stock, or
 low-salt chicken broth
½ cup heavy cream
2 teaspoons whole grain mustard
2 teaspoons minced flat
 leaf parsley

Season the chops with salt and pepper. Heat 1 tablespoon of oil over medium-high heat in a large, heavy skillet (not nonstick). Add the chops and brown lightly, 1 to 2 minutes per side. Lower the heat to medium, cover the pan, and cook for about 6 minutes, turning once. Regulate the heat so that the chops sizzle gently. Remove them from the pan, cover loosely with foil, and let them rest.

Drain the fat from the skillet and return it to the heat. Add the remaining oil and the shallots. Cook, scraping up all of the browned bits, until the shallots have softened. Add the wine and reduce it by half. Add the stock and simmer until reduced by half. Add the cream and simmer until slighty reduced and thickened. Remove the pan from the heat and whisk in the mustard. Season with salt and pepper and add the parsley. Plate the chops, spoon the sauce over them, and serve.

Serves 4

Pork Loin Braised in Milk

Thank the Italians for inventing this method of cooking a pork roast. It results in tender, juicy meat and a wonderful sauce. Serve the sliced pork with rice or potatoes and colorful vegetables.

A 5-pound center-cut pork loin
   roast, trimmed of fat
3 medium garlic cloves, slivered
Salt and white pepper
4 tablespoons vegetable oil
1 large onion, chopped

1 tablespoon finely minced fresh thyme
1 tablespoon finely minced
   fresh rosemary
1 bay leaf
2 to 3 quarts whole milk
1 tablespoon cognac or brandy

Preheat the oven to 375°F. With a small, sharp knife, make several slits in the pork and insert a garlic sliver in each. Season the meat with salt and pepper. Heat 2 tablespoons of the oil in a deep, heavy roasting pan just large enough to hold the meat comfortably. Add the pork and brown well on all sides, regulating the heat so that the drippings do not burn. Remove the meat from the pan and pour off the fat. Add 2 tablespoons of fresh oil to the pan. Add the onions and sauté over medium heat until golden, about 8 to 10 minutes. Add 1½ teaspoons of thyme, 1½ teaspoons of rosemary, and the bay leaf. Place the meat on top of the onions and add enough milk to reach at least halfway up its side. Salt the milk lightly and bring to a boil. Transfer the pan to the oven and roast, uncovered, for 2½ hours. Turn the meat over, being careful not to break the crust, and continue to roast for 30 minutes or until the internal temperature reaches 150 degrees. Remove the meat from the pan and tent with foil while finishing the sauce.

Strain the pan juices into a wide saucepan and skim off the fat. Simmer over medium-high heat until reduced to 2 cups. Add the remaining thyme and rosemary. Add the cognac, salt, and pepper. Slice the pork and overlap the slices on a large serving platter. Pass the sauce separately.

Serves 10

Pork Rib Roast with Apples and Cider Sauce

A Christmas Day favorite worthy of all the trimmings—mashed sweet potatoes, Brussels Sprouts Leaves with Bacon, and corn bread and sausage dressing. Uncork a Pinot Gris from Alsace or a German Reisling.

An 8-rib pork loin roast, bones frenched, chine cracked
2 garlic cloves, thinly sliced
1½ tablespoons fresh thyme leaves, coarsely chopped
1 tablespoon kosher salt
Freshly ground pepper
2 medium onions, peeled, roots trimmed but intact
Olive oil
4 medium cooking apples, peeled, cored, cut into thick wedges

2 cups unsweetened apple cider
1 2-inch piece cinnamon stick
5 whole black peppercorns
1 whole clove
1 sprig thyme
2 tablespoons minced shallots
2 cups brown veal or chicken stock or low-salt chicken broth
3 tablespoons cornstarch or arrowroot dissolved in 4 tablespoons cold water (optional)

Make 12 or more small incisions all over the fatty side of the roast and insert a slice of garlic in each. Sprinkle the roast with thyme leaves, kosher salt, and pepper. Cover and refrigerate overnight.

Preheat the oven to 400°F. Cut the onions into thick wedges, leaving part of the root attached to each. Brush the bottom of a roasting pan with olive oil. Place the roast in the pan, fat side up, and surround it with the onion wedges. Brush the onions lightly with olive oil. Roast for 40 minutes. Add the apples to the pan, turning to coat with the drippings (add broth or water if the pan is dry). Roast for an additional 30 to 40 minutes, or until a thermometer inserted in the center of the roast registers 145 to 150 degrees. Remove the roast to a carving board and let it rest, loosely covered with foil, for 15 to 20 minutes. Keep the apples and onions warm.

While the pork is roasting, combine the cider, cinnamon stick, peppercorns, clove, and thyme sprig in a saucepan. Boil until reduced to 1 cup. Set aside. Heat a saucepan over medium heat and add 1 tablespoon of olive oil. Add the shallots and stir until wilted. Set aside.

Drain the fat from the roasting pan and set it over 2 burners. Add the stock and bring it to a boil, scraping up all of the brown drippings. Strain it into the saucepan with the shallots and boil until reduced to 1½ cups. Add ½ cup of reduced cider and simmer briefly. Add more cider to taste and season with salt and pepper. If desired, add the cornstarch slurry to the simmering sauce, 1 tablespoon at a time, until lightly thickened. Carve the roast into 8 chops. Serve with the apples, onions, and sauce.

Serves 8

Pork Tenderloin with Port and Blueberry Sauce

Perfect for a dinner party, this easy dish looks and tastes like you spent the whole day in the kitchen. Accompany it with a rice pilaf and a bottle of Merlot.

1½ to 2 pounds pork tenderloin, trimmed of all fat and silverskin	2 tablespoons sugar
Salt and freshly ground pepper	¼ cup port
2 tablespoons butter	2 tablespoons balsamic vinegar
2 medium onions, sliced	1 cup fresh or frozen blueberries
	1 cup chopped cherry tomatoes

Preheat the broiler. Season the tenderloin with salt and pepper. Place it on a broiler rack and broil, turning occasionally, until done, about 8 minutes. Remove the meat from the pan and let stand, loosely covered with foil, for 10 minutes.

Meanwhile, melt the butter in a large skillet over medium-high heat. Add the onions and cook until golden. Add the sugar and cook until the onions caramelize, about 3 minutes longer. Add the port, vinegar, blueberries, and tomatoes. Bring to a boil and remove the pan from the heat. Keep warm.

Slice the tenderloin on the bias. Add any juices from the cutting board to the sauce and serve with the pork.

Serves 4

Pork Tenderloin with Prunes

Marinating the prunes and pork overnight adds great depth of flavor to this Swiss specialty. The creamy sauce is best with noodles or rice.

20 to 30 dried, pitted prunes	⅓ to ½ cup olive oil
1 cup red wine	1 tablespoon Dijon mustard
1 tablespoon cinnamon	Salt and freshly ground pepper
Dash pepper	1 cup cream
2 pork tenderloins, each about 1 pound	

Combine the prunes, red wine, cinnamon, and pepper in a nonreactive bowl and steep overnight. Trim all fat and silverskin from the tenderloins and place them in a zip-top bag or a glass or ceramic baking dish. Combine the oil and mustard and pour it over the pork. Refrigerate for several hours or overnight.

Preheat the oven to 450°F. Drain the tenderloins, place them in a shallow roasting pan, and season with salt and pepper. Roast for 10 minutes. Add the prunes, the soaking liquid, and the cream. Roast for 5 to 10 minutes or until a thermometer registers 145 degrees. Remove the pork and let rest, loosely covered, for 10 minutes before slicing.

Pour the liquid from the roasting pan into a small saucepan and simmer until lightly thickened. Add any juices from the cutting board to the sauce and serve with the pork.

Serves 4 to 6

Sausages with Apples and Red Cabbage

This cold-weather skillet supper of smoky sausages, red cabbage, and tart apples is sweetened with a bit of brown sugar offset by a splash of vinegar. It's even better when prepared ahead and reheated. Serve it with boiled potatoes and German or Belgian beer.

1 small head red cabbage
2 medium Granny Smith apples, unpeeled
1½ tablespoons vegetable oil
2 small onions, thinly sliced
3 tablespoons light brown sugar

¼ cup cider vinegar
1 pound smoked sausage, cut
  into 1-inch pieces
1 teaspoon dried thyme
1 teaspoon salt

Core the cabbage and cut it into thin ribbons. Core the apples and cut each into 16 wedges. Heat the oil in a 12-inch skillet. Add the onions and cook over medium-high heat, stirring often, until browned, about 5 minutes. Add the brown sugar and vinegar and cook for one minute. Add the cabbage, apples, sausage, thyme, and salt. Mix well. Cover and cook for 5 minutes. Uncover and cook over high heat until the liquid is syrupy, 4 to 5 minutes longer. Adjust the seasoning and serve immediately, or cool and refrigerate. Reheat gently.

Serves 4

Stuffed Pork Shoulder

Cooked long and slow, this roast is moist on the inside and crisp on the outside. The stuffing is a tasty bonus. Serve it with Garlic and Rosemary Roasted Potatoes and a green vegetable.

STUFFING

4 cups fresh, soft bread crumbs
2 teaspoons salt
4 tablespoons minced green bell pepper
2 tablespoons minced onion

1 14-ounce can whole kernel corn
4 tablespoons butter, melted
2 eggs, beaten

1 6- to 8-pound boneless pork shoulder with a pocket for stuffing
Salt and freshly ground pepper

Preheat the oven to 350°F. Combine the ingredients for the stuffing in a bowl and mix well. Stuff the pocket of the pork shoulder and tie the roast firmly with kitchen twine. Season the meat with salt and pepper and place it on a rack in a shallow roasting pan. Roast for 40 minutes per pound. Remove the roast from the pan and let it rest, loosely covered with foil, for 20 minutes before slicing.

Serves 8 to 10

Braised Lamb Shanks with Orange Gremolata

Serve these meltingly tender shanks with Creamy Parmesan Polenta, baby onions, and carrots. Pour a red wine from the Northern Rhône Valley or a Barbaresco.

2 tablespoons unsalted butter
3 tablespoons vegetable oil
4 lamb shanks, about 1 pound each
Salt and freshly ground pepper
1 large onion, coarsely chopped
1 large leek (white and light green only) coarsely chopped
2 medium carrots, coarsely chopped
2 ribs celery, coarsely chopped
1 large shallot, minced

5 large cloves garlic, lightly crushed
1 pound fresh plum tomatoes, quartered and seeded, or 6 canned plum tomatoes, chopped
3 branches fresh thyme
1 bay leaf
1 strip orange zest (no white pith)
1 cup veal stock (optional)
4 to 6 cups chicken stock or low-sodium broth

Preheat the oven to 350°F. Heat a heavy, nonreactive Dutch oven over medium-high heat. Add 1 tablespoon of butter and 2 tablespoons of oil to the pan. Season the shanks with salt and pepper and brown well on all sides. Regulate the heat so that the shanks sizzle, but the juices do not burn. Remove the shanks to a plate and pour out the fat. Add 1 tablespoon of butter and 1 tablespoon of oil to the pan. Add the onions, leeks, carrots, celery, and shallot. Sauté until lightly colored. Add the garlic, tomatoes, herbs, and zest and cook until the tomatoes release their juices. Return the lamb to the pan and add enough stock to reach three-fourths of the way up their sides. Add pepper, salt lightly, and bring to a simmer. Cover tightly and place the pan in the oven. Braise until the shanks are fork tender, turning once, 1½ to 2 hours. Remove the shanks to a plate and cover with foil. Strain the braising liquid into a bowl and skim off the fat. (The shanks can be prepared 2 days in advance and refrigerated in the braising liquid. Place plastic wrap directly on the shanks before covering the pan. Reheat gently, remove the shanks to a plate and proceed.) Boil the braising liquid until reduced and lightly thickened. Return the shanks to the pan and reheat, basting them with the sauce. Transfer to plates and spoon some of the sauce over them. Serve with the gremolata and the remaining sauce.

GREMOLATA
¼ cup finely chopped parsley
2 teaspoons finely minced garlic
1 to 2 teaspoons finely grated orange zest

Combine the ingredients in a small bowl. The gremolata can be refrigerated for several hours.

Serves 4

Lamb Chops with Pomegranate Sauce

The sweet-tart flavor of pomegranate juice is exquisite with lamb. Reduced to a syrup, it becomes pomegranate molasses. Look for them in Middle Eastern markets, health food stores, and the organic food section of some markets. Serve the chops with Saffron Rice Pilaf and a Merlot or Pinot Noir.

8 thick-cut lamb chops, about
    4 ounces each
1 tablespoon fresh rosemary leaves
Salt and freshly ground pepper

½ cup pomegranate molasses
4 cloves garlic, crushed
½ cup olive oil

SAUCE

1 tablespoon butter
1 tablespoon olive oil
4 shallots, minced
4 cloves garlic, minced
1 cup pomegranate juice

2 tablespoons balsamic vinegar
3 cups lamb or chicken stock or
    low-salt broth
2 tablespoons cornstarch dissolved in
    3 tablespoons cold water (optional)

Place the chops in a glass baking dish and sprinkle them with rosemary leaves, salt, and pepper. Combine the molasses, garlic and olive oil and pour over the chops, turning to coat both sides. Cover and refrigerate for 2 to 4 hours.

In a saucepan, melt half the butter with the olive oil over medium heat. Add the shallots and garlic and sauté for 2 minutes, stirring frequently. Add the pomegranate juice and vinegar and simmer to reduce by half. Add the stock and reduce by half, or until the sauce coats the back of a metal spoon. (If using canned broth, it may be necessary to thicken the sauce with a spoonful or two of the cornstarch slurry.) Strain the sauce into a clean saucepan, add salt and pepper, and set aside.

Prepare a barbecue grill or preheat a grill pan or heavy skillet over medium heat. Remove the lamb from the marinade and season with salt and pepper. Grill or pan cook for about 4 to 5 minutes per side for medium rare. If pan cooking, lower the heat if necessary to prevent the glaze from burning.

Bring the sauce to a simmer. Remove the pan from the heat and swirl in the remaining ½ tablespoon of butter. Serve the sauce with the chops.

Serves 4

Moroccan Lamb Tagine with Dried Fruit, Squash, and Shallots

A tagine takes its name from the exotic earthenware vessel with a conical lid in which it is cooked and served. While not as dramatic in appearance, a Dutch oven works very well. Couscous is the traditional accompaniment to this fragrant dish, but rice is a good alternative.

4 tablespoons olive oil
3 pounds trimmed, boneless shoulder of
    lamb, cut into 1½-inch cubes, plus
    some bone-in pieces
1½ cups finely chopped onion
2 teaspoons ground cumin
2 or 3 cloves garlic, finely minced
2 teaspoons finely minced or grated
    fresh ginger
1 tablespoon flour
2 cups low-salt chicken broth
1 heaping tablespoon tomato paste
Large pinch of saffron threads, crumbled

1 large cinnamon stick, broken in half
1 bay leaf
1 3-inch strip of orange zest
2 tablespoons chopped parsley
Salt and freshly ground pepper
¾ cup dried apricots
1 cup dried pitted prunes
12 shallots
2 cups cubed butternut squash
1 tablespoon honey (optional)
Chopped cilantro or parsley
⅓ cup blanched sliced almonds,
    lightly toasted

Preheat the oven to 350°F. Heat the olive oil in a Dutch oven over medium-high heat. Add the lamb in batches and brown. Do not crowd the pan. Remove to a bowl. Add the onions to the pan and cook until softened. Add the cumin, garlic, and ginger. Stir briefly and add the flour. Cook and stir, scraping the bottom of the pan, for a few moments. Add the broth and stir until smooth. Add the tomato paste, saffron, cinnamon, bay leaf, orange zest, parsley, salt, and pepper. Return the lamb and any juices to the pan. Add water if necessary so that the lamb is half to three-quarters covered with liquid. Cover tightly and transfer to the oven until the lamb is almost tender, about 1 hour.

Meanwhile, cover the apricots and prunes with hot water and let stand for 30 minutes. Drain and set them aside. Blanch the shallots in boiling water for 1 minute. Drop them into ice water and slip off the skins. Steam the squash until barely done and set aside.

When the lamb is almost tender, add the shallots to the pot, pushing them into the sauce. Braise until the shallots and the lamb are tender, about 30 minutes longer.

Remove the lamb and shallots to a bowl and keep warm. Discard the cinnamon stick, bay leaf, and zest. Skim the fat from the sauce. If necessary, boil the sauce until lightly thickened, or add water if too thick. Add the drained fruit and the squash to the pan, cover, and simmer gently for about 5 minutes or until the squash is done. Stir in the honey. Return the lamb and shallots to the pan, cover, and simmer until heated through. Transfer to a serving bowl and garnish with chopped cilantro and sliced almonds.

Serves 6

Moussaka

This variation of the popular Greek casserole incorporates potatoes. Salting and draining the eggplant draws out any bitterness and helps it to absorb less oil. The baked dish freezes well.

3 medium eggplants
Salt and pepper
¼ cup olive oil
6 medium red or Yukon Gold potatoes
    or 3 large baking potatoes, peeled,
    sliced ¼-inch thick
¼ cup butter
1½ cups chopped onion

2 cloves garlic, minced
2 pounds lean ground lamb or beef
1 6-ounce can tomato paste
½ teaspoon cinnamon
2 tablespoons chopped flat
    leaf parsley
1 tablespoon dried mint leaves, crumbled
Cream Sauce

Slice the eggplant into ½-inch thick rounds and sprinkle them generously with salt. Lay the slices on paper towels, cover with more paper towels, and place a weight over them (such as a cutting board). Drain for 30 minutes, rinse, and pat dry. Heat 1 tablespoon of oil in a large skillet. Fry the eggplant slices, a few at a time, until lightly browned on both sides, adding more oil as necessary. Drain on paper towels. Film the bottom of the skillet with olive oil and fry the potato slices until golden. Drain on paper towels. Melt the butter in the skillet and sauté the onions until softened. Add the garlic and sauté briefly. Add the ground meat and sauté until no traces of pink remain. Add the tomato paste, salt, pepper, cinnamon, parsley, and mint. Add ¼ cup water if the mixture looks dry. Combine well.

Preheat the oven to 375°F. Arrange half the eggplant in a 9x13x2-inch baking dish and top with half the potatoes and half the meat. Repeat the layering. Cover with cream sauce and bake until the custard is set and lightly browned, about 45 minutes. Let the moussaka rest for 30 minutes before slicing.

CREAM SAUCE

½ cup (1 stick) butter
¾ cup flour
1 quart warm milk

4 eggs, lightly beaten
Salt and freshly ground pepper

Melt the butter over medium heat and add the flour all at once. Whisk until smooth. Cook, whisking constantly, for 1 to 2 minutes. Do not let the roux color. Gradually add the warm milk and cook, stirring constantly, until smooth. Remove the pan from the heat. Gradually beat ½ cup of the hot sauce into the eggs. Gradually beat the warmed eggs back into the sauce. Cook over medium-low heat until thickened, stirring constantly. Season with salt and pepper. (The sauce can be prepared ahead and refrigerated. Reheat gently, adding milk if too thick.) Makes 4 cups.

Note: For a leaner version, the eggplant can be brushed with oil and carefully broiled until tender and golden or roasted in a 450°F oven. Grated Parmesan cheese (about ¾ cup) can be sprinkled between the layers and over the top before baking. A sprinkling of ground nutmeg over the top is traditional.

Serves 8

Rack of Lamb with Herb and Goat Cheese Crust

Nothing is more elegant than rack of lamb. This preparation needs no sauce. Serve it with a potato gratin, colorful vegetables, and a red Burgundy or Pinot Noir.

2 lamb racks, about 1¼ to 1½ pounds each, well-trimmed, bones frenched
½ cup olive oil
4 cloves garlic, coarsely chopped
Several sprigs each fresh thyme and rosemary, lightly crushed
4 tablespoons olive oil
½ cup minced shallots
4 cloves garlic, finely minced
1 tablespoon minced fresh thyme leaves

2 tablespoons minced fresh rosemary leaves
3 tablespoons minced flat leaf parsley
2 cups fine, fresh bread crumbs, made from crustless, slightly stale French or Italian bread
Salt and freshly ground pepper
About ¼ cup pesto or Dijon mustard
About ½ of a small log of fresh goat cheese, at room temperature

Place the lamb in a plastic freezer bag and add the olive oil, garlic, and herb sprigs. Refrigerate for several hours or overnight. Let the lamb stand at room temperature for 30 minutes before cooking.

Heat 4 tablespoons of olive oil in a heavy skillet. Add the shallots and cook for 30 seconds. Stir in the garlic and rosemary and cook for a few seconds. Add the thyme, parsley, and bread crumbs. Combine well. Transfer the topping to a bowl and season with salt and pepper. Set aside or refrigerate until needed.

Position a rack in the middle of the oven and preheat to 475°F. Heat a heavy skillet over medium-high heat. Drain the lamb, scraping off the herbs and garlic, and season with salt and pepper. When the skillet is hot, add the lamb and brown on all sides. Transfer the racks to a rimmed baking sheet, bone side down, and let them rest for 5 minutes. Spread the tops of the racks with pesto or mustard, and press on a layer of the herbed bread crumbs. Crumble the goat cheese and press a thin layer onto the bread crumbs. Cover the goat cheese with a thin layer of bread crumbs, pressing firmly. (Leftover bread crumbs can be frozen.) Roast the racks for 15 to 20 minutes, or until a meat thermometer registers 125 to 130 degrees for medium rare. Remove the racks to a carving board and let them rest, loosely covered, for 10 minutes. Carve into single or double-cut chops.

Serves 4

Roast Leg of Lamb with Garlic and Herbs

A favorite from childhood that perfumes the kitchen with the heady aromas of garlic and herbs. Accompany the lamb with vegetables and Garlic and Rosemary Roasted Potatoes or a rice pilaf. Uncork a Gigondas, Pinot Noir, or Australian Shiraz.

A 6- to 7-pound bone-in leg of lamb
3 cloves garlic, cut into slivers
Olive oil
Coarse salt and freshly ground pepper
2 tablespoons finely chopped rosemary
2 tablespoons chopped thyme

2 or 3 carrots, peeled and cut into large chunks, thick parts split in half
2 ribs celery, each cut into 2 or 3 pieces
1 large onion, peeled and cut into wedges
1½ cups meat or chicken stock or canned low-salt broth

Preheat the oven to 450°F. Make small incisions all over the lamb and insert a sliver of garlic in each. Rub the lamb with olive oil, and sprinkle generously with salt, pepper, and herbs. Place the lamb on a rack in a large, shallow roasting pan and strew the vegetables around the pan. Roast for 10 minutes. Reduce the heat to 350°F and roast until a thermometer inserted in the thickest part of the leg reads 130 to 135 degrees for medium, about 1¼ hours longer. (Add a little water or broth to the pan if the vegetables appear to be burning.) Remove the roast to a carving board, cover loosely, and let it rest for 20 minutes.

Discard the vegetables and pour the fat out of the roasting pan. Place the pan over 2 burners on medium-high heat. Add the stock or broth and bring it to a simmer, scraping up all of the brown drippings. Simmer for a minute or two and strain the jus into a small saucepan. If necessary, boil to reduce and intensify the flavor. Season with salt and pepper and keep warm. Carve the lamb across the grain in fairly thin slices. Serve with the jus.

Note: Never discard jus from roasted meats or poultry. Freeze it in small containers and add leftover jus as accumulated. Thaw and use for deglazing or to enrich pan sauces. It makes all the difference in the world!

Serves 8

Shish Kebabs

Grilling the meat and vegetables separately is the secret to success with this dish. Serve the kebabs with herbed or saffron rice and a red Zinfandel.

3 large lemons
¾ cup olive oil
¼ cup dry white wine
2 to 3 cloves garlic, coarsely chopped
Dried Greek oregano
1 bay leaf
3 to 4 pounds trimmed boneless leg
   of lamb, cut into 2-inch cubes

2 to 3 large sweet onions, sliced
   ½-inch thick
2 red bell peppers, cut into squares
1 green bell pepper, cut into squares
24 medium cherry tomatoes
Coarse salt and freshly ground pepper
24 medium mushroom caps, cleaned

In a large freezer bag or nonreactive container, combine the juice from 1 lemon with the olive oil, white wine, garlic, 2 teaspoons of oregano, and the bay leaf. Add the lamb and refrigerate for several hours or overnight.

Prepare a charcoal grill and let it burn down to medium-hot coals. Slowly grill the onion slices over indirect heat until caramelized and softened, up to 1 hour. Add more coals as necessary.

Drain the lamb and thread the pieces onto long metal skewers. Do not pack the cubes together too tightly. Let the meat stand at room temperature for 30 minutes. Thread the peppers and cherry tomatoes onto separate skewers. When the onions are almost done, season the lamb generously with oregano and salt. Sprinkle with pepper. Grill over direct heat, turning as necessary, until done, but still pink and juicy. Do not overcook or the meat will be dry. Brush the tomatoes and peppers with olive oil. Grill the peppers until they have softened and charred a bit around the edges. Grill the tomatoes just until heated through. Thread the mushrooms onto skewers, brush with olive oil and grill until tender, or sauté them whole with a little butter.

Remove the lamb from the skewers and arrange on a large platter. Squeeze ½ a lemon over the lamb, cover loosely, and let it rest for several minutes. Surround the lamb with the vegetables. Squeeze the remaining lemon half over the vegetables and sprinkle with oregano. Cut the remaining lemon into wedges and place around the platter.

Serves 8

Aunt Edith's Brisket

An old family favorite that never fails to satisfy a hungry crowd. Carrots and potato pancakes with applesauce are the traditional accompaniments, but roasted potatoes are a good alternative.

A 5- to 6-pound first cut brisket
of beef, trimmed
3 to 4 cloves garlic, slivered
1 teaspoon kosher salt
Freshly ground pepper
1 bottle Bennett's Chili Sauce
1 whole clove garlic, peeled

2 large Spanish onions, cut in
thick wedges
2 to 3 carrots, peeled, and cut
into pieces
2 ribs celery, cut into pieces
2 bay leaves

Preheat the oven to 350°F. Make small incisions all over the meat and insert a sliver of garlic in each. Line a roasting pan with heavy duty foil, leaving generous overhangs. Place the brisket in the foil and season with salt and pepper. Pour the chili sauce into a small bowl. Put the peeled garlic clove through a garlic press into the bowl and combine. Spread the sauce over the brisket. Scatter the vegetables around the brisket and place the bay leaves on top. Fold the edges of the foil together tightly, forming a sealed envelope that completely encloses the meat and vegetables. Leave some airspace between the foil and the meat. Place in the oven for 2½ hours. Carefully open the foil (the steam will be very hot) and check the meat. It should be fork tender. If not, reseal and continue to bake.

Remove the brisket to a platter and cover it with plastic wrap. Remove the vegetables and bay leaves from the pan. Strain the pan juices into a bowl or a fat separator reserving the solids. Skim off the fat and pour the juices into a saucepan. Bring to a boil and reduce slightly to intensify the flavor. Add some or all of the solids from the sieve, as desired. Thinly slice the brisket across the grain on the bias and arrange on a platter. Pour some of the juices over the meat and pass the remainder.

Note: The brisket is easier to slice when chilled. Wrap it well and refrigerate for several hours or up to 2 days. Slice the meat and overlap the slices in a foil-lined pan. Moisten with a little of the braising liquid, cover tightly, and reheat in a 325°F oven. Add the juices to the sauce.

Serves 8

Carne Con Papas
(Beef Stew with Potatoes)

The green olives and paprika add piquant flavor to this Cuban stew. It's traditionally served with rice.

¼ cup olive oil
2 pounds boneless chuck, cut
    into cubes
1 large onion, finely chopped
1 medium green bell pepper,
    finely chopped
4 cloves garlic, finely chopped
2 teaspoons salt
1 tablespoon paprika

2 to 3 bay leaves
1 cup chopped tomatoes
1 cup dry sherry
1 cup water
4 large potatoes, peeled and cut up
¼ cup pimento-stuffed Spanish olives,
    or unpitted, green Spanish olives
¼ cup chopped parsley
½ cup baby sweet peas, blanched

In a large, heavy-bottomed saucepan or Dutch oven, heat the oil over medium-high heat. Add the beef, in batches if necessary, and brown on all sides. Do not crowd the pan. Lower the heat and add the onion, bell pepper, and garlic. Cook, stirring occasionally, until the onions have softened. Add the salt, paprika, bay leaves, tomatoes, sherry, and water. Cover and simmer for 1 hour. Add the potatoes and olives. Simmer for 45 minutes to 1 hour, or until the meat and potatoes are tender. Add equal parts water and dry sherry if the stew seems dry. Transfer to a serving bowl and garnish with the chopped parsley and peas.

Serves 4

Chili with a Kick

The name says it all! Cold beer will hit the spot.

1 pound chorizo sausage
2 tablespoons olive oil
1 sweet onion, finely chopped
2 pounds coarsely ground beef chuck
2 tablespoons chili powder
1 tablespoon ground cumin
1 teaspoon salt
1 teaspoon dried oregano
1 teaspoon dried basil
1 teaspoon freshly ground pepper
2 cloves garlic, minced

½ cup chopped fresh jalapeño
    peppers
2 teaspoons Worcestershire sauce
1 teaspoon Tabasco
1 cup dry red wine
1 28-ounce can tomato puree
2 14-ounce cans tomato sauce
    with tomato bits
⅓ cup chopped fresh cilantro
1 or 2 cans black beans, drained
    and rinsed (optional)

Remove the casing from the chorizo and crumble. Heat the olive oil in a large saucepan or Dutch oven. Add the onions and cook until browned. Add the chuck and chorizo and cook until no traces of pink remain. Add the spices, garlic, jalapeños, Worcestershire, and Tabasco. Combine well. Stir in the wine, tomato puree, and tomato sauce. Cover and simmer for 2 hours or more, stirring occasionally. Add the cilantro and beans during the last 30 minutes.

Serves 8 to 10

Jon's Hungarian Pot Roast

Caramelized onions add sweet, rich flavor as the meat cooks slowly to succulent perfection. The pot roast can be made in advance and reheated gently. Serve it with spaetzle or noodles.

A 5-pound top round of beef
4 cloves garlic, slivered
Salt and freshly ground pepper
Vegetable or corn oil
2 large onions, quartered and sliced
1 28-ounce can whole, peeled
   tomatoes, including the juice

8 to 12 carrots, peeled and
   sliced lengthwise
3 tablespoons flour
Gravy Master or Kitchen Bouquet
   (optional)

Make small incisions all over the meat and insert a sliver of garlic in each. Season with salt and pepper. Film the bottom of a large, heavy Dutch oven or electric skillet (with a cover) with oil and place over medium-high heat. When the oil is hot, add a small handful of the onions and cook until browned. Push them to the side of the pan, add the meat and brown slowly on all sides, about 10 minutes. Gradually add the remaining onions, taking care to keep them around, not under, the meat. Remove any onions that are in danger of blackening. Add more oil if necessary. When the meat and onions are thoroughly browned, reduce the heat to a low simmer, add the whole tomatoes with their liquid and cover the pan tightly. (If the lid is not tight, first cover the pan with foil and add the lid.) Simmer gently for 1 hour. Uncover the pan, break the tomatoes into smaller pieces, and turn the meat over. Cover and continue to simmer for about 2½ hours longer. The meat should be almost tender. If so, turn it over, add the carrots, cover, and cook until the meat is fork tender and the carrots are done, about 30 minutes longer.

Remove the pot roast and carrots from the pan. Mash most of the remaining tomato pieces. Combine 3 tablespoons of flour with ½ cup cold water. Gradually add enough of the slurry to the simmering juices to thicken. If desired, add a few drops of Gravy Master or Kitchen Bouquet to deepen the color of the gravy. Slice the pot roast and serve with the carrots and gravy.

Serves 8

Peppered Filets Mignon with Balsamic Sauce

The sauce is super easy to make and is superb with the filets. Serve them with wild rice and sautéed vegetables. Open a good Zinfandel or a Cabernet Sauvignon.

4 tablespoons black peppercorns
4 1½-inch thick filets mignon,
   7 to 8 ounces each
2 tablespoons canola or vegetable oil

Coarse salt
½ cup aged balsamic vinegar
¼ cup demi-glace
Sprigs of fresh thyme or rosemary

Preheat the oven to 450°F. Place the peppercorns in a plastic bag and coarsely crush them with a rolling pin or a heavy skillet. Rub the filets with oil, season with salt, and press some of the cracked pepper on one side of each steak. Heat a heavy, oven-proof skillet (not nonstick) over medium-high heat until hot. Add the steaks, pepper-coated sides down, and cook for 1 minute. Turn and cook until nicely crusted, about 3 minutes. Do not move the steaks around in the pan. Transfer the skillet to the oven and roast for 7 to 8 minutes for medium rare. Remove the steaks from the skillet and cover loosely with foil. Let the skillet cool for a minute, pour in the vinegar, and place the pan over medium-high heat. Bring to a boil, scraping up the browned bits from the bottom of the pan. The vinegar will foam and give off strong fumes at first. Boil until reduced to 4 or 5 tablespoons. Stir in the demi-glace and any accumulated juices from the steaks and simmer briefly. Spoon the sauce over the filets and garnish with the herb sprigs.

Serves 4

Not My Mom's Meatloaf

Hands down, meatloaf is America's favorite comfort food. This one is worth making just for the cold leftovers. It's terrific with scalloped potatoes and corn.

2 tablespoons olive oil
⅓ cup finely diced poblano pepper
¼ cup finely diced red bell pepper
1 jalapeño pepper, seeded
  and minced
¼ cup finely diced carrot
¼ cup finely diced celery
1½ cups finely chopped onion
2 cloves garlic, minced
½ cup Italian seasoned bread crumbs
½ cup whole milk
1 pound ground round

½ pound ground veal
½ pound ground pork
⅓ cup minced flat leaf parsley
1½ teaspoons salt
½ teaspoon freshly ground pepper
1 teaspoon dry mustard
1 teaspoon coarsely chopped
  fresh thyme
1½ teaspoons dried Greek oregano
2 eggs
1 tablespoon Worcestershire sauce
Barbecue sauce

Heat the olive oil in a medium skillet. Add the peppers, carrots, celery, onions, and garlic, and cook until softened. Transfer to a large bowl and cool.

Preheat the oven to 350°F. Soak the bread crumbs in the milk. Add the soaked crumbs and all the remaining ingredients, except the barbecue sauce, to the bowl. Mix and knead until everything is well incorporated. The mixture should hold its shape, but should not be stiff. Add more milk or bread crumbs as necessary. Turn the mixture into a 9x13-inch baking pan and shape into a loaf, about 3-inches thick in the center. Spread the top and sides with barbecue sauce and bake for 1½ hours. Let the meatloaf rest for 15 to 30 minutes before slicing.

Serves 6 to 8

Korean Barbecued Skirt Steaks

Skirt steak is chewier than more expensive cuts, but has superb flavor, especially in this Asian preparation. Be careful not to overcook it, and slice it across the grain or it will be tough. Rice, broccoli, and Chinese or Japanese beer are ideal accompaniments.

1½ to 2 pounds skirt steak, well-trimmed, cut into 6 to 8 serving pieces
3 tablespoons light brown sugar
6 tablespoons soy sauce
1 tablespoon sake, dry sherry, dry white wine, or dry white vermouth

5 large cloves garlic, minced
6 scallions (white part only), minced
3 teaspoons fresh ginger, minced
1 tablespoon Asian sesame oil
Freshly ground pepper
1 to 2 tablespoons peanut oil if pan searing the steak

Place the steak on a plate. Combine all the ingredients, except the peanut oil and pepper, and pour over the meat. Turn to coat both sides. Marinate at room temperature for 30 minutes, turning after 15 minutes.

Prepare a barbecue grill. Drain the steak and season with pepper. Grill over hot coals for 2 to 3 minutes per side for medium rare. (Alternatively, heat a large, heavy skillet over high heat. When hot, add 1 tablespoon peanut oil, turn the heat down to medium high, add the steak, in two batches if necessary, and sear for 2 or 3 minutes per side. Do not crowd the pan or the meat will steam rather than brown.) Transfer the steak to a cutting board and let it rest, loosely covered with foil, for 5 minutes. Slice the steak across the grain on the bias in ¼-inch thick slices and serve.

Serves 4

Picadillo

This aromatic Cuban dish is full of zesty flavor. Delicious right out of the pan, it's even better the next day. Serve it as they do in Miami's Little Havana, with rice, black beans, and fried plantains.

2 tablespoons olive oil
2 cups finely chopped onions
½ cup diced red bell pepper
½ cup diced green bell pepper
2 pounds ground round
2 or 3 garlic cloves, minced
1 teaspoon ground cumin
1 teaspoon chili powder
1 teaspoon sweet paprika
½ teaspoon ground cinnamon
2 Turkish bay leaves

2 teaspoons dried oregano
¾ cup low-salt beef broth
½ cup tomato paste
¼ cup dry sherry
Salt and freshly ground pepper
½ cup sliced pimento stuffed green olives
½ cup golden raisins
¼ cup chopped parsley
½ cup slivered almonds, toasted (optional)

In a large skillet or Dutch oven, heat the oil over medium-high heat. Add the onions and bell peppers and cook until softened. Add the meat and cook until no traces of pink remain, breaking it up with a wooden spoon. Stir in the garlic, cumin, chili powder, paprika, cinnamon, bay leaves, and oregano and cook for about 1 minute. Add the beef broth, tomato paste, and sherry, and stir well. Season with salt and pepper, cover, and cook for 20 minutes. Add the olives, raisins, and parsley and cook, uncovered, for 5 minutes or until moderately thick. Add the almonds. Serve immediately or refrigerate for up to 3 days.

Serves 8 or more

Roast Tenderloin of Beef Stuffed with Lobster

No doubt about it, this is an extravagant, pull-out-all-the-stops dish. Accompany the beef with Bernaise sauce, wild rice, Herbed Tomatoes, and a green vegetable. Open a fine Burgundy or Cabernet Sauvignon.

3 small lobster tails
1 6-pound beef tenderloin, trimmed
3 tablespoons butter, melted
Salt and freshly ground pepper

Garlic powder
6 slices bacon
Parsley sprigs

Have the fishmonger run wooden skewers through the lobster tails to keep them straight, or tie them securely to butter knives. Drop the tails into a large pot of boiling water. Simmer for 5 minutes and drain. When cool enough to handle, remove the tail meat in one piece.

Preheat the oven to 400°F. Trim the tip end from the beef (save it for a quick stir fry). Beginning and ending ½ inch from the ends, slice the tenderloin lengthwise to form a deep pocket. Be careful not to cut through the bottom. Place the lobster tails in the pocket end to end. Slice the tails in half if necessary to fill the entire length of the pocket. Drizzle the lobster with melted butter. Pull the opening closed and tie the tenderloin with kitchen twine at 2-inch intervals. Season the meat with salt, pepper, and garlic powder and place it on a rack in a large, shallow roasting pan. Top with the bacon slices. Roast for 30 to 40 minutes or until a meat thermometer inserted in the thickest part of the roast registers 120 degrees for rare, 125 for medium rare, or 130 for medium. (Take care not to push the thermometer through the meat and into the lobster.) The meat will continue to cook as it rests. Remove the pan from the oven and transfer the beef to a carving board. Discard the bacon and let the meat rest, loosely covered with foil, for 15 to 20 minutes. Remove the twine, slice the tenderloin, and arrange it on a platter. Garnish with parsley sprigs and serve.

Serves 4

Rosemary Strip Steak with Arugula and Blue Cheese Salad

This dish is based on a rosemary infused steak once served at a New York bistro. It was love at first bite. The salad is a delicious addition. Pair the steak with a good Cabernet Sauvignon.

STEAK

⅓ cup olive oil
2 sprigs fresh rosemary
1 large clove garlic, peeled and sliced
1 boneless New York strip or ribeye
  steak 1¼- to 1½-inches thick (about 1 pound)

Coarse salt and freshly
  ground pepper
Lemon wedges

SALAD

Rosemary oil
1 small clove garlic, put through a press
1 to 2 tablespoons balsamic vinegar
About 4 cups mixed arugula and frisée
1 Belgian endive, sliced crosswise
Thinly sliced red onion, to taste

6 cherry tomatoes, halved, or
  diced tomato
Freshly ground pepper
3 to 4 tablespoons crumbled
  blue cheese

Place the olive oil, rosemary sprigs, and garlic in a small saucepan and warm over very low heat. When the rosemary begins to sizzle, remove the pan from the heat and set aside to cool. Strain the oil into a small bowl. Discard the rosemary and garlic. Place the steak on a plate and drizzle with a little of the rosemary oil. Rub the oil over both sides. Cover the steak with plastic wrap and let stand at room temperature for 1 hour.

Place the remaining rosemary oil in a small bowl. Put the garlic clove through a press into the bowl and whisk in 1 tablespoon of balsamic vinegar. Add more vinegar to taste. Set the vinaigrette aside.

Preheat the oven to 400°F. Heat a heavy, ovenproof skillet over medium-high heat until hot. Season the steak with coarse salt and pepper. Place it in the pan and cook until well-browned, 2 to 3 minutes. Turn it over and transfer the skillet to the oven for 6 to 7 minutes for medium rare. Remove the steak to a cutting board and let it rest, covered loosely with foil, for 10 minutes before slicing.

In a bowl, combine the arugula, frisée, endive, onions, and tomatoes and sprinkle with pepper. Toss with enough vinaigrette to coat lightly. Add the cheese and toss again. Mound the salad on 2 plates. Slice the steak on the bias and arrange on the plates. Sprinkle the slices lightly with coarse salt and serve with lemon wedges and any remaining dressing.

Serves 2

Sautéed Beef and Vegetables

This quick sauté was the first "fancy" dish attempted by a young bride. To her relief, it was a great success and is still a favorite. Serve it with rice or buttered noodles and a dry, full-bodied red wine.

1 medium onion, halved lengthwise
4 tablespoons olive oil
2 green bell peppers, cut into 1½-inch squares or 1-inch wide strips
2 red bell peppers, cut into 1½-inch squares or 1-inch wide strips
1 large clove garlic, slivered
Salt and freshly ground pepper
2 teaspoons dried Greek oregano
2 tablespoons unsalted butter

1 pound mushrooms, trimmed and thickly sliced
1½ pounds skirt steak or beef tenderloin, cut into strips, about 1-inch wide by 2½-inches long
1 large clove garlic, finely minced
⅓ cup dry or sweet sherry or sauterne
½ to ¾ cup chicken stock or broth
2 to 3 tablespoons tomato paste
2 medium tomatoes, cut in wedges

Separate the onion into leaves and slice them into strips about ¾-inches wide. Heat 2 tablespoons of oil in a large, heavy skillet over medium heat. Add the peppers, a sliver or two of garlic, a pinch of salt and pepper, and ½ teaspoon of oregano. Sauté for a minute or so, cover the pan and cook for a few minutes, stirring often. Remove the peppers from the pan as soon as they are crisp-tender. Repeat with the onions and add them to the peppers. Add 1 tablespoon of oil and the butter to the pan and heat until the butter is foaming. Add the mushrooms and a pinch of salt. When the mushrooms begin to cook down, add ½ teaspoon of oregano and one or two slices of garlic. Sauté until the mushrooms are lightly browned. Add them to the peppers and onions. Turn the heat up to high, add the remaining tablespoon of oil and heat until very hot, but not smoking. Add the meat, in batches if necessary, a pinch of salt and pepper, ½ teaspoon of oregano, and sauté until browned. Do not crowd the pan. Turn the heat down to medium. (If the meat was sautéed in batches, add it all to the pan.) Add the minced garlic and stir briefly. Add the sherry or sauterne, ½ cup of broth, and the tomato paste. Stir well, cover and cook, stirring occasionally, for 2 to 3 minutes. The meat should still be pink in the center. Remove to a serving platter. Add the peppers, onions, and mushrooms to the pan and place the tomato wedges over the top. Add more broth if the pan is dry. Cover and cook just long enough to heat the vegetables through. Surround the meat with the vegetables and spoon the sauce over the top.

Serves 4

Southwestern Black Bean Chili with Seared Sirloin

Chipotle and pasilla chilies add smoky flavor to this southwestern-style chili. Make it a day ahead for best flavor. The amounts called for produce a spicy, but not fiery, chili. Serve it with Mexican Confetti Cornbread and cold beer.

1 pound dried black beans
4 tablespoons olive oil
3 cups finely chopped onions
6 cloves garlic, finely minced
  (about 2 tablespoons)
3 teaspoons dried oregano
2 teaspoons paprika
½ teaspoon cayenne pepper
3 to 4 tablespoons ground cumin,
  or to taste
2 bay leaves

1 teaspoon pasilla chili powder
2 to 3 tablespoons ancho
  chili powder
1 canned chipotle chili in adobo,
  minced
1 28-ounce can tomatoes, drained
  and chopped, juice reserved, or
  tomato puree
Salt and freshly ground black pepper
1 tablespoon white or cider vinegar
2 to 3 pounds sirloin steak

GARNISH
Chopped cilantro
Sour cream
Salsa

Grated Monterey Jack cheese
Chopped onions or scallions
Tabasco or other hot sauce

Pick over the beans to check for stones. Place them in a bowl or saucepan, cover with cold water by 2 inches and soak overnight, or boil for 2 minutes, cover, remove from the heat, and soak for 1 hour. Drain. Heat the oil in a large, heavy saucepan and sauté the onions until wilted. Add the garlic and cook for a few seconds. Add the oregano, paprika, cayenne, cumin, and bay leaves and stir for 2 minutes. Add the beans, the chili powders, minced chipotle, and enough water to cover by 3 inches. Combine well and bring to a boil. Lower the heat, cover, and simmer for 1 hour. Add the tomatoes, reserved juice (or puree), and salt and pepper. Continue to simmer until the beans are very tender, 1 hour or longer, adding more water if necessary. Stir in the vinegar. Taste and adjust the seasoning.

Grill, pan-cook, or broil the steak to your liking. Let it rest, loosely covered with foil, for 10 minutes before cutting into bite-sized pieces. Ladle the chili into bowls, top with the steak, and sprinkle with chopped cilantro. Serve it with bowls of sour cream, salsa, grated cheese, chopped onions or scallions, and hot sauce.

Serves 8

Herb Crusted Filets Mignon with Shallot and Red Wine Sauce

Filets mignon are easy to cook and always impressive. Serve the filets with rice or potatoes, sautéed mushrooms, a green vegetable, and a good bottle of Cabernet Sauvignon.

2 tablespoons minced fresh thyme
2 tablespoons minced fresh rosemary
1 tablespoon minced fresh marjoram
4 filets mignon, 1½- to 2-inches thick,
   7 to 8 ounces each
Coarse salt and freshly ground pepper
3 tablespoons canola or vegetable oil
2 large shallots, thinly sliced
1 clove garlic, minced

2 level teaspoons tomato paste
2 tablespoons cognac
¾ cup dry red wine, such as zinfandel
1 cup veal or chicken stock, demi-glace,
   or low-sodium beef broth
1 tablespoon arrowroot or cornstarch
   dissolved in 2 tablespoons
   cold water (optional)

Preheat the oven to 450°F. Combine the herbs. Pat the filets dry and season them with salt and pepper. Heat a heavy, ovenproof skillet (not non-stick) over medium-high heat until hot. Add 2 tablespoons of the oil. Add the filets and cook for 1 minute. Turn and cook until nicely browned and crusted, about 3 minutes longer. Press the herbs onto the tops of the steaks. Transfer the skillet to the oven and roast the filets for 7 to 8 minutes for medium rare. Remove the filets from the skillet and tent them with foil.

Add the remaining tablespoon of oil to the skillet and sauté the shallots until wilted. Add the garlic, stir for a few seconds, and stir in the tomato paste. Cook, stirring constantly, until the tomato paste darkens. Add the cognac and red wine and simmer until almost syrupy. Add the stock or demi glace and simmer to reduce and thicken lightly. (If using beef broth, reduce it to about ½ cup. Add the cornstarch slurry, one teaspoon at a time, until lightly thickened.) Transfer the filets to warm plates and top with the sauce.

Serves 4

Zinfandel Braised Short Ribs

These succulent short ribs can be made a day or two ahead. Serve them with horseradish mashed potatoes or Creamy Parmesan Polenta, glazed carrots, and Balsamic Glazed Onions. Open a Zinfandel.

6 pounds beef short ribs
Salt and freshly ground pepper
3 tablespoons olive oil
2 medium onions, chopped
2 carrots, chopped
2 ribs celery, chopped
6 shallots, peeled and coarsely chopped
1 medium leek (white and light green parts only), chopped
2 tablespoons tomato paste
2 tablespoons flour

½ cup ruby port
4 cups red zinfandel
1 or 2 small sprigs rosemary, 8 sprigs flat leaf parsley, 6 sprigs thyme, and 2 bay leaves, tied together with kitchen twine
6 to 8 cloves garlic, lightly crushed
2 to 4 cups veal stock, or 2 cups each canned low-salt beef and chicken broth
Chopped flat leaf parsley

Preheat the oven to 325°F. Tie each short rib in 1 or 2 places with kitchen twine and season with salt and pepper. Heat the olive oil in a heavy, nonreactive Dutch oven over medium-high heat. Add the short ribs in a single layer, in batches if necessary, and brown on all sides. Do not crowd the pan. Remove to a plate. Pour off all but 3 tablespoons of fat from the pan. Lower the heat to medium and add the onions, carrots, celery, shallots, and leeks. Sauté until the onions turn golden. Add the tomato paste and flour and cook, scraping the bottom of the pan, for 1 minute. Add the port and zinfandel. Return the ribs to the pot and bring to a boil. Boil until the wine is reduced to about 1½ cups. Add the herb bundle, garlic, and 2 cups of stock or broth. Bring to a simmer. Add enough additional stock to reach about ¾ of the way up the side of the ribs. Bring to a boil, cover the pan tightly, and transfer it to the oven. (If the cover isn't tight, cover the pan with foil before putting on the lid.) Braise the ribs until they are fork tender and almost falling off the bone, 2½ to 3 hours, turning them over occasionally. Remove the ribs and keep warm. Strain the sauce into a fat separator or directly into a large saucepan. Skim off the fat and reduce if necessary until lightly thickened and full-flavored. Adjust the seasoning. Remove the strings and arrange the short ribs on plates. Spoon the sauce over them and sprinkle with chopped parsley.

Note: If preparing in advance, refrigerate the ribs in the defatted liquid. Place plastic wrap directly on top of the ribs before covering the pot. Reheat slowly. Reduce the sauce if necessary.

Serves 6

Veal Provençal

This warming dish fills the kitchen with a mouthwatering aroma. Cut the meat into chunks to turn it into a fabulous stew. Serve it with buttered noodles, carrots, and sautéed mushrooms. Pour a dry white wine.

2 tablespoons olive oil
1 3-pound boneless veal shoulder roast, tied
Salt and freshly ground pepper
1 cup chopped onion
½ cup chopped carrot
½ cup sliced leek (white part only)
2 tablespoons flour
1½ cups dry white wine or dry white vermouth

½ cup chicken stock or canned low-salt broth
1 cup canned tomatoes, drained and well-crushed
2 branches fresh thyme
4 large fresh basil leaves
3-inch strip of orange zest (no white pith)
2 cloves garlic, smashed
Chopped parsley

Preheat the oven to 350°F. Heat the olive oil in a heavy Dutch oven just large enough for the meat to fit comfortably over medium-high heat. Season the veal with salt and pepper and brown it slowly on all sides. Remove it to a plate. Add the onions and carrots to the pan and sauté for 2 minutes. Add the leeks and cook until the vegetables have softened. Add the flour and cook, scraping the bottom of the pot, for about 1 minute. Add the wine and bring to a simmer, scraping up any browned bits. Add the stock and simmer, stirring well, until the flour is thoroughly incorporated. Add the tomatoes, herbs, orange zest, garlic, salt, and pepper. Return the veal to the pot. Cover the pot with foil and add the lid. Transfer it to the oven and braise until the meat is fork tender, about 1½ to 2 hours, turning the veal over once or twice.

Remove the veal to a plate and tent with foil. Strain the braising liquid and skim off the fat. Return the liquid to the pot and boil until lightly thickened. Slice the veal and arrange it on a platter. Spoon some sauce over the slices and sprinkle with chopped parsley. Serve with the remaining sauce.

Note: Braised meats and poultry give their all to the braising liquid and dry out quickly when exposed to the air. Be sure to keep the surface moistened or well covered with plastic wrap or foil.

Serves 6

Veal Scaloppine with Lemon, Parmesan, and Asparagus

This light, fresh-tasting veal is based on a dish enjoyed on a sunny terrace in Florence. Pour a crisp Italian Sauvignon Blanc.

1½ pounds veal scaloppine, cut thin
1 pound slender asparagus
Olive oil
Unsalted butter
Salt and freshly ground pepper
2 cloves garlic, minced
½ cup dry white wine or dry
   white vermouth

1 cup chicken stock or low-salt broth
2 tablespoons butter, softened
¼ cup fresh lemon juice
2 teaspoons chopped flat
   leaf parsley
¼ cup freshly grated Parmesan cheese
Lemon wedges

Pound the scaloppine between two sheets of plastic wrap to a thickness of ⅛ inch. Wrap and refrigerate until needed. Snap off the woody stems from the asparagus stalks. (If the stalks are thick, peel them with a vegetable peeler.) Cook the asparagus until crisp-tender, drain, and keep warm.

Meanwhile, heat a large, heavy skillet over medium-high heat until very hot. Add 1½ tablespoons of oil and 1 tablespoon of butter to the pan. Season the scaloppine with salt and pepper. In batches, add as many scaloppine as will fit comfortably without touching and cook until lightly browned, about 1 minute. Add 2 or 3 small pieces of butter to the pan, turn, and cook the second side. Remove from the pan and keep warm. If the butter has burned, pour it out and heat a spoonful of fresh oil. Stir in the garlic. Add the wine and let it reduce until slightly syrupy. Add the stock and boil until reduced to about ¾ cup. Add the softened butter, the lemon juice, parsley, and any accumulated juices from the veal. Simmer until the sauce thickens lightly. Spoon the sauce onto warm plates. Arrange the asparagus over the sauce and top with the veal. Sprinkle the scaloppine evenly with grated Parmesan and serve with lemon wedges.

Serves 4

Veal Scaloppine Puttanesca

This modified version of puttanesca sauce is delicious with veal and chicken breasts. Don't omit the anchovies. They add depth but not fishiness to the sauce. Pour a crisp white or a lighter red wine.

½ cup sun-dried tomatoes
1½ pounds veal scaloppine, cut thin
Olive oil
Freshly ground pepper
2 anchovy fillets, chopped
2 cloves garlic, minced

½ cup dry white wine
1 cup veal or chicken stock
¼ cup brine-packed capers, drained
12 imported black olives
Chopped parsley

Soak the sun-dried tomatoes in hot water to soften, drain, and cut them into pieces. Pound the scaloppine between two sheets of plastic wrap to a thickness of ⅛ inch.

Heat a large, heavy skillet over medium-high heat. When the pan is very hot, add 1½ tablespoons of oil. Season the scaloppine with pepper. In batches, add as many scaloppine as will comfortably fit in the pan without touching, and cook until lightly browned, about 1 minute per side. Remove to a plate and keep warm. Lower the heat and add a little fresh oil to the pan. Add the anchovies and cook until they dissolve. Stir in the garlic. Add the wine and reduce until syrupy. Add the stock and tomatoes. Simmer until reduced to about ¾ cup. Add the scaloppine, turn to coat with the sauce, and add the capers and olives. Simmer just until the scaloppine is reheated. Divide the scaloppine and sauce among 4 plates and garnish with chopped parsley.

Serves 4

Züri Gschnetzlets
(Zurich-Style Veal in Cream Sauce)

Chicago's Swiss Consul General shared the recipe for this traditional dish. It's wonderful with buttered noodles or rice, a green salad, and a lightly chilled, dry white wine. For real drama, prepare it table-side in a chafing dish or an electric skillet.

1½ pounds veal, sliced thin
¼ cup butter
4 green onions, chopped
¼ cup flour
¼ teaspoon salt

¼ teaspoon freshly ground pepper
1 teaspoon dried rosemary, crumbled
½ cup dry white wine, warmed
½ cup half & half, warmed

Pound the veal between sheets of plastic wrap to a thickness of ⅛ inch. Slice it against the grain into strips, ¼-inch wide by 1-inch long. Wrap and refrigerate until needed. Melt the butter in a heavy skillet over medium-high heat until foamy. Add the onions and sauté until softened, about 2 minutes. Add the veal and stir for 3 minutes. Sprinkle the flour, salt, pepper, and rosemary over the meat. Add the wine and half & half and stir until smooth. Lower the heat, cover, and simmer gently for 3 minutes, or until the sauce is lightly thickened.

Note: In lieu of flour, 2 tablespoons of cornstarch dissolved in 3 tablespoons of cold water can be added to the simmering sauce, a spoonful at a time, until it reaches the desired consistency.

Serves 4 to 6

Slimmed-Down Veal Parmesan

Here's a lightened, fresher-tasting version of the popular Italian-American dish. The fresh mozzarella can be omitted to trim calories even further. Serve it with sautéed spinach or chard instead of pasta. Pair it with a light red wine, such as Valpolicella.

TOMATO SAUCE

2 pounds ripe garden tomatoes, or 1 28-ounce can plum tomatoes in juice, drained and chopped
1 tablespoon olive oil

3 cloves garlic, minced
Salt and freshly ground pepper
¼ cup chopped fresh basil

VEAL

8 to 12 veal cutlets (about 3 to 4 ounces each)
Olive oil
Salt and freshly ground pepper

½ cup freshly grated Parmesan cheese
6 ounces fresh mozzarella cheese, coarsely grated or thinly sliced

Cut an "X" across the stem ends of the tomatoes and blanch them in boiling water for 10 seconds. Plunge them into ice water and slip off the skins. Working over a sieve suspended over a bowl, cut the tomatoes in half and scoop out the seeds. Discard the seeds. Dice the tomatoes and transfer them to the bowl. Heat the oil and garlic in a large skillet over medium heat. When the garlic begins to sizzle, add the tomatoes, salt and pepper. Simmer until the sauce thickens lightly, about 20 to 30 minutes. Remove the sauce from the heat and stir in the basil. Set aside.

Preheat the oven to 350°F. Pound the veal between sheets of plastic wrap to a thickness of ¼ inch. Heat a large, heavy skillet over medium-high heat until very hot. Add 3 tablespoons of olive oil. Season as many cutlets as will fit in the pan without touching with salt and pepper. Sear the veal, turning once, for 1 to 2 minutes per side. Repeat with the remaining cutlets. Spread a little sauce in the bottom of a large baking dish and add the veal, overlapping slightly. Lightly cover the cutlets with sauce, sprinkle evenly with Parmesan, and top with mozzarella. Cover with foil and bake for 30 minutes or until the veal is tender. The dish can be assembled ahead and baked before serving.

Note: The light, fresh tomato sauce is wonderful on pasta or in any recipe calling for tomato sauce. The amounts given will make about 2 cups of sauce. It freezes well.

Serves 4

Osso Buco
(Braised Veal Shanks)

Comfort food at its very best! Risotto Milanese is traditionally served with this hearty dish but Creamy Parmesan Polenta or mashed potatoes are also excellent. The gremolata adds a final burst of fresh flavor. Pour a Barolo, Brunello di Montalcino, or a Chianti Classico Riserva.

VEAL

4 to 6 pieces veal shank, each
    about 2 inches thick
Salt and freshly ground pepper
Olive oil
Flour
1½ cups dry white wine or dry
    white vermouth
1½ cups finely chopped onions
¾ cup finely chopped carrots
¾ cup finely chopped celery
4 cloves garlic, minced

1½ cups canned plum tomatoes,
    drained and well crushed,
    ⅓ cup juice reserved
2 strips lemon zest (no white pith)
1 large sprig fresh thyme
1 large sprig fresh basil (about 6 leaves)
2 Turkish bay leaves
3 large sprigs flat leaf parsley
1 to 2 cups veal or beef stock, or
    canned low-salt beef broth

GREMOLATA

1 tablespoon grated lemon zest
¾ teaspoon finely minced garlic
3 tablespoons finely chopped parsley

Tie each piece of veal tightly around the middle with kitchen twine and season with salt and pepper. Heat 3 tablespoons of olive oil in a heavy skillet over medium-high heat. Flour as many pieces of veal as will fit in the skillet without touching. Add the veal in batches and brown well on all sides, regulating the heat so that the drippings do not burn. Remove to a plate. Add the wine to the skillet and boil for 2 or 3 minutes, scraping up all of the browned bits. Set aside.

Preheat the oven to 350°F. Heat 2 tablespoons of oil in a heavy Dutch oven large enough to hold the veal in one layer. Add the onions, carrots, and celery, and cook until softened. Add the garlic and cook until fragrant. Add the wine from the skillet, the tomatoes, reserved juice, lemon zest, and herbs. Season lightly with salt and pepper. Place the shanks on the vegetables and add enough broth to reach ¾ of the way up their sides. Bring to a simmer, cover tightly, and transfer the pan to the oven. Braise until the veal is very tender, turning once or twice, about 2 hours. Remove to a plate and tent with foil. Strain the braising liquid into a bowl (or a fat separator) and skim off the fat. Return the liquid and vegetables to the pan and cook at a lively simmer until it has reduced and thickened lightly. Taste for seasoning. (The shanks can be prepared a day or two in advance. Place plastic wrap directly on the surface of the meat and refrigerate in the sauce. Reheat gently, adding a little water if necessary.)

Meanwhile, combine the ingredients for the gremolata in a bowl and set aside or refrigerate for several hours. Remove the strings from the veal and transfer to plates. Spoon some sauce over the shanks and serve with the remaining sauce and the gremolata.

Serves 4

Veal Chops Marsala

This is a marvelous dish for a chilly evening. Serve the chops with Creamy Parmesan Polenta and cherry tomatoes sautéed with garlic and minced parsley. Pour a Barbera d'Alba or a Chianti Classico.

½ cup olive oil
3 cloves garlic, coarsely chopped
Several thyme and rosemary sprigs,
   lightly crushed
4 veal rib chops, ¾- to 1-inch thick,
   bones frenched
3 tablespoons unsalted butter
1 tablespoon olive oil
1 pound mixed mushrooms
   (such as chanterelles, morels, shitakes,
   cremini), sliced

Coarse salt and freshly ground pepper
2 cloves garlic, finely minced
1 shallot, minced
½ cup dry Marsala wine
1 cup veal or chicken stock or canned
   low-salt broth
2 tablespoons cornstarch or arrowroot
   mixed with 3 tablespoons water
   (optional)
1 sprig fresh thyme or rosemary
Chopped flat leaf parsley

Combine the olive oil, garlic, and herb sprigs and pour over the chops. Cover and refrigerate for several hours or overnight. Let the chops stand at room temperature for 30 minutes before cooking.

Preheat the oven to 400°F. Heat a heavy, ovenproof skillet over medium-high heat. Drain the chops and sear on one side until browned, about 2 minutes. Turn the chops, transfer the skillet to the oven, and roast for about 8 minutes for medium. Heat 3 tablespoons of butter and 1 tablespoon of olive oil in a large skillet over medium-high heat. Add the mushrooms and salt lightly. Sauté until lightly browned. Make an opening in the center of the pan and add a spoonful of oil. Add the garlic, stir briefly, and combine with the mushrooms. Remove the pan from the heat.

Remove the chops to a platter and let them rest, loosely covered with foil, for 5 minutes. Pour off any fat and let the skillet cool slightly. Add a spoonful of fresh oil to the skillet and heat over medium-high heat. Add the shallot, cook briefly, and stir in the remaining garlic. Add the wine and reduce until almost syrupy. Add the stock and boil until it reduces to about ⅔ cup. If necessary, add the cornstarch mixture, one spoonful at a time, until the sauce is lightly thickened. Add the thyme or rosemary sprig and remove the pan from the heat. Season the sauce with salt and pepper and add any accumulated juices from the veal. Reheat the mushrooms if necessary. Remove the herb sprig from the sauce and spoon it onto warm plates. Add the chops and top with the mushrooms. Sprinkle with chopped parsley.

Serves 4

Rack of Venison with Tart Cherry and Red Wine Sauce

The tart cherry sauce is a perfect foil to the richness of the venison in this elegant dish. Accompany the venison with mashed sweet potatoes, Balsamic Glazed Onions, and Brussels Sprouts with Bacon. Pour a fine Chateauneuf du Pape. Finish with Poached Pears with Raspberry Coulis.

1½ cups red zinfandel
½ cup dried tart cherries
1 8- or 9-rib rack of cervena venison
    (about 2½ pounds), top flap, sinew,
    silverskin, and all fat removed, bones
    frenched (about 2 pounds trimmed
    weight) trimmings reserved
Olive oil
1 teaspoon tomato paste

⅓ cup peeled, sliced shallots
1 bay leaf
4 sprigs parsley
½ cup ruby port
4 cups brown veal stock or
    brown chicken stock
Salt and freshly ground pepper
2 tablespoons cornstarch combined
    with 4 tablespoons cold water

In a small saucepan, bring the zinfandel and dried cherries to a boil. Remove the pan from the heat and cool. Strain the wine into a small bowl. Reserve the cherries.

Cut most of the fat from the reserved venison trimmings and cut the meat into small chunks. Heat a saucepan over medium-high heat until very hot and add 1 tablespoon of olive oil. Add the chopped meat and brown very well. Add the tomato paste and cook, stirring, until it darkens. Add the shallots, bay leaf, and parsley and cook, stirring, for 1 minute. Add the port and strained zinfandel. Turn the heat to high and boil until syrupy, scraping up all of the browned bits. Add the stock, lower the heat, and simmer gently until reduced by half. Strain the sauce and discard the solids. Return the sauce to the pan and add the cherries. Simmer for 3 or 4 minutes, season with salt and pepper and set aside. (The sauce can be prepared a day ahead. Leftover sauce can be frozen to serve with duck or pork.)

Preheat the oven to 450°F. Heat a large, heavy skillet over high heat (not nonstick). Rub the venison with olive oil and season with salt and pepper. Sear the rack on all sides until well-browned. Transfer the rack, bones down, to a shallow roasting pan or rimmed sheet pan and roast until a thermometer registers 125° to 130°F for medium rare, about 20 minutes. (Venison cooked beyond medium will be dry.) Meanwhile, place the skillet over medium-high heat and deglaze with a little stock, scraping up the browned bits. Strain it into the sauce and set the sauce aside. When the venison is done, remove it to a carving board and let it rest, loosely covered with foil, for 15 minutes. Reheat the sauce and add any accumulated juices from the resting meat. If desired, add the cornstarch mixture to the simmering sauce, 1 tablespoon at a time, until the desired consistency is reached. Carve the venison into single chops and serve with the sauce.

Serves 4

Vegetables & Sides

Baked Butternut Squash and Apples

Winter squash and apples have a natural affinity, and both are enhanced by autumn spices. Serve this fragrant dish warm from the oven with pork, duck, turkey, or game.

½ cup unsalted butter, melted
2 butternut squash (about 4 pounds), peeled, halved, seeded, and sliced ½-inch thick
4 or 5 baking apples, peeled, cored, and sliced ½-inch thick

¾ cup firmly packed light brown sugar
1 teaspoon salt
1 teaspoon cinnamon
½ teaspoon nutmeg
½ teaspoon ground ginger

Preheat the oven to 350°F. Brush a large baking dish with a little of the melted butter. Layer the squash in the dish and top with the apples. Sprinkle with the brown sugar, salt, and spices. Drizzle with the remaining melted butter and bake until the squash and apples are tender, about 40 minutes.

Serves 12

Balsamic Glazed Onions

Richly glazed, these sweet and sour onions are wonderful with meats, poultry, or salmon. They can be prepared in advance and quickly finished before serving.

16 to 20 cipollini, or small boiling onions
2 tablespoons unsalted butter

2 tablespoons balsamic vinegar
Unsalted chicken stock or water
1½ teaspoons sugar

Drop the onions into boiling water for 10 seconds. Drain, plunge them into cold water, and slip off the skins. Trim, but do not completely remove the root ends.

Choose a skillet just large enough to hold the onions comfortably in a single layer. Add the butter and melt it over medium heat. Add the peeled onions and cook until they brown lightly on all sides. Add the vinegar and enough chicken stock or water to reach halfway up their sides. Partially cover the pan and simmer gently for about 20 minutes or until the onions are tender but still firm. The liquid should not be syrupy. Add water or stock if necessary. Uncover the pan and set aside for an hour or two, or refrigerate.

To serve, cover the pan and reheat gently. Uncover, raise the heat and stir in the sugar. Boil the liquid, turning the onions over, until it is syrupy and the onions are glazed. Serve hot.

Serves 4

Black Bean Stew

Hearty enough to ladle over rice as a main course, the stew is a great side dish for pork, beef, poultry, or fish. Make it in advance to allow the complex flavors to blend.

2 cups dried black beans
4 cups chicken stock or canned
   low-salt chicken broth
4 cups water
¼ pound smoked bacon, diced
2 cups finely chopped onions
2 ribs celery, cut into ½-inch dice
1 medium poblano or green
   bell pepper, seeded and cut
   into ½-inch dice
1 tablespoon ground cumin
2 teaspoons dried oregano

3 garlic cloves, finely minced
2 medium tomatoes, peeled,
   seeded, and cut into ½-inch dice
1 bay leaf
Salt and freshly ground pepper
1 small butternut squash (about 1
   pound), peeled, seeded, and cut
   into 1-inch dice
1 to 2 tablespoons sherry vinegar
   or lime juice
¼ cup chopped cilantro

Check the beans for pebbles. Place them in a bowl or saucepan, cover them with cold water by 2 inches and soak overnight, or boil for 2 minutes, cover, remove from the heat, and soak for 1 hour. Drain. Place the beans in a large saucepan, add the chicken stock and water, and bring to a boil. Lower the heat and simmer, partially covered, until tender, but not quite done, about 1 hour. The stew should be moist, but not soupy. Add more water to thin, or drain excess liquid and reserve.

Fry the bacon in a large skillet until lightly browned and drain on paper towels. Pour off all but 2 tablespoons of the drippings. Add the onions, celery, and poblano pepper to the skillet and sauté until wilted, about 5 minutes. Stir in the cumin, oregano, and garlic and cook until fragrant. Add the tomatoes, bay leaf, and bacon. Season with salt and pepper. Cook, stirring frequently, for 5 minutes. Set aside.

When the beans are tender, but not quite done, add the sautéed vegetables and the diced squash. Partially cover the pan and cook over medium-low heat until the squash is tender, about 15 to 20 minutes. The beans should be fully cooked. Add water or reserved cooking liquid to keep the stew moist. Stir in the vinegar and chopped cilantro. Taste for seasoning. Serve immediately, or cool and refrigerate for a day or two.

Serves 4

Brandied Cranberries

These cranberries shine like jewels and taste heavenly. A perfect accent to poultry, pork, or game, they are equally delicious over cheesecake or ice cream. Packed into clear jars, they make pretty holiday gifts.

3 12-ounce packages fresh cranberries
3 or more cups granulated sugar
½ to ⅔ cup good brandy or cognac

Preheat the oven to 350°F. Rinse and dry the cranberries. Place them in a single layer on 1 or 2 rimmed sheet pans. The pans should be full. Add enough sugar so that the cranberries "peek" out of the sugar. Cover the pans tightly with foil and bake for 1 hour. Remove the pans from the oven and carefully loosen the foil from a corner to allow steam to escape. Be careful—the steam will be very hot. Uncover the pans and stir the cranberries. Transfer them to a bowl and pour brandy or cognac over the top. Cool.

Pack the cranberries into clean jars (run the jars and lids through the dishwasher). Store in a cool, dark place for up to 1 month. Refrigerate for longer storage.

Makes about 6 cups

Brussels Sprouts Leaves with Bacon

Even those who claim to hate Brussels sprouts have changed their minds when they tried this dish. The secret? Quick cooking doesn't allow a strong, cabbagey flavor to develop. Try it!

1½ pounds Brussels sprouts
3 slices bacon or pancetta,
  finely diced
¼ to ⅓ cup finely diced
  onions or shallots

¼ cup water
1 to 2 tablespoons balsamic
  vinegar (optional)
Salt and freshly ground pepper

Trim the Brussels sprouts, cut out the cores, and separate the leaves. Thinly slice the centers crosswise if they won't come apart. Rinse the leaves and drain.

In a large skillet, cook the bacon or pancetta until lightly browned. Drain on paper towels. Add the onions or shallots to the drippings and cook until softened. Add the Brussels sprouts leaves and ¼ cup of water. Sauté until the leaves are just tender and most of the moisture in the pan has evaporated. Do not overcook. Remove from the heat and stir in the vinegar and bacon. Season with salt and pepper and serve hot.

Serves 6

Corn and Okra Stew

The flavor of this summery side dish shines when prepared a day in advance. It's especially good with chicken, lamb, or fish. It freezes well.

2 to 3 tablespoons olive oil
2 cups chopped onions
1 cup chopped leeks
  (white and light green parts only)
1 pound okra, tops trimmed,
  sliced ½-inch thick
3 cloves garlic, finely minced

1 cup low-salt chicken broth
Salt and freshly ground pepper
Kernels from 3 ears fresh corn
6 medium plum tomatoes, peeled,
  seeded, and diced
⅓ cup sliced green onions
¼ cup chopped fresh basil

Heat the olive oil in a large skillet or Dutch oven. Add the onions and leeks and sauté until wilted, about 5 minutes. Add the okra and sauté for 2 minutes. Make a space in the center of the pan and add the garlic (add a spoonful of oil if the pan is dry). Sauté briefly and combine with the okra. Add ½ cup of the broth and season with salt and pepper. Add more broth as necessary if the pan seems dry. Cover and simmer gently for 2 to 3 minutes, or until the okra is almost tender. Add the corn. Cover and cook until the corn and okra are just done, about 2 minutes. Uncover the pan and add the tomatoes, green onions, and basil. Stir to combine and remove the pan from the heat. Taste for seasoning. Serve the stew warm, at room temperature, or lightly chilled.

Serves 8

Spiced Peaches

Prepare these aromatic peaches several days in advance. They really dress up poultry, game, fowl, or pork.

3 29-ounce cans cling peach halves
1 cup vinegar
1¾ cups sugar

10 to 12 whole cloves
½ teaspoon ground cinnamon
2 tablespoons bourbon

Drain the peaches and place them in a bowl. Combine the vinegar, sugar, cloves, and cinnamon in a saucepan. Simmer for 10 minutes and add the bourbon. Pour the liquid over the peaches and let stand until cool. Refrigerate, covered, for several days. Serve the peaches lightly chilled.

Serves 6 to 8

Spinach and Mushroom Casserole

Mushroom cream sauce and a cheese topping turn ordinary creamed spinach into something special. The spinach is wonderful with steak, roast beef, meatloaf, or poultry.

3 tablespoons butter
¼ cup grated onion
1 pound mushrooms, sliced or diced
3 tablespoons flour
1 teaspoon salt
Freshly ground pepper

¼ teaspoon nutmeg
2 cups half & half
2 10-ounce packages frozen chopped
   spinach, thawed and drained well
⅓ cup grated Gruyère cheese

Preheat the oven to 325°F. Butter a 1-quart baking dish or gratin. In a large skillet, melt the butter and add the onion and mushrooms. Sauté until the mushrooms are beginning to color and any liquid has evaporated. Sprinkle the flour, salt, pepper, and nutmeg over the mushrooms. Blend well and cook for a moment or two, stirring constantly and scraping the bottom of the pan. Gradually stir in the half & half and bring to a simmer. Remove the pan from the heat and taste the sauce for seasoning. Spread half of the spinach in the casserole and cover with half of the mushroom cream sauce. Add the remaining spinach and top with the remaining sauce. Sprinkle the grated cheese over the casserole. Place the dish in a larger baking pan and add enough boiling water to reach half way up the side of the dish. Bake for 40 to 45 minutes, or until hot.

Serves 6

Herbed Tomatoes

This simple side dish delivers lots of flavor and dresses up simply cooked meats and poultry.

2 medium-size, ripe garden tomatoes
Butter
Dried oregano

Salt and freshly ground pepper
Grated Parmesan cheese

Preheat the oven to 350°F. Cut the tomatoes in half and place them on a baking sheet. Top each with a pat of butter and sprinkle with oregano, salt, pepper, and grated cheese. Bake, uncovered, for 20 minutes. The tomatoes can also be grilled for 5 minutes.

Serves 4

Grilled Artichokes with Sun-Dried Tomato Aioli

Serve these delicious artichokes as a first course or as part of a casual buffet. The aioli is fabulous on its own with fish and shrimp, or as a dip for raw vegetables.

3 lemons, halved
6 large, fresh artichokes

Olive oil
Salt and freshly ground pepper

Fill a large bowl with cold water and add the juice and rinds from 2 of the lemons. One at a time, snap off the small, lower leaves from the artichokes. With a heavy knife, slice about 1 inch off the top. With kitchen shears, cut off the tips of the remaining leaves. Cut off the stem at the base of the artichoke and trim the bottom evenly with a small, sharp knife. Rub the cut surfaces with the third lemon and drop the artichoke into the bowl. Repeat with the remaining artichokes. Place a steamer rack in a large, non-aluminum pot and add water. Steam the artichokes upside down until the bottoms are tender when tested with a small knife, about 25 to 30 minutes. Remove them from the steamer and drain. (The artichokes can also be boiled, covered, in a large, non-aluminum pot. Drain them upside down.) When cool enough to handle, halve the artichokes lengthwise, pull out the inner cone of pointed leaves, and scrape away the hairy choke with a teaspoon. The artichokes can be refrigerated overnight.

Brush the artichokes lightly with olive oil and season with salt and pepper. Grill them over hot coals, or on a preheated, ridged grill pan, until heated through and marked on both sides. Serve them hot with the aioli, or grill them in advance and serve at room temperature.

Aioli

1 large egg yolk
2 tablespoons cider vinegar
2 to 4 cloves garlic, chopped
½ cup olive oil combined with
  ½ cup canola oil

3 tablespoons sun-dried tomato
  paste from a tube
Salt and freshly ground pepper
Snipped chives

Process the egg yolk, vinegar, and garlic in a food processor or blender for 10 seconds. With the machine running, slowly dribble in oil until the mixture emulsifies. Add the remaining oil in a thin stream. Transfer the aioli to a bowl, add the sun-dried tomato paste and season with salt and pepper. The aioli can be refrigerated for several hours. Sprinkle with snipped chives before serving. Makes about 1 cup.

Serves 6 to 12

Hungarian Potatoes

Make plenty of these fabulous potatoes 'cause they'll be coming back for seconds!

6 medium potatoes, parboiled
4 hard-cooked eggs, peeled
¼ pound butter, melted
1 pint sour cream

Salt and freshly ground pepper
½ cup bread crumbs
Additional butter for the top of
   the potatoes

Preheat the oven to 325°F. Slice the potatoes and eggs. In a bowl, combine the melted butter with the sour cream. In a 1- or 2-quart casserole, depending on how many layers are desired, alternate layers of potatoes, eggs, and sour cream. Season each layer with salt and pepper. Scatter the bread crumbs evenly over the top and dot with butter. Bake until bubbly, about 45 minutes. Serve immediately.

Serves 4 to 6

Make-Ahead Mashed Potato Casserole

The note added to this recipe said, "I made this the first time I cooked for my husband. Not having spent much time in the kitchen, I was timid about altering the recipe. I made the full five pounds of potatoes—just for the two of us. Lots of leftovers!"

5 pounds russet or Yukon Gold
   potatoes, peeled
½ cup butter, softened
6 ounces cream cheese, softened
4 ounces sharp Cheddar cheese, shredded

½ cup grated Parmesan cheese
4 green onions, chopped
1 tablespoon salt
1 teaspoon freshly ground pepper

Cut the potatoes into large chunks, place them in a large pot, and cover with cold water. Bring the water to a boil and boil gently until the potatoes are tender. Drain. Mash the potatoes and fold in the remaining ingredients. Don't work them too much or they will be gluey. Turn the potatoes into a 3-quart casserole, cover with plastic wrap, and refrigerate for up to 2 days.

Let the casserole stand at room temperature for 1 hour before baking. Preheat the oven to 350°F. Fluff the potatoes with a fork and bake, covered, for 1 hour. Serve hot.

Serves 12 or more

Maple and Rum Baked Beans

Move over Boston! This unusual recipe from New Hampshire gives baked beans a whole new concept!

2 cups dried navy beans
6 cups water
½ cup maple syrup
¼ cup dark rum
1 tablespoon salt
1 medium onion, chopped

½ teaspoon dry mustard
¼ cup maple sugar or light
  brown sugar
3 tablespoons butter
4 unpeeled apples, cored

Check the beans for pebbles. Cover them with cold water by 2 inches and soak overnight. Drain and cover the beans with fresh water by 2 inches. Bring to a boil and boil, uncovered, until some of the skins start to fall off. Preheat the oven to 125°F. Transfer the beans and cooking liquid to a bean pot or a heavy kettle. Add the maple syrup, rum, and salt. Toss the chopped onions and dry mustard together and bury them in the middle of the beans. Bake for 3 to 4 hours.

In a bowl, cream the maple sugar and butter together. Place the whole apples on top of the beans as close together as possible and spread the creamed mixture over the top. Return the pot to the oven and bake for 1 hour.

Serves 4 to 6

Salsa Verde

Add this piquant, green herb sauce to your repertoire. It adds real spark to fish, chicken, vegetables, or meats. The bread produces a thicker sauce and can be omitted.

½ cup chopped flat leaf parsley
½ cup lightly packed fresh basil or
  arugula leaves
3 tablespoons chopped fresh chives
1 teaspoon chopped fresh thyme
1 teaspoon chopped fresh oregano
2 tablespoons capers, drained
1 slice firm white sandwich bread,
  crust removed

1 anchovy, mashed (optional)
2 tablespoons fresh lemon juice, or
  1 tablespoon white wine or sherry
  wine vinegar
1 to 2 teaspoons Dijon mustard
⅓ to ½ cup good quality extra-virgin
  olive oil
Salt and freshly ground pepper

Mince the herbs. Coarsely chop the capers. Tear the bread into the bowl of a food processor and add the anchovy, lemon juice, and mustard. Process until smooth. With the machine running, add the oil in a thin stream through the feed tube. Turn the sauce into a bowl, stir in the minced herbs and capers, and season with salt and pepper. The salsa can be refrigerated for up to 2 days. Bring it to room temperature before serving.

Makes about 1 cup

Roasted Broccoli with Sesame Dressing

Roasting vegetables concentrates their natural sugars and results in exceptional flavor. Asparagus are a good alternative to the broccoli in this Asian-inspired dish.

1 pound broccoli florets	2 teaspoons white sesame seeds, lightly toasted
3 tablespoons olive oil	3 tablespoons vegetable oil
4 tablespoons fresh lemon juice	1 teaspoon freshly ground pepper
2 teaspoons Asian sesame oil	½ teaspoon minced garlic
4 teaspoons soy sauce	

Preheat the oven to 500°F. Place the broccoli on a rimmed baking sheet, drizzle with the olive oil, and toss to coat. Roast, turning frequently, for 10 to 12 minutes, or until the broccoli is crisp-tender. Do not overcook. Process the remaining ingredients in a blender until smooth. Transfer the broccoli to a platter. Pour on the dressing and serve.

Serves 4

Savory Bread Pudding

To those who think of bread pudding only in terms of dessert, this savory version will come as a revelation. It's a superb alternative to potatoes.

4 tablespoons olive oil	½ cup plus 2 tablespoons grated Parmesan cheese
6 ounces fresh mushrooms, quartered	1 cup milk
1 large leek (light green and white parts only), diced	2 cups whipping cream or half & half
½ cup diced roasted red pepper	6 large eggs
½ loaf Vienna bread, cut into 1-inch cubes	1 teaspoon each salt and pepper

Preheat the oven to 350°F. Heat the olive oil over medium-high heat in a large, oven-proof skillet. Add the mushrooms and leeks and sauté until lightly browned, 5 to 7 minutes. Add the roasted peppers, bread cubes, and ½ cup of Parmesan cheese. Combine well. In a bowl, whisk together the milk, cream, eggs, salt, and pepper. Pour the mixture over the bread. Let stand until the liquid is absorbed. Sprinkle the pudding with the remaining 2 tablespoons of Parmesan cheese and bake until lightly browned and a knife inserted in the center comes out clean, about 1 hour. Serve hot.

Serves 6

Spa-Style Leek and Potato Gratin

Not only is there no cream in this flavorful, reduced-fat gratin, it can be made with skim milk! It's a fine accompaniment to roast lamb or beef.

½ cup fresh bread crumbs
2 teaspoons olive oil
1 clove garlic
3 pounds medium-size baking potatoes, peeled and sliced ⅛-inch thick
1½ cups whole, reduced-fat, or skim milk
Salt and freshly ground pepper

2 large leeks (white and light green parts only), halved, washed, dried, and thinly sliced
6 ounces (approximately) fresh, soft goat cheese
¼ cup freshly grated Parmesan cheese

Place the oven rack in the middle of the oven and preheat to 350°F. In a bowl, toss the bread crumbs with 2 teaspoons of olive oil until lightly moistened. Butter a 3-quart gratin or baking dish. Put the garlic through a garlic press into the milk.

Arrange a single, slightly overlapping layer of potatoes in the bottom of the prepared dish. Drizzle with some of the milk and season lightly with salt and pepper. Add a layer of leeks and dot with goat cheese. Repeat until all of the potatoes and leeks are used, ending with a layer of potatoes. Drizzle with milk and dot with goat cheese (all of the milk and goat cheese may not be needed). Cover the dish with foil and bake for 30 minutes or until the potatoes are somewhat tender. Uncover, sprinkle the top of the gratin with the bread crumbs and dust with Parmesan. Bake uncovered for another 30 minutes, or until the crumbs are browned and a knife can easily pierce through all of the layers. Cover with foil if the crumbs darken too much before the potatoes are tender. Remove the gratin from the oven and let it rest for 10 to 15 minutes before serving.

Serves 8

Mango-Peach Salsa

This tropical salsa is especially good with grilled chicken and seafood.

1 large mango, peeled and cut into small dice
1 large peach, peeled and cut into small dice
⅓ cup diced red onion
1 or 2 plum tomatoes, seeded and diced
1 small jalapeño pepper, seeded and minced

½ teaspoon grated orange zest
½ teaspoon ground cumin, or more to taste
1 to 2 tablespoons fresh orange juice
1 tablespoon fresh lime juice
2 tablespoons chopped cilantro

Combine all the ingredients in a bowl and let stand for 15 to 30 minutes, or cover and refrigerate for several hours.

Makes about 2 cups

Stuffed Baby Eggplants

The Greeks whimsically call these "papoutsakia," or "little shoes." Delicious as a side dish with roast lamb, beef, or chicken, they are also a good addition to a buffet.

4 small eggplants, 4- to 5-inches long
Olive oil
½ cup finely minced onion
½ pound lean ground beef or lamb
2 cloves garlic, minced
1 to 2 tablespoons chopped flat leaf parsley
1 teaspoon dried mint, crushed

1 teaspoon dried Greek oregano
2 plum tomatoes, peeled, seeded, and chopped
1 tablespoon tomato paste dissolved in ¼ cup water
Salt and freshly ground pepper
½ cup cooked rice
½ cup grated Parmesan cheese

Preheat the oven to 375°F. Line a rimmed baking sheet with kitchen parchment. Halve the eggplants lengthwise and scoop out most of the pulp, leaving a thin shell. Lightly brush the shells with oil, place them on the baking sheet, and roast until they have softened slightly but still hold their shape. Cool.

Dice the eggplant pulp. Heat a skillet over medium-high heat and add 2 tablespoons of olive oil. Sauté the diced eggplant until lightly browned and remove to a bowl. Add 1 tablespoon of olive oil to the pan. Add the onions and sauté until wilted. Add the ground meat and cook until it is beginning to brown. Make an opening in the center of the pan, add the garlic and stir until fragrant. Return the diced eggplant to the pan and add the parsley, mint, oregano, chopped tomato, tomato paste, salt, and pepper. Cook the filling over moderate heat until fairly dry. The eggplant should be tender. Remove the pan from the heat and add the rice and ¼ cup of the cheese. Taste and adjust the seasoning. Lightly mound the filling in the eggplant shells. Sprinkle with the remaining cheese and bake for about 15 minutes. Serve hot, warm, or at room temperature.

Serves 8

Ray's Soufflé

This homey corn pudding can be assembled several hours in advance and refrigerated.

4 eggs
2 cups milk (fat-free is fine)
4 15-ounce cans cream-style corn
1⅓ cups crushed crackers or bread crumbs

1 teaspoon salt
½ teaspoon pepper
2 teaspoons sugar
1 tablespoon minced onion

Preheat the oven to 350°F. Grease a 13x9-inch baking dish. In a large bowl, beat the eggs and add all the remaining ingredients. Combine well. Pour the mixture into the prepared dish and bake for 50 to 60 minutes, or until set and lightly browned. Let stand for 10 minutes before serving.

Serves 10 to 12

Stuffed Artichokes

These are a bit of work, but well worth the effort! The artichokes can be stuffed and refrigerated for several hours before baking. Smaller artichokes make a delightful first course.

1 lemon
2 large (or 4 medium) artichokes
4 tablespoons olive oil
⅓ cup chopped Italian salami, pancetta, or bacon
½ cup finely chopped onions
½ pound small raw shrimp, peeled, deveined, and cut into pieces
3 cloves garlic, finely minced
3 cups fresh breadcrumbs made from slightly stale, French or Italian bread whirled in a food processor
⅓ cup freshly grated Parmesan cheese

1 tablespoon lemon juice
1 teaspoon grated lemon zest
½ cup halved and thinly sliced green onions
Salt and freshly ground pepper
1½ teaspoons dried oregano
3 tablespoons minced parsley
2 teaspoons finely chopped fresh thyme
3 teaspoons finely chopped fresh rosemary
Lemon wedges for garnish

Squeeze the lemon into a large pot of salted water, cover, and bring to a boil. Snap off the small leaves from the base of each artichoke and cut about 1½ inches off the top. With kitchen shears, cut off the pointed ends of the remaining leaves. When the water comes to a boil, cut off the artichoke stems and trim the bases smooth. Drop them into the pot and simmer, partially covered, until the bottoms are tender when pierced with a small knife, about 20 to 25 minutes. Do not overcook. Remove the artichokes from the water and drain them upside down. When they are cool enough to handle, spread open the centers, pull out the inner leaves, and gently scrape away the choke with a teaspoon. Rinse the inside of the artichoke and drain again.

While the artichokes are cooking, heat 2 tablespoons of olive oil in a skillet over medium heat. Add the salami, pancetta or bacon, and cook until lightly browned. Drain on paper towels. Add the onions to the pan and sauté until wilted. Add the shrimp and sauté until they are pink. Stir in the garlic and cook until fragrant. Transfer the mixture to a bowl and cool. In a large bowl, toss the breadcrumbs with 3 to 4 tablespoons of olive oil until lightly moistened. Add the remaining ingredients along with the salami and the shrimp mixture. Combine well.

Preheat the oven to 400°F. Spoon some of the stuffing into the cavity of each artichoke. Gently pull back the leaves and spoon a little stuffing into the spaces. The stuffed artichokes should look like open roses. Place them in a baking dish just large enough to hold them and drizzle each with 1 teaspoon of olive oil. Add enough water to cover the bottom of the dish and bake until the crumbs are golden brown, about 20 minutes. Serve warm (not hot) or at room temperature with lemon wedges.

Serves 2 as a light entrée, 4 as a first course

Curried Vegetables

This northern India-style curry is an excellent side dish with simply cooked meats, poultry, or fish. Almost any combination of vegetables can be used. Look for garam masala in the spice aisle.

1½ pounds mixed vegetables, such as cauliflower florets, carrots, and potatoes
4 tablespoons vegetable oil
1 teaspoon ground cumin
1 teaspoon ground coriander
¼ teaspoon ground turmeric
1-inch piece fresh ginger, peeled and minced
4 cloves garlic, minced
2 tablespoons grated onion

1 jalapeño pepper, seeded and finely minced
2 medium tomatoes, peeled and finely chopped
1 cup water
1 teaspoon salt
Dash cayenne pepper
1½ tablespoons fresh lemon juice
½ teaspoon garam masala
Chopped fresh cilantro

Trim, peel, and cut up the vegetables as appropriate. In a wide, heavy skillet, heat the oil over medium heat. Add the ground spices and stir for a few moments. Add the ginger, garlic, grated onion, and jalapeño and stir for about half a minute. Add the tomatoes and cook for about 2 minutes, mashing them with the back of a spoon. Add the vegetables, water, salt, cayenne pepper, and lemon juice. Bring to a simmer, cover, and cook until the vegetables are tender and most of the water has been absorbed. Stir in the garam masala. Turn the curry into a serving dish and sprinkle with chopped cilantro.

Serves 4 as a side dish

Garlic and Rosemary Roasted Potatoes

Crisp, tender, and deliciously flavored, these may be the best roasted potatoes you've ever had.

2 pounds red potatoes, scrubbed, peeled if desired, and cut into chunks
Salt and freshly ground pepper

Olive oil
2 cloves garlic, minced
2 teaspoons chopped fresh rosemary

Preheat the oven to 375°F. Place the potatoes in a saucepan and add enough cold water to cover by 2 inches. Bring to a simmer and add salt. Simmer until they are just tender, about 15 minutes. Drain and place them in a bowl. Drizzle the potatoes with olive oil (about 2 to 3 tablespoons) and toss. Transfer them to a shallow baking pan just large enough to hold them comfortably in one layer. Season with salt and pepper. Roast, turning once or twice, until golden and crisp, about 30 minutes. Push the potatoes to one side and tip the pan so that the oil collects. Add the garlic and rosemary to the oil and stir for a moment or two. Do not let the garlic brown. Combine the garlic and rosemary with the potatoes and transfer to a serving bowl. Serve hot.

Serves 4

Sweet Potato Casserole with Whiskey Sauce

This family favorite is served every year with the Thanksgiving turkey. It's equally good with pork, game, or other fowl.

2½ pounds cooked sweet potatoes
2 tablespoons butter
½ teaspoon ground cloves
½ teaspoon ground nutmeg
½ teaspoon ground allspice
1 cup brown sugar

½ cup butter
1 egg, lightly beaten
¼ cup whiskey
⅓ cup lightly toasted
   pecans (optional)

Preheat the oven to 350°F. Place the potatoes in a bowl and mash. Add the butter and spices and beat until smooth. Transfer to a greased casserole or soufflé dish. Make a large indentation in the center for the sauce. Bake for 45 minutes.

Combine the brown sugar, butter, and egg in the top of a double boiler. Cook, stirring constantly, until the mixture has thickened slightly. Remove the pan from the heat and add the whiskey.

Remove the casserole from the oven and pour the sauce into the indentation. Garnish with the pecans and serve hot. (If desired, the pecans can be coarsely chopped and folded into the potatoes before baking.)

Serves 6

Tangy Tomato-Glazed Green Beans

Haricots verts—small, slender French green beans—make this zingy, sweet-and-sour dish extra special.

2 pounds fresh green beans or
   haricots verts
½ cup balsamic vinegar
½ cup sun-dried tomatoes (not
   oil-packed)

8 slices bacon
4 tablespoons minced shallots
3 tablespoons brown sugar
½ teaspoon salt
¼ teaspoon cracked pepper

Rinse and trim the beans. Steam or boil them in plenty of salted water until crisp-tender. Drain and plunge them into cold water to stop the cooking and set their color. Drain again and pat dry. (The beans can be prepared several hours ahead.)

In a saucepan, bring the vinegar to a boil. Remove the pan from the heat. Add the tomatoes and let stand for 15 minutes. Drain the tomatoes, reserving the vinegar, and chop them coarsely. Set aside.

Cook the bacon in a large skillet over medium heat until crisp. Drain on paper towels and crumble. Drain all but 2 tablespoons of the bacon drippings from the pan. Place the pan over medium heat and add the shallots. Sauté until tender, stirring constantly. Add the reserved vinegar, chopped tomatoes, brown sugar, salt, and pepper. Cook over low heat until the sugar melts, stirring occasionally. Add the beans to the skillet and toss gently until heated through. Transfer to a serving bowl, sprinkle with the bacon, and serve.

Serves 6

Virginia Spoonbread Soufflé

Spoonbread is one of America's oldest traditional dishes. The recipe for this elegant version of the Southern favorite was acquired on a trip to Williamsburg. It's especially good with baked ham.

4 cups milk	¼ cup butter
1¼ cups cornmeal	2 tablespoons sugar
2 teaspoons baking powder	4 eggs, separated
½ teaspoon salt	

Preheat the oven to 350°F. Butter a 1½-quart soufflé dish or baking dish. Combine 1 cup of milk with the cornmeal. Scald the remaining milk in the top of a double boiler. Add the cornmeal mixture and cook until it becomes a thin mush, about 10 minutes. Remove the pan from the heat and add the baking powder, salt, and butter. Beat the egg yolks and gradually beat them into the batter. With an electric mixer, beat the egg whites on medium speed until foamy. Add a pinch of salt, increase the speed to high, and beat until the whites stand in fairly firm peaks. Stir a large spoonful of the whites into the batter to lighten it. Fold in the remaining whites. Pour the batter into the prepared dish and bake for 40 to 45 minutes, or until the soufflé is golden brown and a knife inserted near the center comes out clean. Serve immediately.

Serves 4 to 6

Pineapple-Orange Relish

Serve this fresh-tasting relish with pork, fish, or chicken breasts.

2 cups diced fresh pineapple, or canned pineapple packed in juice	2 tablespoons chopped cilantro
1 cup diced fresh orange segments	1 tablespoon chopped fresh basil
½ cup diced red onion	½ teaspoon grated lime zest
Pinch salt	2 tablespoons orange juice
1 small jalapeño pepper, seeded and minced	Juice from 1 to 2 limes

Combine all of the ingredients in a bowl and let stand for 15 to 30 minutes or cover and refrigerate for several hours.

Makes about 3½ cups

Chestnut Dressing

The recipe for this unique stuffing has been passed down for four generations and is served every year with the holiday turkey. It's equally delicious with chicken, capon, or Cornish hens.

1½ pounds fresh, firm chestnuts
2 tablespoons vegetable oil
1 large Spanish onion, finely chopped
3 pounds ground round or chuck
3 tablespoons tomato paste
Salt and freshly ground black pepper

½ teaspoon cinnamon
½ cup pine nuts (pignoli)
1 cup golden raisins
⅔ cup raw converted rice (such as
   Uncle Ben's)

With a chestnut knife (available in cookware stores) or a small paring knife, cut a large "X" through the shell on the flat side of each chestnut. Cover with water by 3 inches, bring to a boil, and boil gently until tender but still firm, about 10 minutes. While still very hot, remove them from the water one at a time with a slotted spoon. Hold the chestnut with a dishcloth and use the knife to pull away the shell and the bitter, brown skin. Bring the water back to a boil if the chestnuts become hard to peel. Break about two-thirds of the chestnuts into large pieces and leave the rest whole. They can be refrigerated for 2 days or frozen.

Heat the oil in a large Dutch oven over medium-high heat. Add the onions and sauté until wilted, about 5 minutes. Add the ground meat and sauté until no traces of pink remain, breaking it up with a wooden spoon. Do not brown. Drain off the fat. Add the tomato paste, salt, pepper, and cinnamon. Stir well and taste for seasoning. The cinnamon should be barely discernable. Remove the pan from the heat and add the pine nuts, raisins, rice, and chestnuts. Cool prior to stuffing the bird or refrigerate overnight. (There is enough stuffing for a 20-pound turkey.)

Just prior to roasting, loosely stuff the body and neck cavities of the turkey. Refrigerate any remaining dressing in a casserole while roasting the bird. While the turkey rests, lightly baste the dressing in the casserole with some of the pan juices. Cover and place in a 325°F oven until hot, about 20 to 30 minutes. Remove all of the stuffing from the turkey to a large serving bowl and combine with the contents of the casserole. If desired, all of the dressing can be baked separately.

Serves 14 to 16

Desserts

Almond Torte

Serve this rich, European-style cake in thin slices with raspberry puree or lightly poached cherries or apricots.

½ cup unsalted butter
7 ounces almond paste
¾ cup sugar
3 eggs
¼ teaspoon baking powder

½ teaspoon vanilla
1 tablespoon Kirsch (optional)
¼ cup flour
Confectioners' sugar

Preheat the oven to 350°F. Butter an 8-inch round cake pan. In a bowl, cream the almond paste with the butter. Beat in the sugar. Scrape down the bowl and continue beating until well blended. Add the eggs one at a time, beating well after each addition. Add the baking powder, vanilla, and Kirsch. Fold in the flour by hand and spread the batter in the pan. Bake for 30 to 35 minutes or until the center feels firm. Cool in the pan on a wire rack. Turn the torte out of the pan and dust with confectioners' sugar.

Serves 6

Babi's Whiskey Cake

Illinois State Treasurer Judy Baar Topinka sent us the recipe for her grandmother's whiskey cake. One bite and you'll understand why it's a family favorite.

1 pound butter
3 cups sugar, divided
8 eggs, separated
2 teaspoons vanilla

2 teaspoons almond extract
⅓ cup bourbon
3 cups all-purpose flour
½ cup chopped pecans

Preheat the oven to 350°F. Butter a 10-inch tube or Bundt pan. In the bowl of an electric mixer, cream the butter with 2 cups of sugar until light and fluffy. Add the egg yolks one at a time, beating thoroughly after each addition. Combine the vanilla and almond extract with the bourbon. Add the flour alternately with the bourbon in three additions, beginning and ending with flour. Beat until smooth after each addition.

In a large bowl with clean beaters, beat the egg whites until they hold soft peaks. Gradually add the remaining sugar and beat until the meringue is glossy and stands in firm peaks. Gently fold the batter into the beaten whites. Sprinkle the pecans in the bottom of the prepared pan, or fold them into the batter. Turn the batter into the pan and bake for 1 to 1½ hours, or until a tester comes out clean. Transfer to a wire rack and cool before turning out of the pan.

Serves 12 to 14

Belle Reve Pecan Cake

This cake is mostly fruit and nuts and proves that there really is such a thing as a good fruitcake! Serve it in thin slices.

1 pound pecan halves (about
    4 cups)
½ pound candied pineapple (about
    1 cup), diced
½ pound candied cherries (about
    1 cup), halved

¾ cup flour
¾ cup sugar
½ teaspoon baking powder
½ teaspoon salt
3 large eggs
1 teaspoon vanilla

Preheat the oven to 300°F. Line a 9x5x3-inch loaf pan (or two 7x3x2-inch loaf pans) with foil and grease the foil. Combine the pecans, pineapple, and cherries in a large bowl. Sift the flour with the sugar, baking powder, and salt. Add the flour to the pecans and fruit and toss to coat evenly. Beat the eggs and add the vanilla. Pour over the fruit and mix thoroughly. The dough will be stiff. Press the dough into the prepared pan. Bake for 1¾ hours (bake smaller loaves for 1 hour). Transfer to a wire rack and cool completely. Turn the cake out of the pan and wrap it in heavy duty foil. Store in the refrigerator.

Makes one large or 2 small loaves

Lemon Pudding Cake

This super easy cake separates in the oven into a light, fluffy cake on top of lemon curd sauce. It's lovely served warm with fresh berries and a dollop of whipped cream.

2 large eggs, separated
1 cup milk
Juice from 1 large lemon (about ¼ cup)
1 tablespoon finely grated lemon zest

1 cup sugar
3 tablespoons flour
½ teaspoon salt

Preheat the oven to 350°F. Bring a kettle of water to a boil. Butter a 1-quart baking dish. In a bowl, whisk the egg yolks and add the milk, lemon juice, and grated zest. In a small bowl, combine ¾ cup of the sugar with the flour and salt. Add to the egg mixture, whisking just until combined. In another bowl, beat the egg whites with an electric mixer to soft peaks. Gradually add the remaining sugar and beat until the whites are fairly stiff. Whisk a large spoonful of the whites into the batter. Fold in the remaining whites and pour the batter into the baking dish. Set the dish in a larger, shallow pan and place it on the oven rack. Carefully pour boiling water into the larger pan until it reaches halfway up the side of the baking dish. Bake for about 35 minutes, or until puffed, lightly browned, and the cake springs back when pressed. Serve warm or chilled.

Serves 6

Caramel Glazed Pear Cake

A simple, easy, and delicious cake that you'll make again and again.

4 ripe Bartlett pears, peeled and diced (about 3 cups)	1 teaspoon salt
3 large eggs	1 teaspoon baking soda
2 cups plus 1 tablespoon sugar	2 teaspoons vanilla
1¼ cup vegetable oil	1½ cups chopped pecans
3 cups all-purpose flour	Caramel Glaze

Preheat the oven to 350°F. Butter and flour a 10-inch Bundt pan. In a bowl, toss the pears with 1 tablespoon of sugar and let stand for five minutes. In the bowl of an electric mixer, beat the eggs with 2 cups of sugar at medium speed. Add the vegetable oil and beat until blended. Combine the flour, salt, and baking soda. Turn to low speed and add the flour in 2 additions, beating until each addition is incorporated. Add the vanilla. Fold in the pears and chopped pecans. Pour the batter into the pan and bake for 1 hour or until a toothpick inserted in the center comes out clean. Turn the cake out of the pan onto a serving plate. Cool slightly. Drizzle with the caramel glaze while still warm.

CARAMEL GLAZE
    1 cup brown sugar
    ½ cup butter
    ½ cup evaporated milk

Stir the ingredients together in a saucepan over medium heat. Bring to a boil and stir for 2½ minutes, or until the sugar dissolves.

Serves 12

Chocolate Macadamia Nut Cake

This superb cake has deep chocolate flavor. It can stand alone with a simple dusting of confectioners' sugar, but forgoing the fabulous macadamia-fudge glaze is unthinkable!

¼ cup cocoa	1½ teaspoons instant coffee
¾ cup sour cream	½ teaspoon baking soda
1 egg	¼ teaspoon salt
½ teaspoon vanilla	½ cup unsalted butter, softened
1 cup flour	Macadamia-Fudge Glaze
¾ cup sugar	

Preheat the oven to 350°F. Butter a 9-inch round cake pan and line the bottom with waxed paper. In a medium bowl, whisk together the cocoa, sour cream, egg, and vanilla until smooth. In a large bowl, combine all of the dry ingredients and mix on low speed with an electric mixer to combine. Add the butter and half the cocoa mixture. Mix until the dry ingredients are moistened. Increase the speed to medium (high if using a hand mixer) and beat for 1 minute. Scrape down the sides of the bowl. Add the remaining cocoa mixture in 2 additions, beating for 30 seconds after each. Scrape the batter into the pan and smooth the top. Bake for 30 to 35 minutes or until a toothpick inserted near the center comes out clean. Cool on a wire rack for 10 minutes and turn out of the pan. Peel off the paper and cool completely, top side up. Place the rack with the cake on a rimmed baking sheet.

Prepare the glaze and pour it quickly over the cake, allowing some to run down the sides. Refrigerate until the glaze is firm, about 1 hour.

MACADAMIA-FUDGE GLAZE

1 cup heavy cream	4 squares semisweet chocolate
½ cup sugar	1 teaspoon vanilla
2 tablespoons unsalted butter	1 cup macadamia nuts,
1 tablespoon corn syrup	coarsely chopped

Place all the ingredients except the vanilla and nuts in a 2-quart saucepan. Bring to a boil over medium heat, stirring constantly. Remove the saucepan from the heat and add the vanilla. Cool for 10 minutes and stir in the nuts. Use warm.

Serves 6 to 8

Holiday Cheesecake

Do you like dense, creamy, New York–style cheesecake? If so, this cake's for you! Try it with poached cherries or blueberries on the side.

1 cup graham cracker crumbs	1 tablespoon lemon juice
3 tablespoons margarine, melted	1 teaspoon grated lemon zest
1 cup plus 1 tablespoon sugar	3 eggs
1½ pounds cream cheese, softened	1 cup sour cream

Preheat the oven to 325°F. Combine the graham cracker crumbs, margarine, and 3 tablespoons of sugar in a bowl. Press the mixture over the bottom of a 9-inch springform pan. Bake for 10 minutes. Remove the pan from the oven and lower the heat to 300°F.

Beat the cream cheese in the bowl of an electric mixer. Add ¾ cup of sugar, the lemon juice, and grated zest, and beat until blended. Add the eggs one at a time, beating well after each addition. Pour the filling into the crust and bake for 55 minutes. Combine the sour cream and remaining 2 tablespoons of sugar and carefully spread it over the cheesecake. Return the cake to the oven for 10 minutes. Place the pan on a wire rack and run a knife around the edge to loosen the cake. Cool completely and refrigerate for several hours or overnight before slicing.

Serves 12

Marbled Chocolate and Cream Cheese Brownies

So rich and delicious, these brownies ought to be illegal!

4 ounces unsweetened chocolate	½ teaspoon salt
1 cup unsalted butter, softened	2 teaspoons vanilla
4 eggs	1 cup chopped walnuts
2½ cups sugar	8 ounces cream cheese, softened
1 cup all-purpose flour	

Preheat the oven to 350°F. Grease and flour a 9x13-inch baking pan. Chop the chocolate into small pieces. Place the chocolate and butter in a small, heavy saucepan and melt over low heat, stirring constantly. Remove the pan from the heat and set aside.

Beat 3 eggs in the bowl of an electric mixer on medium speed until well blended. Slowly beat in 2 cups of the sugar. Beat in ½ cup of flour. Add the remaining flour along with the salt, 1 teaspoon of the vanilla, and the nuts. Scrape down the sides of the bowl. Add the melted chocolate and mix well. Spread half of the batter in the prepared pan. In a separate bowl, beat the cream cheese with the remaining ½ cup of sugar until smooth. Add the remaining egg and 1 teaspoon vanilla and beat until thoroughly blended. With a spoon, drop half of the cream cheese mixture in dollops over the chocolate batter. Lightly swirl the cream cheese into the chocolate batter with the tip of knife. Add the remaining chocolate batter, top with dollops of the remaining cream cheese, and swirl them together. Bake for 20 minutes. Lower the oven temperature to 325°F and continue to bake until a toothpick inserted in the center comes out clean, about 20 minutes longer. Transfer the pan to a wire rack and cool. Cut into squares.

Makes 30

Cherry and Almond Picnic Cake

With its buttery flavor and velvety texture, this cherry-studded cake is a treasure. Pack it into your picnic hamper or serve it with a scoop of ice cream at a backyard barbecue.

1 pound pitted sour cherries, unthawed if frozen	1½ sticks unsalted butter, softened
1 cup plus 2 tablespoons all-purpose flour	¾ cup plus 1 tablespoon sugar
1 teaspoon baking powder	3 large eggs, separated
¼ teaspoon salt	1 teaspoon vanilla
¼ pound blanched almonds	2 teaspoons almond extract
	Confectioners' sugar

Place an oven rack in the center of the oven and preheat to 375°F. Butter a 9-inch round cake pan, line the bottom with parchment, butter the paper, and flour the pan. If using fresh cherries, pit them over a bowl. Combine the flour, baking powder, and salt in a bowl. Grind the almonds fine with a nut grinder or, for more texture, grind the nuts in the food processor with the dry ingredients. In the bowl of an electric mixer, cream the butter with ¾ cup of the sugar until light and fluffy. Add the egg yolks one at a time, beating well after each addition. Stir in the flour mixture, vanilla, and almond extract. Drain the juice from the cherries and add it to the batter. Set aside.

With clean beaters, beat the egg whites in a bowl until they barely hold stiff peaks. Stir ¼ of the whites into the batter to lighten it. Gently fold in the remaining whites. Pour the batter into the pan and scatter the cherries evenly over the top, pressing them into the batter slightly. Sprinkle with the remaining 1 tablespoon of sugar. Bake the cake until golden brown and a tester comes out clean, 45 minutes to 1 hour. Remove the pan to a wire rack and cool for 10 minutes. Turn the cake out of the pan, return it to the rack, top side up, and cool completely. Dust the top with confectioners' sugar before serving.

Serves 8

Hummingbird Cake

Moist and absolutely delicious, this luscious cake is a Southern favorite.

3 cups all-purpose flour	1½ cups vegetable oil
2 cups sugar	1½ teaspoons vanilla
1 teaspoon salt	1 8-ounce can crushed pineapple,
1 teaspoon baking soda	undrained
1 teaspoon cinnamon	2 cups chopped bananas
3 eggs, beaten	2 cups chopped pecans

Preheat the oven to 350°F. Butter and flour three 9-inch cake pans. Combine the dry ingredients in a large bowl. Add the eggs and oil and stir by hand until moistened. Do not beat. Stir in the vanilla, undrained pineapple, bananas, and 1 cup of the nuts. Divide the batter among the cake pans and bake for 25 to 30 minutes. Transfer the pans to wire racks and cool completely before turning out the layers. Fill and frost the cake and sprinkle the top with the remaining cup of pecans. Store in the refrigerator.

FILLING AND FROSTING

1 cup butter, softened	1 teaspoon vanilla
8 ounces cream cheese, softened	1 16-ounce box confectioners' sugar

Cream the butter and cream cheese in the bowl of an electric mixer until smooth. Add the vanilla. Gradually add the confectioners' sugar and beat until fluffy.

Serves 8 to 10

English Toffee Cheesecake

Everybody gives rave reviews to this cheesecake. To really put it over the top, sprinkle the finished cake with more toffee bits and toasted, sliced almonds. It's best when made a day or two ahead.

CRUST

1½ cups graham cracker crumbs
½ cup toasted almonds, finely chopped or ground
½ cup English toffee bits (such as Skor)

2 tablespoons packed dark brown sugar
¼ teaspoon salt
6 tablespoons unsalted butter, melted

FILLING

4 8-ounce packages cream cheese, at room temperature
1 cup packed dark brown sugar
4 large eggs
1 tablespoon vanilla

¼ teaspoon almond extract
8 ounces chocolate-covered English toffee (such as Skor or Heath bars), cut into ½-inch pieces

TOPPING

16 ounces full fat sour cream
½ cup sugar
1 teaspoon vanilla

Preheat the oven to 350°F. For the crust, combine the dry ingredients in a bowl and add the melted butter. Stir until moistened. Press onto the bottom and 1 inch up the sides of a 10-inch springform pan. Bake until just set, about 5 minutes. Set aside. Reduce the oven temperature to 325°F.

In a large bowl, beat the cream cheese and brown sugar with an electric mixer until well blended. Beat in the eggs one at a time. Beat in the vanilla and almond extract. Pour half of the mixture into the pan and sprinkle with the toffee pieces. Add the remaining batter and bake until the edges of the cake are puffed, but the center is barely set, 55 minutes to 1 hour.

While the cake bakes, mix together the sour cream, sugar, and vanilla. Stir until smooth. Pour the mixture over the hot cheesecake and return it to the oven until the topping is just set, about 5 to 6 minutes. Transfer the cake to a rack and cool for 10 minutes. Run a knife around the inside edge of the pan to loosen the cake. Cool completely and refrigerate overnight, uncovered, before slicing.

Serves 12 to 15

Plum Crisp

Plums do a star turn in this simple, not-too-sweet crisp. Red-fleshed plums are especially good, but any variety can be used. A scoop of ice cream makes it even better.

1 cup flour
¼ teaspoon salt
⅓ cup light brown sugar
5 tablespoons unsalted butter, cut into small pieces and softened slightly
½ teaspoon cinnamon

½ cup coarsely chopped walnuts
2½ pounds plums, pitted and quartered
1 tablespoon cornstarch
1 teaspoon vanilla
⅓ cup sugar

Preheat the oven to 375°F. Combine the flour, salt, and brown sugar in a medium bowl. With your fingertips, rub in the butter until the mixture is crumbly. Stir in the cinnamon and nuts. Refrigerate while preparing the fruit.

In a large bowl, toss the plums with the cornstarch, vanilla, and sugar. Let stand, tossing occasionally, until the sugar dissolves. Pour the fruit into an 11x7-inch glass baking dish. Scatter the topping over the plums and bake for 40 minutes, or until the topping is browned and the fruit is bubbling. Cool for 20 to 30 minutes before serving.

Serves 6

Chocolate Toffee Squares

Rich and positively addicting, these are for sharing—if there are any left to share.

1 cup butter, softened
1 cup light brown sugar
1 teaspoon vanilla
1 egg yolk
¼ teaspoon salt

2 cups flour, sifted
1 large chocolate bar, or 6 ounces semisweet chocolate morsels
¾ cup walnuts or pecans, coarsely chopped

Preheat the oven to 350°F. Grease a 9x13-inch pan. In the bowl of an electric mixer, cream together the butter and brown sugar until fluffy. Add the vanilla, egg yolk, and salt and blend well. Add the flour and beat just until incorporated. Spread the dough evenly in the pan and bake for 20 minutes or until golden brown. Remove the pan from the oven. Place the chocolate on top and let stand until melted. Spread the chocolate evenly over the top and sprinkle with nuts. Cut into squares while warm.

Makes 32

Ricotta Cheesecake

This light, lemony-flavored Italian cheesecake is especially appealing after a heavy meal. It's delicious on its own, but fresh or lightly stewed berries are a nice accompaniment.

2 pounds whole milk ricotta cheese
   (or 2 15-ounce containers)
½ cup heavy cream
6 large eggs, separated, whites at
   room temperature
⅔ cup sugar
2 teaspoons vanilla
¼ cup fresh lemon juice

Grated zest of 1 orange
Grated zest of 1 lemon
½ cup golden raisins tossed with 1
   teaspoon flour (optional)
⅛ teaspoon cream of tartar
Fresh or lightly stewed berries
   for garnish
Confectioners' sugar

Line a sieve with a double layer of cheesecloth, suspend it over a bowl, and add the ricotta. Cover the ricotta with the ends of the cheesecloth and refrigerate for several hours to drain. If the ricotta is very loose, drain it overnight. For a smoother texture, turn the ricotta into the bowl of a food processor and blend for a minute or two. Pour the cheese into a bowl and stir in the cream.

Preheat the oven to 325°F. Butter and flour a 9-inch springform pan. Place the egg yolks in the bowl of an electric mixer and beat until thick and sticky. Gradually add the sugar and beat at a high speed until pale and thick, about 3 minutes. Turn the mixer to low speed and add the vanilla, lemon juice, grated zests, and ricotta cheese. Fold in the raisins with a rubber spatula and set aside.

In a large bowl with clean beaters, beat the egg whites on medium speed until frothy. Add ⅛ teaspoon cream of tartar, increase the speed to high, and beat until firm peaks form. Stir ⅓ of the whites into the ricotta mixture to lighten it. Gently fold in the remaining whites. Pour the mixture into the prepared pan and bake until the top is golden brown, the cake is fairly firm in the center, and a toothpick inserted near the center comes out clean, about 1½ hours. Transfer the cake to a wire rack and run a knife around the edge to loosen it from the pan. Cool completely. Chill the cheesecake for several hours or overnight before removing it from the pan. (Cover the cake after it is thorougly chilled.) Serve it in fairly thin slices with berries and a sprinkling of confectioners' sugar.

Serves 10 to 12

Strawberry Glacé Cheesecake

With its glistening, ruby-red topping, this gorgeous cheesecake looks like a photograph straight out of a gourmet cookbook—and tastes like one too!

CRUST

⅓ cup butter

⅓ cup sugar

1 egg

1¼ cups flour

FILLING

3 8-ounce packages cream cheese, softened

¾ cup sugar

2 tablespoons flour

1 teaspoon vanilla

3 eggs

2 tablespoons milk

TOPPING

1 10-ounce jar strawberry jelly

1 tablespoon cherry brandy

Whole strawberries, as evenly sized as possible

Preheat the oven to 450°F. For the crust, cream the butter with the sugar in the bowl of an electric mixer until light and fluffy. Beat in the egg. Add the flour and mix well. With a spatula, spread the dough over the bottom and ½ inch up the sides of a 9-inch springform pan. Bake for 5 minutes and remove from the oven.

In a large bowl, beat the cream cheese with an electric mixer at medium speed. Add the sugar, flour, and vanilla and beat until well blended. Add the eggs one at a time, beating well after each addition. Blend in the milk. Pour the mixture into the crust and bake for 10 minutes. Reduce the heat to 250°F and continue to bake for an additional 30 minutes. Remove the cheesecake from the oven and place it on a cooling rack. Run a knife around the inside edge of the pan to loosen the cake. Cool completely in the pan. Refrigerate, uncovered, for several hours or overnight (cover after the cake is chilled).

Several hours before serving, melt the strawberry jelly in a saucepan over low heat. Cool slightly and stir in the brandy. Wash the strawberries, pat them dry, and remove the stems. Remove the cake from the pan and arrange the strawberries over the top, stem side down. Spoon the warm jelly over the berries. Chill well before slicing.

Serves 8 to 10

Sunken Chocolate Cakes with Coffee Ice Cream

These luscious little cakes sink back upon themselves, resulting in a rich texture. If coffee ice cream isn't a favorite, try cherry or raspberry swirl.

8 tablespoons butter, cut into pieces
5 ounces bittersweet chocolate, coarsely chopped
4 large egg yolks

¼ cup sugar
2 large egg whites
1 pint coffee ice cream

Preheat the oven to 350°F. Lightly butter 4 jumbo, nonstick muffin cups leaving the 2 center cups empty. Coat lightly with sugar.

Place the butter and chocolate in a heat-proof bowl and set it over a pan of simmering water until the chocolate is melted. Remove from the heat and stir until the chocolate and butter are thoroughly combined. In the bowl of an electric mixer, beat the egg yolks with 2 tablespoons of sugar at medium high speed until pale yellow and thick. Stir in the melted chocolate.

In a small bowl, with clean beaters, beat the egg whites until soft peaks form. Sprinkle on the remaining 2 tablespoons of sugar and continue to beat until the whites stand in fairly firm peaks. Fold into the chocolate mixture. Fill the prepared muffin cups and bake until set and slightly springy to the touch, about 25 minutes. Transfer the pan to a wire rack. Cool the cakes in the pan for 15 minutes. Carefully run a knife around the edges of the cakes and unmold. Serve the cakes warm with a scoop of ice cream.

Serves 4

Chinese Chews

These yummy date-nut bars really are wonderfully chewy.

3 eggs
1 teaspoon vanilla
1 cup sugar
Pinch salt
1 cup flour, sifted

1 cup ground or finely chopped walnuts
1 cup ground or finely chopped dates
Confectioners' sugar

Preheat the oven to 350°F. Grease an 8x12-inch baking pan. In a large bowl, beat the eggs with an electric mixer on medium speed until fluffy. Add the vanilla. Gradually beat in the sugar and salt. Add the flour ¼ cup at a time, beating just until incorporated. With a rubber spatula, fold in the walnuts and dates. Spread the batter in the prepared pan and bake for 25 to 30 minutes. Remove the pan from the oven and cut the cookie into finger-sized pieces while still hot. Immediately roll the pieces in confectioners' sugar. Cool completely. Sift additional confectioners' sugar over the cookies. Store in an airtight container.

Makes about 32

Walnut Meringue Torte

Layers of cake separated by walnut meringue make this elegant torte special. The cake is light, but rich. Serve it in thin slices.

1 cup all-purpose flour
¼ teaspoon salt
1 teaspoon baking soda
1 stick unsalted butter
¾ cup plus 2 tablespoons sugar
½ teaspoon vanilla

4 large eggs, separated, whites at
   room temperature
⅓ cup whole milk
⅛ teaspoon cream of tartar
¾ cup chopped walnuts

FROSTING
⅓ cup unsweetened cocoa
2 cups heavy whipping cream
¼ cup sugar

GARNISH
Fresh mint leaves
Fresh raspberries or cherries

Butter two 8-inch cake pans, line the bottoms with parchment, butter the parchment, and flour the pans. Position a rack in the center of the oven and preheat to 300°F. Sift the flour with the salt and baking soda. In the bowl of an electric mixture, beat the butter on medium speed. Gradually add ½ cup of sugar and cream well. Beat in the vanilla. Add the egg yolks one at a time, beating to incorporate after each addition. Turn the speed to low and incorporate half the flour. Add the milk. Add the remaining flour and beat until blended. Divide the batter evenly between the prepared pans.

In a medium bowl with clean beaters, beat the egg whites on medium speed until foamy and add the cream of tartar. Raise the speed to high and beat until soft peaks form. Gradually add the remaining 6 tablespoons of sugar and beat until the meringue stands in firm peaks. Gently fold in the walnuts with a rubber spatula. Divide the meringue between the pans, spreading it evenly over the batter. Bake for 1 hour. Transfer the pans to a wire rack and cool the layers completely.

Meanwhile, whisk the cocoa with a little of the cream in a metal bowl until smooth. Whisk in the sugar and the remaining cream. Place the beaters in the bowl and refrigerate for at least 1 hour.

Turn the layers out of the pans and peel off the parchment. Beat the cream until stiff. Fill and frost the cake with the chocolate cream, placing the meringue sides together. Refrigerate for several hours or overnight. Garnish with mint leaves and fresh raspberries or cherries.

Serves 8 to 10

Warm Chocolate Torte with Bananas and Pecans

Light, moist, and not too sweet, this European-style torte has real chocolate flavor. Wonderful warm, it's also delicious at room temperature with a sprinkling of confectioners' sugar, a dollop of whipped cream, and fresh raspberries.

3 large egg yolks
1⅓ cups whole milk
⅓ cup heavy cream
6 ounces bittersweet or semisweet
    chocolate, shaved or chopped
1½ cups cake flour

1 teaspoon baking powder
½ teaspoon salt
1½ sticks unsalted butter, softened
1⅓ cups sugar
2 large eggs
1 teaspoon vanilla

GARNISH

Sliced bananas tossed with a little
    confectioners' sugar and a spoonful
    of orange juice

Toasted pecan halves
Lightly sweetened whipped cream

In a medium-size, heat-proof bowl, whisk the egg yolks and add ⅓ cup of milk and the cream. Set the bowl over a pan of simmering water, making sure that the bottom does not touch the water. Whisking constantly, cook until the mixture thickens and coats the back of a metal spoon. Remove the bowl and add the chocolate, whisking until melted and smooth. Set aside to cool.

Preheat the oven to 350°F. Butter a 10-inch round cake pan, line the bottom with parchment, butter the parchment, and flour the pan. In a bowl, sift together the flour, baking powder, and salt. In a medium bowl, beat the butter with an electric mixer on medium speed and gradually add the sugar. Beat until the butter is very pale, about 6 minutes, scraping the sides of the bowl occasionally. Add the eggs one at a time, beating to incorporate after each addition. Add the vanilla and continue to beat until the mixture is fluffy, about 5 minutes longer. Turn the mixer to low and add the cooled chocolate. Add the flour alternately with the remaining 1 cup of milk in 3 additions, beginning and ending with flour. Beat after each addition until incorporated. Pour the batter into the prepared pan.

Meanwhile, heat a kettle of water. Place the cake pan in a larger, shallow pan. Place the pan on the oven rack and add enough hot water to reach halfway up the side of the cake pan. Bake for 60 to 70 minutes, or until the cake feels fairly firm to the touch and a tester inserted into the center comes out with a few moist crumbs attached. Remove from the water bath and cool on a wire rack for 10 minutes. Remove the cake from the pan and peel off the parchment. Cool completely, top side up. (The cake may be wrapped well in plastic and refrigerated for up to 2 days or frozen. Thaw in the refrigerator.) When ready to serve, cut the number of slices needed and place them on a foil-lined baking sheet. Cover with foil and place in a 325°F oven until warm. Transfer the slices to plates. Garnish each serving with bananas, toasted pecans, and sweetened whipped cream.

Serves 8

Zucchini and Pineapple Cake

A moist, fragrant, triple-layer cake tangy with pineapple, crowned with fluffy frosting that's flavored with more pineapple. Better make two!

3 cups all-purpose flour
½ teaspoon baking powder
1 teaspoon baking soda
¼ teaspoon salt
1 teaspoon ground cinnamon
2 cups grated zucchini
3 large eggs

1½ cups sugar
1 tablespoon vanilla
1 cup vegetable oil
1 cup pecan halves, chopped
½ cup raisins
1 15-ounce can crushed pineapple, undrained

Preheat the oven to 325°F. Grease and flour three 8-inch round cake pans. Combine the flour, baking powder, baking soda, salt, and cinnamon in a bowl. Drain the zucchini well and press it between layers of paper towels to remove as much excess liquid as possible. Set aside.

In the bowl of an electric mixer, beat the eggs at medium speed until thick. Gradually add the sugar, vanilla, and oil and beat well. Add the grated zucchini. Gradually add the flour mixture. Stir in the pecans, raisins, and undrained pineapple. Pour the batter into the pans and bake for 35 minutes, or until a toothpick inserted in the center comes out clean. Transfer the pans to wire racks and cool for 10 minutes. Turn the layers out of the pans and cool completely. Fill the cake and frost only the top. (The frosting is soft and tends to slide off the sides.) Store, covered, in the refrigerator.

PINEAPPLE–CREAM CHEESE FROSTING

1 8-ounce can crushed pineapple, drained
1 8-ounce package cream cheese, softened

¼ cup butter, softened
1 16-ounce box confectioners' sugar

Place the pineapple in a wire-mesh strainer and press with the back of a spoon to squeeze out excess juice. In a bowl, beat the cream cheese and butter with an electric mixer on medium speed until fluffy. Gradually stir in the confectioners' sugar and drained pineapple. The frosting can be refrigerated for 1 hour before using.

Serves 8

Apple Bars

Pitted sour cherries can be substituted for the apples in these moist treats.

TOPPING

½ cup flour
⅓ cup packed light brown sugar
¼ teaspoons cinnamon

¼ teaspoon salt
½ cup butter
1 cup chopped walnuts

CRUST

1½ cups flour
⅓ cup sugar
1½ teaspoons cinnamon

¾ teaspoon salt
½ cup butter
2 tablespoons orange juice

APPLE FILLING

1 whole egg
1½ cups sour half & half (See note)
2 teaspoons vanilla
1 teaspoon lemon juice

⅓ cup plus 1 tablespoon sugar
¼ cup flour
½ teaspoon salt
4 cups peeled, chopped apples

Preheat the oven to 350°F. Grease a 13x9-inch pan. For the topping, combine the flour with the brown sugar, cinnamon, and salt in a bowl. Cut in the butter until it is the size of peas. Stir in the walnuts. Refrigerate while preparing the bars.

For the crust, combine the flour, sugar, cinnamon, and salt in a large mixing bowl. Cut in the butter until the mixture resembles cornmeal. Stir in the orange juice. Pat the dough into the bottom of the prepared pan and set aside.

For the filling, place the egg in a bowl and beat with an electric mixer on medium speed. Add the sour half & half and vanilla. Beat in the lemon juice and sugar. Add the flour and salt and beat until smooth. Fold in the apples. Spread the filling over the dough and bake for 30 minutes.

Remove the pan from the oven and sprinkle the topping evenly over the filling. Return to the oven and bake for 10 to 15 minutes. Cool on a wire rack for at least 45 minutes before cutting into bars. Cover and store in the refrigerator or freeze.

Note: For sour half & half, combine the half & half with 1 tablespoon lemon juice. Let stand for 15 minutes.

Makes 20 bars

Cinnamon-Almond Mondel Bread

These crumbly, cookie-like biscuits are perfect with an afternoon cup of coffee or tea.

3½ cups flour
¼ teaspoon salt
2 teaspoons baking powder
⅔ cup slivered almonds, chopped
3 eggs

1 cup sugar
1 teaspoon vanilla
2 teaspoons almond extract
1 cup vegetable oil

TOPPING
½ cup granulated sugar
Cinnamon, to taste

Combine the flour, salt, baking powder, and almonds in a bowl and stir with a wire whisk. In another bowl, beat the eggs with an electric mixer until foamy. Gradually add the sugar. Beat in the vanilla and almond extract. Add the oil in a thin stream. Add the dry ingredients one cup at a time, beating to incorporate after each addition. Scrape down the sides of the bowl. Place plastic wrap directly on the surface of the dough and chill for at least 30 minutes.

Position a rack in the center of the oven and preheat to 350°F. Have two baking sheets at hand. Divide the dough into four pieces and form each into an 11-inch long roll. Place 2 rolls on each baking sheet and pat them into logs, about 2½ inches wide x ½-inch thick, with flat bottoms and gently arched tops. Bake until lightly browned, about 30 minutes. (Refrigerate 1 baking sheet while baking the first 2 rolls.)

While the rolls bake, combine the granulated sugar with cinnamon to taste. Remove the pan from the oven and cool for 2 or 3 minutes. With a serrated knife, cut the rolls into ½-inch thick slices. (For larger biscuits, slice the rolls on the diagonal.) Lay the slices on their sides and sprinkle with cinnamon sugar. Return to the oven until lightly browned, about 6 minutes. Turn, sprinkle with cinnamon sugar, and return to the oven to brown the second side. Cool completely on wire racks. Store in an airtight container for up to 3 weeks.

Makes about 6 dozen

Citrus Bars

This is not your ordinary lemon bar. The wheat germ in the crust adds a nutty taste and subtle crunch, and the lemon-lime filling is sublime. Good thing this recipe makes lots!

CRUST

3½ cups all-purpose flour
½ cup wheat germ
½ cup confectioners' sugar

½ teaspoon salt
2 cups (4 sticks) chilled, unsalted butter, cut into small pieces

FILLING

8 large eggs
4 cups granulated sugar
⅔ cup all-purpose flour
¾ cup freshly squeezed lemon juice

¾ cup freshly squeezed lime juice
1 tablespoon finely grated lemon zest
1 tablespoon finely grated lime zest
1 teaspoon salt

Preheat the oven to 350°F. In a large bowl, whisk together the flour, wheat germ, confectioners' sugar, and salt. Using a pastry cutter, or your fingertips, cut in the butter until it is the size of peas. Press the dough into a 12x17-inch rimmed baking sheet. Bake until golden, 20 to 30 minutes. Transfer the pan to a wire rack and cool completely.

In a medium bowl, whisk together the eggs, sugar, and flour. Whisk in the lemon and lime juices, zests, and salt. Pour the filling over the crust and bake until the center is set, about 30 minutes. Transfer to a rack and cool. Cut into 2-inch squares. Store the bars in an airtight container at room temperature for up to 2 days.

Makes 4 dozen bars

Pecan Temptations

If you like pecan pie but find a whole slice too rich, try these decadent little morsels.

CRUST

1 cup flour
½ cup packed light brown sugar

½ cup unsalted butter, softened
⅛ teaspoon salt

TOPPING

¾ cup packed light brown sugar
½ cup maple syrup
2 large eggs
2 tablespoons flour
6 tablespoons unsalted butter, melted

⅛ teaspoon salt
1 teaspoon bourbon
1 teaspoon vanilla
1¼ cups coarsely chopped pecans

Preheat the oven to 350°F. In a mixing bowl or in the bowl of a food processor, combine the flour, brown sugar, butter, and salt. Beat with an electric mixer on low speed, or process in a food processor using on-off turns, until crumbly. Press firmly into an ungreased 8-inch square cake pan. Bake until lightly browned, about 18 minutes.

While the crust bakes, combine all the ingredients for the topping except the pecans in a bowl. Beat or process well. Stir in the pecans.

Remove the pan from the oven and spoon the topping evenly over the crust. Return to the oven and bake until the topping is set and lightly browned, about 35 minutes. Transfer the pan to a rack and cool completely. Refrigerate until firm, about 1 hour. Cut into squares.

Makes 16 2-inch bars

Persian Slices

The recipe for these delicious, easy-to-make pinwheel cookies was passed from mother (who made them for over forty years) to daughter. You may well pass it on yourself.

¼ pound butter, softened	8 ounces apricot jam
1 cup flour	⅔ cup shredded coconut
½ cup sour cream	½ cup slivered almonds

Combine the butter, flour, and sour cream in a bowl and mix well. Form the dough into a ball and wrap it well in plastic. Chill for 6 hours or overnight.

Preheat the oven to 350°F. On a floured surface, roll the dough into a rectangle ⅛-inch to ¼-inch thick. Spread with the apricot jam and sprinkle with the coconut and nuts. Starting at a long edge, roll up the dough jelly-roll fashion. Transfer the roll to an ungreased cookie sheet and bake for 25 minutes or until lightly browned. Remove to a wire rack and cool. Cut into ¾-inch thick slices. The cookies are best on the day they are baked.

Makes about 1½ dozen

Pineapple Cookies

The sweet, tropical flavor of pineapple is in every bite.

1½ cups plus 2 tablespoons flour	1 cup sugar
¼ teaspoon baking soda	2 eggs
⅛ teaspoon salt	¼ teaspoon vanilla
1½ teaspoons baking powder	⅔ cup crushed pineapple, drained
½ cup shortening	

Preheat the oven to 375°F. Combine the flour, baking soda, salt, and baking powder in a bowl. In the bowl of an electric mixer, cream the shortening with the sugar until light. Add the eggs and vanilla and beat well. Gradually add the dry ingredients. With a rubber spatula, fold in the pineapple. Drop well-rounded teaspoons of dough onto ungreased cookie sheets. Bake for 10 minutes or until lightly colored. Cool on wire racks.

Makes about 4 dozen

Rocky Road S'mores

Kids of all ages love these S'mores! For a grown-up version, use bittersweet chocolate.

1 cup flour
½ cup graham cracker crumbs
1 stick butter, softened

½ cup packed light brown sugar
6 ounces semisweet chocolate pieces
2 cups mini-marshmallows

Preheat the oven to 375°F. Grease a 9-inch square cake pan. Combine the flour and graham cracker crumbs in a bowl. In another bowl, cream the butter and brown sugar with an electric mixer on medium speed until light and fluffy. Add the dry ingredients in 2 or 3 additions and mix well. Press the dough over the bottom of the prepared pan. Top with the chocolate and marshmallows. Bake for 15 to 20 minutes, or until the topping is golden brown. Transfer to a wire rack and cool completely. Cut into squares.

Makes 12 to 16 bars

Sage and Apricot Cornmeal Cookies

Sage adds an herbal note, cornmeal adds subtle crunch, and apricots add sweet chewiness to these unique cookies.

2 tablespoons finely chopped fresh
  sage leaves
¾ cup plus 2 tablespoons
  all-purpose flour
⅓ cup white cornmeal
½ teaspoon baking soda

½ teaspoon salt
½ cup unsalted butter, softened
¾ cup sugar
1 egg
½ cup finely chopped
  dried apricots

Position a rack in the middle of the oven and preheat to 350°F. Lightly grease a baking sheet. Process the sage and 2 tablespoons of flour in a food processor. In a bowl, combine the remaining flour with the cornmeal, baking soda, and salt. In the bowl of an electric mixer, cream the butter and sugar. Add the egg and beat until smooth. Add the flour mixture, beating just until incorporated. Add the apricots and the sage. Drop the batter by tablespoonfuls, about 1 inch apart, and immediately transfer the baking sheet to the oven. Bake for about 10 minutes. Cool on the baking sheet for a minute or so until the cookies firm up enough to be transferred to a cooling rack. Cool completely before storing in an airtight container.

Makes about 3½ dozen

Swedish Wafer Sandwich Cookies

Crisp and buttery with a vanilla cream filling, these delicate cookies are melt-in-your-mouth delicious.

1 cup unsalted butter, softened
⅓ cup whipping cream, at
   room temperature

2 cups flour
Granulated sugar

FILLING

¼ cup unsalted butter, softened
¾ cup confectioners' sugar

1 egg yolk
1 teaspoon vanilla

Cream the butter in the bowl of an electric mixer until light. Beat in the whipping cream. Gradually add the flour. Scrape down the sides of the bowl, cover, and refrigerate until the dough is firm.

Preheat the oven to 375°F. Roll out the dough to a thickness of about ⅛ inch. Cut into 1½-inch rounds. Sprinkle the cookies with sugar and prick each several times with the tines of a fork. Bake on ungreased cookie sheets until barely brown. Cool on wire racks.

With an electric mixer, cream together the butter and confectioners' sugar. Add the egg yolk and vanilla and blend well. Sandwich the filling between the bottom sides of the cookies. Store the filled cookies in the refrigerator. Serve at room temperature.

Makes about 30

Brownie Drops

An easy cookie to make with children, these rich and chocolaty morsels are a holiday favorite.

2 4-ounce bars German's chocolate
1 tablespoon unsalted butter
¼ cup flour
¼ teaspoon baking powder
¼ teaspoon ground cinnamon

⅛ teaspoon salt
2 large eggs
6 tablespoons sugar
½ teaspoon vanilla
¾ cup finely chopped pecans

Preheat the oven to 350°F. Break the chocolate into pieces and melt it with the butter over barely simmering water. Stir well and cool to room temperature. Combine the flour, baking powder, cinnamon, and salt. In a bowl, beat the eggs with an electric mixer until foamy. Add the sugar 2 tablespoons at a time. Beat until the mixture thickens. Add the chocolate and vanilla and combine well. On low speed, blend in the flour. Stir in the nuts. Drop the batter by teaspoonfuls onto a greased baking sheet. Bake for 8 to 10 minutes. Cool on wire racks. Store the cookies in an airtight container or freeze.

Makes about 4 dozen

Tri-Level Brownies

Three yummy layers—brown sugar and oatmeal, chocolate-walnut, and chocolate frosting—oh my!

OATMEAL

½ cup sifted all-purpose flour
¼ teaspoon baking soda
¼ teaspoon salt

1 cup quick-cooking rolled oats
½ cup packed light brown sugar
½ cup butter, melted

CHOCOLATE

1 ounce unsweetened chocolate, melted
4 tablespoons butter, melted
¾ cup granulated sugar
1 egg
½ teaspoon vanilla

⅔ cup flour
¼ teaspoon baking powder
¼ teaspoon salt
¼ cup milk
½ cup chopped walnuts

FROSTING

1 ounce unsweetened chocolate
2 tablespoons butter

1½ cups sifted confectioners' sugar
1 teaspoon vanilla

Preheat the oven to 350°F. In a bowl, sift together the flour, baking soda, and salt. Stir in the oats and brown sugar. Stir in the butter. Pat the mixture into an 11x7x1½-inch pan and bake for 10 minutes.

Combine the chocolate, butter, sugar, and egg in the bowl of an electric mixer and beat well. Add the vanilla. Sift together the flour, baking powder, and salt. Add the flour alternately with the milk to the chocolate mixture, beginning and ending with flour. Beat after each addition to incorporate. With a spatula, fold in the chopped nuts. Spread the batter over the oatmeal base and return to the oven for 25 minutes. Cool completely.

For the frosting, place the chocolate and butter in a small saucepan and stir over low heat until melted. Remove the pan from the heat and stir in the confectioners' sugar and vanilla. Stir in hot water (about 2 tablespoons) until the mixture is pourable. Spread the frosting over the brownies. Cool until the frosting is firm. Cut the brownies into squares.

Makes about 15

World's Best Sugar Cookies

The original recipe for these drop cookies belonged to a lady from Wisconsin who was born in 1879 and lived to be over one hundred years old. Her recipe has been handed down by generations of family and friends.

5 cups flour
1 teaspoon cream of tartar
1 teaspoon baking powder
2 eggs
2 teaspoons vanilla
1 teaspoon almond extract

1 cup butter, softened
1 cup granulated sugar
1 cup confectioners' sugar
1 cup corn or vegetable oil
Granulated sugar

Preheat the oven to 350°F. In a bowl, combine the flour, cream of tartar, and baking powder. In another bowl, beat the eggs and add the vanilla and almond extract. In the bowl of an electric mixer, cream the butter and sugars together until light and fluffy. Lower the speed and gradually add the oil. Beat in the egg mixture. Add the flour mixture one cup at a time, beating just to incorporate each addition. Drop the dough by rounded teaspoonfuls onto ungreased cookie sheets. Dip the bottom of a glass in sugar. Flatten the cookies with the glass, dipping the bottom in sugar each time. Bake for 8 to 10 minutes. Do not brown. Transfer the cookies to wire racks and cool.

Makes many

Creamy Tapioca Pudding

Creamy and satisfying, this homey dessert was often prepared by a great uncle who was a talented cook. Delicious chilled, it's even better when it's still warm.

1 quart whole milk
¾ cup sugar
5 tablespoons tapioca
3 eggs, separated

¼ teaspoon salt
Cinnamon
Whipped cream (optional)

In a heavy saucepan, bring the milk to a simmer. Add the sugar and stir until it dissolves. Slowly add the tapioca, stirring constantly. Simmer for 4 minutes, stirring occasionally. Meanwhile, beat the egg yolks. Beating constantly, slowly add ½ cup of the hot tapioca mixture to the yolks to warm them. Reverse the process, and slowly add the yolks to the tapioca mixture, stirring constantly. Simmer for an additional 4 minutes and remove the pan from the heat. Beat the egg whites until foamy. Add the salt and beat until they hold firm peaks. Fold the whites into the pudding with a rubber spatula. Pour the pudding into a small pan or baking dish, or individual cups. Cool for several minutes and sprinkle with cinnamon. Serve warm or cool to room temperature and refrigerate. If serving chilled, garnish with a dollop of whipped cream.

Serves 6

Yiayia's Kourambiedes
(Grandmother's Butter Cookies)

These melt-in-your-mouth cookies have been made by at least four generations of grandmothers in the family. The dough is traditionally shaped into crescents, but the plump discs are more delicate and far less messy to eat!

1 pound unsalted butter, softened
2 teaspoons sugar
1 egg yolk
1½ ounces cognac or brandy

2½ ounces freshly squeezed orange juice
4 to 5 cups sifted, bleached,
   all-purpose flour
1 16-ounce box confectioners' sugar

In the bowl of an electric mixer, cream the butter on medium speed until pale and fluffy. Add the sugar and beat well. Add the egg yolk, cognac, and juice. Turn the mixer to low and add 4 cups of flour, one cup at a time, beating to incorporate after each addition. The dough should be light and soft, but not sticky. Add more flour, ¼ cup at a time, if necessary.

Preheat the oven to 350°F. Pinch off about 1½ teaspoons of dough for each cookie and gently pat into a plump disc, about 1 inch in diameter. Space the cookies 1½ inches apart on ungreased baking sheets. Bake until the tops are a pale sand color and the bottoms are lightly browned.

While the cookies bake, place 2 or 3 sheets of foil or waxed paper on a flat surface. Sieve confectioners' sugar evenly over the foil, covering it fairly well. Transfer the hot cookies to the sugar-coated foil and sieve confectioners' sugar over them, covering lightly. Cool completely and sprinkle again until the cookies are completely covered with a layer of sugar. Transfer the cookies to mini-paper muffin cups and layer them between sheets of waxed paper in an airtight container. The cookies will keep for up to 2 weeks.

Makes 8 dozen

Scruppino
(Venetian Lemon Slush)

This refreshing dessert is often prepared tableside in Venetian restaurants. The proportions are up to you.

2 scoops softened lemon sorbet
   (do not use sherbet)
1 cup very ripe, sweet strawberries,
   cored, sliced if large

8 to 12 ounces Prosecco (Italian
   sparkling wine)
2 whole strawberries for garnish

Let the sorbet stand until slightly softened. In a bowl, mash the strawberries into a coarse puree with a fork. Add the sorbet and mash together until the mixture is slushy. Pour in the Prosecco. Ladle the Scruppino into goblets or bowls and garnish each with a whole strawberry.

Serves 2

Baklava Cigarettes

If you find Baklava too heavy and sweet, try these impossibly light, crisp rolls. Make them with fresh phyllo if at all possible. It's much easier to work with and results in superior texture. Look for it in Greek and Middle Eastern markets.

SYRUP

1 cup sugar
1¼ cups water

⅓ cup honey
1 teaspoon lemon juice

ROLLS

1 pound walnuts, chopped
Cinnamon

1 pound unsalted butter, melted
1 pound phyllo, fresh preferred,
    thawed if frozen

Combine the syrup ingredients in a saucepan and boil until lightly thickened. Cool to room temperature. In a bowl, combine the walnuts with cinnamon to taste. Have the nuts, melted butter, a pastry brush, baking sheets, plastic wrap, and damp kitchen towels at hand.

Place a sheet of plastic wrap on the counter. Working quickly, unroll the phyllo on a cutting board and cut it lengthwise into thirds. Place it on the plastic and immediately cover with more plastic. Cover the plastic with dampened kitchen towels. Redampen the towels as necessary. Remove 2 strips of phyllo at a time and place them on a flat surface with the short ends facing you. Brush each lightly with butter, taking care to cover the edges. Fold them in half, bottom to top, and brush with butter. Place a heaping teaspoon of filling across the strip, about 1 inch from the bottom and ½ inch from each side. Fold the bottom over the filling, fold the sides inward, and roll into snug "cigarettes." Transfer to a baking sheet, seam side down, and brush the top with butter. Repeat with the remaining phyllo. (The rolls can be frozen, in single layers, at this point. Transfer the frozen rolls to a container, keeping sheets of waxed paper between the layers, and store for up to 2 months. Do not thaw before baking.)

Preheat the oven to 350°F. Bake the rolls until golden brown, about 30 minutes. Remove them from the oven and baste lightly with the cooled syrup. Serve them slightly warm or at room temperature with a small pitcher of syrup.

Note: The cigarettes are best when freshly baked, but they are also very good reheated in a 350°F oven.

Makes about 75

Frozen Lemon-Lime Soufflés
with Bittersweet Chocolate Sauce

These elegant little desserts are really frozen mousses. Light and tangy, they are a perfect ending to a special meal. The delicious sauce adds a lovely accent, but the soufflés are fine on their own.

SOUFFLÉS

1 cup sugar

½ cup water

2 teaspoons light corn syrup

6 egg yolks

2 tablespoons lemon juice

4 tablespoons lime juice

½ teaspoon finely grated lemon zest

½ teaspoon finely grated lime zest

2 cups heavy cream

CHOCOLATE SAUCE (Makes about 1½ cups)

¾ cup whipping cream

2 tablespoons dark corn syrup

8 ounces bittersweet chocolate, chopped

GARNISH

Whipped cream

Candied lemon or lime zest (optional)

Cut foil into 4-inch wide strips and fold the strips lengthwise in half. Tie or tape them around eight, 4-ounce ramekins so that the foil extends 1½ inches above the rims. Set aside. In a small saucepan, combine the sugar, water, and corn syrup. Stir until the sugar dissolves. Clip a candy thermometer to the side of the pan and bring the mixture to a boil without stirring. Boil until the syrup reaches 234°F (soft-ball stage). Remove from the heat and use immediately. While the syrup comes to a boil, beat the egg yolks in the bowl of an electric mixer on medium-high speed until thick. Gradually add the lemon and lime juice and beat for several more minutes. With the mixer running, add the hot syrup in a thin stream. Continue beating until the mixture cools to room temperature. Add the lemon and lime zests. In a separate bowl with clean beaters, whip the cream to soft peaks. Fold a large spoonful of the cream into the egg yolk mixture to lighten it. Pour the mixture over the remaining whipped cream and gently fold together until no white streaks remain. Spoon the mousse into the prepared ramekins, swirling the tops, and freeze for at least 4 hours or up to 3 days. Remove the collars and cover when frozen.

To prepare the chocolate sauce, heat the cream and corn syrup in a saucepan until it comes to a simmer. Remove the pan from the heat and add the chocolate. Stir until melted. Let stand to cool and thicken, about 15 minutes. Serve warm. (The sauce can be prepared 3 days ahead and refrigerated. Stir over low heat until warm.)

To serve, allow the soufflés to stand at room temperature for about 10 minutes to soften slightly. Garnish with whipped cream and candied lemon or lime zest. Serve the sauce alongside the ramekins in small, individual containers, such as egg cups.

Serves 8

Lemon Mousse

Serve this airy mousse with whipped cream, fresh berries, and crisp cookies.

1 package unflavored gelatin
  (1 tablespoon)
Juice from 3 lemons
Finely grated zest from 2 lemons

3 eggs, separated
½ cup plus 3 tablespoons sugar
1½ cups heavy cream

Sprinkle the gelatin over the lemon juice in a nonreactive saucepan and set aside to soften. Place the pan over low heat and stir constantly until the gelatin is completely dissolved. Do not allow it to boil. Remove the pan from the heat and add the lemon zest. In the bowl of an electric mixer, beat the egg yolks with ½ cup of sugar until pale and thick. Gradually beat in the hot gelatin mixture. Place the bowl in a larger bowl filled with water and ice and cool, stirring occasionally, until the mixture begins to mound softly when dropped from a spoon. Do not allow it to set. Remove the bowl from the ice bath. With clean beaters, beat the egg whites in a bowl until soft peaks form. Gradually add 3 tablespoons of sugar and beat until the whites hold firm peaks. In a separate bowl with clean beaters, whip the cream to soft peaks. Stir a large spoonful of whipped cream into the lemon base to lighten it. Fold in the egg whites. Fold in the remaining whipped cream. Spoon the mousse into stemmed glasses, cover, and chill for several hours or overnight.

Serves 8

Poppy Seed Torte

The recipe for this custard dessert was handed down by a grandmother. For some reason, she called it "Poppy Seed Torte." The name stuck. It's a great family favorite.

1½ cups graham cracker crumbs
¼ cup margarine, melted
1 cup plus 2 rounded tablespoons sugar
4 eggs, separated
3 cups milk

2 tablespoons flour
2 tablespoons cornstarch
½ cup dry poppy seeds
1 teaspoon vanilla

Preheat the oven to 350°F. Combine the graham cracker crumbs, margarine, and ¼ cup of the sugar in a bowl. Reserve ¼ cup of the mixture for the topping and press the remainder over the bottom of a 9x13-inch pan.

Beat the egg yolks. In a saucepan, combine the beaten yolks, milk, flour, cornstarch, ¾ cup of sugar, and the poppy seeds. Stirring constantly, bring to a simmer and cook until thickened. Remove from the heat and add the vanilla. Pour the custard into the pan.

Beat the egg whites in the bowl of an electric mixer until soft peaks form. Add the remaining 2 tablespoons of sugar and beat until the whites stand in firm peaks. Spread the meringue over the custard and sprinkle with the reserved graham cracker mixture. Bake for 20 minutes. Cool and refrigerate until well chilled before cutting into squares.

Serves 12

Lychee Sorbet with Tropical Fruit Salsa

The vodka helps prevent this refreshing tropical sorbet from freezing too hard. Serve it in martini or marguerita glasses with crisp ginger cookies.

SORBET

¼ cup water
½ cup sugar
1 tablespoon finely grated
   fresh ginger

2 20-ounce cans lychees in heavy
   syrup, drained, ½ cup syrup
   reserved
2 tablespoons fresh lemon juice
1 tablespoon vodka

TROPICAL FRUIT SALSA

3 cups finely diced mixed fruits, such as:
Mango
Kiwi
Pineapple
Honeydew, cantaloupe, or other
   melon (do not use watermelon)

Passionfruit
Papaya
Strawberries
Slices of carambola (star fruit)
   for garnish

In a small saucepan, bring the water, sugar, and ginger to a boil. Remove the pan from the heat and let the syrup cool. Strain it through a fine sieve and discard the ginger. Puree the lychees in a blender or food processor with the reserved lychee syrup until smooth. Strain the puree through a fine sieve into a bowl. Discard any pulp. Add the ginger syrup, lemon juice, and vodka. Chill the mixture for at least 4 hours. Freeze in an ice cream maker according to manufacturer's directions. The sorbet can be served soft, right out of the machine, or, for firmer sorbet, freeze it for 2 hours or up to 1 week. Let stand at room temperature to soften if necessary. (Makes 1 quart)

Finely dice enough fruit to measure about 3 cups. Cover and chill for up to 3 hours.

To serve, spoon the fruit salsa into stemmed glasses. Top with a scoop of sorbet and garnish with a slice of carambola. Alternatively, slice or cut the fruit into chunks, spoon it into bowls, and top with sorbet.

Serves 6 to 8

Poached Pears with Raspberry Coulis

This is a gorgeous dessert. The poaching liquid can be strained and frozen to be used again and again for poaching any fruit. It tastes better with each batch. Crème Anglaise or chocolate sauce can be substituted for the coulis.

1 bottle fruity California Sauvignon Blanc
1 whole nutmeg
1 whole cinnamon stick
1 large bay leaf
4 whole cloves
2 whole star anise pods
1 vanilla bean, split lengthwise, or
   2 teaspoons vanilla extract

1 teaspoon cardamom seeds or
   ½ teaspoon ground cardamom
4 whole black peppercorns
1 tablespoon chopped fresh ginger
6 strips lemon zest (no white pith)
1½ cups sugar
8 ripe but firm Bosc pears

RASPBERRY COULIS
2 10-ounce packages frozen red
   raspberries in syrup, thawed
Few drops lemon juice

Mint sprigs
Whipped cream

Combine all the ingredients for the poaching liquid in a deep, non-aluminum pot large enough to hold the pears in one layer. Simmer for 30 minutes. Peel the pears and carefully core them from the bottom, leaving the stems attached. Cut a thin slice from the bottom of each pear so that it will stand upright. Place the pears in the poaching liquid and weight them with a heat-resistant plate to keep them submerged. Simmer gently, uncovered, until tender, but not mushy, 10 to 20 minutes depending on ripeness. Remove the pears to a plate. Place the pot in a sink filled with water and ice and cool the poaching liquid. Refrigerate the pears overnight or up to 2 days in enough poaching liquid to cover.

Drain the raspberries and reserve ½ cup of syrup. Puree the berries in a food processor or blender and force the puree through a sieve to remove seeds. Add a few drops of lemon juice and/or reserved syrup to taste. Refrigerate until well chilled or up to 2 days.

Shortly before serving, remove the pears from the liquid and drain. With a toothpick, make a small hole next to each stem and insert a mint sprig. Spoon coulis onto 8 plates. Tip and rotate the plates to cover the entire center portion with coulis. Place a large dollop of whipped cream in the center of the coulis, spread it slightly, and stand a pear in the center.

Serves 8

Poached Figs
with Port Syrup and Crème Anglaise

Fresh figs come into the markets in June and are available through late summer. When fully ripe, they are honey-sweet and luscious. Try this easy, sophisticated dessert with black or green figs.

1 750 ml bottle ruby or tawny port
12 to 16 fresh black or green figs with stems

CRÈME ANGLAISE

2 cups milk
1 vanilla bean, split lengthwise
   (use ½ of the bean)

4 egg yolks
½ cup sugar
Mint sprigs for garnish

Bring the port to a boil in a 2-quart, non-aluminum saucepan. Add the figs (they should be completely covered), reduce the heat, and simmer gently until soft, but not mushy, about 4 to 6 minutes, depending on ripeness. Do not let them fall apart. With a slotted spoon, gently remove them to a plate. Increase the heat and boil the port until syrupy. There should be about ¾ cup of syrup. Set aside to cool. (The figs can be refrigerated.)

Pour the milk into a saucepan. With a small knife, gently scrape the vanilla "caviar" from the inside of the vanilla bean half. Add it to the milk along with the scraped pod and slowly bring it to a boil. Meanwhile, beat the eggs and sugar in the bowl of an electric mixer until the mixture falls back on itself in a ribbon when the beaters are lifted. Beating constantly, slowly add the hot milk to the eggs. The milk can be added faster after the eggs have warmed. Return the mixture to the saucepan and cook over medium heat, stirring constantly, until it coats the back of a metal spoon. Remove from the heat and immediately strain the custard through a fine sieve into a bowl. Set aside to cool. Add ¼ cup of the custard to the port syrup. (The syrup and the Crème Anglaise can be refrigerated.)

To serve, spoon the Crème Anglaise onto individual serving plates. Place 2 figs in the center of each plate and drizzle with the port-syrup. Garnish with mint sprigs.

Serves 6 to 8

Really Good Holiday Mincemeat

This delicious variation on an old English recipe makes very nice holiday gifts. It's a wonderful filling for pies or small tarts.

1 pound dried tart cherries or currants
1 pound raisins
½ pound golden raisins
1 pound Granny Smith apples, peeled and diced
1 pound dark brown sugar
Scant ½ pound candied lemon or orange peel, or candied citron, finely chopped
2 ounces almonds, chopped
2 ounces walnuts, chopped
Grated zest and juice from 2 lemons
Grated zest and juice from 1 orange
1 teaspoon finely grated nutmeg
¼ teaspoon ground cloves
¼ teaspoon ground cinnamon
⅛ teaspoon ground mace
⅛ teaspoon ground ginger
¼ cup dark rum
5 ounces Drambuie or cognac

Run 6 or 7 pint-sized jars and lids through the dishwasher. Combine all the ingredients in a large bowl. Spoon into the clean jars, cover, and store at room temperature, turning the jars upside down occasionally, for at least 3 weeks and up to 1 year. Traditionally, mincemeat is allowed to stand for at least 1 month before using.

Note: Two teaspoons Penzey's Baking Spice can be substituted for the spices listed.

Makes enough for 6 or 7 pint jars

Roasted Pears with Goat Cheese and Honey

A simple, elegant, and not-too-sweet finale to any meal. The pears can be roasted several hours in advance and reheated in the oven. Blue cheese is a delicious alternative to the goat cheese.

4 tablespoons unsalted butter
4 large, firm Bosc or Anjou pears
6 tablespoons balsamic vinegar
An 8-ounce log of fresh goat cheese, at room temperature
½ cup toasted pecans, coarsely chopped
Honey

Place a rack in the middle of the oven and preheat to 400°F. Place the butter in a 9x13-inch glass baking dish and melt in the preheated oven. Peel the pears, cut them in half, and scoop out the seeds with a melon baller. Place the pears in a single layer, cut sides down, in the baking dish. Bake until the pears are just tender, about 20 minutes. Drizzle the vinegar over the pears and return them to the oven for about 5 minutes. To serve, place a pear half on each plate, cut side up. Crumble the cheese into the cavities. Spoon some of the cooking juices over each pear, sprinkle with pecans, and drizzle with honey. Serve warm.

Serves 8

Summer Pudding

An English creation, summer pudding is a luscious melange of juicy, ripe berries layered with bread. The bread soaks up the delicious juices and lightly binds the whole together. It's a perfect summer dessert.

2 pints ripe strawberries, hulled
  and sliced
1 pint red currants, stems removed
1 cup granulated sugar
¼ cup water
½ pint blueberries
1 pint blackberries
2½ pints red raspberries

1 tablespoon raspberry liqueur
  (optional)
1 loaf dense, homemade-style
  white bread
1 cup heavy cream
1 teaspoon confectioners' sugar
½ teaspoon vanilla extract

Combine the strawberries, currants, sugar, and water in a nonreactive saucepan and cook over medium-low heat until they begin to release their juices, about 5 minutes. Add the blueberries, blackberries, and 1½ pints of raspberries. Bring to a bare simmer and stew until they release their juices, 1 to 2 minutes. Remove from the heat and stir in the liqueur and the remaining pint of raspberries. Cool to room temperature.

Trim the crust from the bread and cut it into ½-inch thick slices. Drain the juices from the berries into a bowl. Place a layer of bread in the bottom of a 9-inch square glass baking dish, cutting it to fit snugly with no gaps. Spoon half of the berries over the bread and drizzle with some of the juices. Add another layer of bread, spoon on the remaining berries, and drizzle with a little juice. Dip the bread for the top layer in the remaining juice and arrange over the berries. Drizzle any remaining juice over the top of the pudding. Cover the dish with plastic wrap and place it on a rimmed baking sheet to catch any drips. Place a slightly smaller pan on top of the pudding and weight with moderately heavy canned goods. Refrigerate overnight. Remove the weights in the morning.

Just before serving, whip the cream until it begins to hold its shape. Add the sugar and vanilla and whip until soft peaks form. Cut the pudding into squares and garnish with whipped cream.

Note: If red currants are unavailable, increase the amount of raspberries and add a spoonful of red currant jelly to the saucepan. The pudding can be assembled in a 1½-quart soufflé dish or bowl lined with plastic wrap. Line the bottom (and sides, if desired) of the mold with bread and proceed as above. Invert the mold onto a deep platter and peel away the plastic.

Serves 8

Tropical Fruit Pavlovas

This stunning dessert of crisp meringue shells filled with whipped cream and fruit was created in Australia and named for the famous Russian ballerina. Any combination of fruit and berries can be substituted.

MERINGUE

4 egg whites, at room temperature
¼ teaspoon cream of tartar
½ teaspoon vanilla

1 cup sugar
2 teaspoons cornstarch

FRUIT AND CREAM TOPPING

About 4 cups mixed, fresh tropical fruits,
    such as:
Mango
Kiwi
Strawberries
Pineapple
Bananas

1 cup whipping cream
½ teaspoon vanilla
1 teaspoon sugar
2 to 3 passionfruit (optional)

Place a rack in the center of the oven and preheat to 200°F. Line a baking sheet with kitchen parchment. Using a small bowl or mold and a pencil, trace 6 circles about 4 inches in diameter on the parchment. Turn the parchment over, pencil side down, and set aside.

In the bowl of an electric mixer, beat the egg whites on medium speed until frothy. Add the cream of tartar, raise the speed to medium-high (high on a hand mixer), and continue to beat until soft peaks form. Add the vanilla. Gradually add the sugar and beat until the meringue is glossy and stands in stiff peaks. Beat in the cornstarch. With a large spoon, drop mounds of meringue on the parchment, using about ½ cup for each. With the back of a small spoon, shape the meringue into "nests," using the pencil outlines as guides. Bake for 1½ hours. Turn off the heat and let the meringues dry in the oven for 1½ hours. Do not open the oven door during this time. The meringues should be white, dry, and crisp. Cool them completely on a wire rack. Store at room temperature in an airtight container between sheets of waxed paper for up to 1 day.

Up to 4 hours before serving, slice the fruit into wedges or chunks and combine in a bowl. Slice strawberries or bananas just before serving and combine with the other fruit. In a bowl, whip the cream with the vanilla and sugar until soft peaks form. Spoon large dollops of whipped cream over the meringue shells. Using a slotted spoon, top with fruit. Cut the passionfruit in half and spoon some of the pulp on top of each dessert. Drizzle some of the juices over the fruit and serve immediately.

Serves 6

Williamsburg Sherry Trifle

English in origin, this glorious dessert has been a favorite in Williamsburg since its colonial beginning. The recipe has been shared over the years and has become a favorite everywhere.

CUSTARD

1½ tablespoons cornstarch
2 cups light cream
4 egg yolks
½ cup sugar

1 teaspoon unflavored gelatin softened
   in ¼ cup cold water (optional)
1 teaspoon vanilla

TRIFLE

2 dozen ladyfingers or sponge cake
   cut into finger-size pieces
1 cup strawberry jam
Grated zest from 1 lemon
1 cup dry sherry
3 tablespoons brandy

4 cups fresh fruit, such as peaches
   and/or berries
1 dozen macaroons, crushed
2 cups Custard
2 cups whipping cream
½ cup blanched sliced almonds

Combine the cornstarch and ¼ cup of the cream and stir until smooth. In a bowl, beat the egg yolks until light and add the cornstarch. In a small saucepan, heat the remaining cream, add the sugar, and stir until dissolved. Do not allow the cream to come to a boil. Remove the pan from the heat. Beating constantly, gradually add 1 cup of the hot cream to the eggs. Return the saucepan to low heat and, stirring constantly, slowly add the warmed eggs to the pan. Still stirring, continue to cook the custard for 5 minutes, or until it is lightly thickened. Do not boil. (If using gelatin, add it now and stir until completely dissolved.) Remove the pan from the heat and add the vanilla. Strain the custard through a fine sieve into a bowl. Set the bowl in a larger bowl of ice and water and cool, stirring occasionally. Cover and refrigerate until needed.

Spread half of the ladyfingers with ½ cup of strawberry jam and arrange in the bottom of a trifle bowl. Sprinkle with half the lemon zest, ½ cup of sherry, and half of the brandy. Arrange half the fruit in the bowl and top with half of the macaroons. Let stand for an hour or so.

Pour half of the cooled custard over the trifle. Repeat the layers and top with the remaining custard. Cover the bowl and chill for several hours.

When ready to serve, whip the cream to soft peaks in a large, chilled bowl, spread it over the trifle, and sprinkle with sliced almonds.

Serves 10 to 12

Apple-Cranberry Crostata

Crisp, flaky pastry, tender apples, and fragrant spices make this rustic tart memorable. Make it in the fall when new-crop apples are in the markets. In summer, use plums, apricots, or peaches.

PASTRY

1¼ cups bleached all-purpose flour
1 tablespoon sugar
Pinch salt

8 tablespoons (1 stick) unsalted butter,
    cut into ½-inch cubes and chilled well
3 to 6 tablespoons ice water
2 tablespoons melted butter

FILLING

1 pound crisp cooking apples
½ cup dried cranberries or tart cherries
1 to 2 tablespoons flour, depending on
    the juiciness of the apples

1 to 3 tablespoons granulated sugar,
    depending on the sweetness of the apples
½ teaspoon each ground cinnamon,
    nutmeg, and ginger (omit for stone fruit)

Whisk the flour, sugar, and salt together in a bowl. Cut the butter into the flour with a pastry blender until evenly distributed, but still in chunky pieces. Add 4 tablespoons of ice water and toss with a fork. Add more water, 1 tablespoon at a time, just until the dough holds together when pinched. Turn the dough out onto a sheet of plastic wrap, gather it together, and press it into a flattened disk. Wrap in the plastic and refrigerate for 1 hour or overnight. (The dough can be frozen for 2 months. Thaw in the refrigerator.)

Preheat the oven to 400°F. Roll out the dough between sheets of plastic wrap into a 14-inch circle. Transfer to a rimless cookie sheet lined with kitchen parchment. Cover loosely with the plastic and refrigerate while preparing the fruit.

Peel, core, and slice the apples ½-inch thick. Place them in a bowl and add the cranberries, flour, sugar, and spices. Toss to combine. Arrange the fruit in the center of the pastry, leaving a 2-inch border all around. Fold the dough over the fruit and pleat as necessary to form a rustic tart with an open center. Brush the pastry with the melted butter and sprinkle with granulated sugar. Drizzle any remaining butter over the apples. Bake until the crust is golden brown, about 30 to 35 minutes. Remove from the oven and cool on the baking sheet for a minute or two, then slide the tart off the parchment onto a cooling rack. Cool for 15 minutes before slicing. Serve the tart warm with a scoop of ice cream. The pastry is best when it is still warm from the oven, but it is also very good at room temperature or even reheated.

Note: If using stone fruit that is very juicy, scatter 3 tablespoons of crushed vanilla wafers over the pastry before adding the fruit.

Serves 6 to 8

Candy Cream Tart

This dreamy dessert is rich and creamy and crunchy—and good!

¾ cup shortbread cookies (about 12),
  finely crushed
¼ cup finely crushed graham crackers
3 tablespoons butter, melted
1 8-ounce package cream cheese,
  softened
3 tablespoons butter, softened
½ cup light cream

3 eggs
¼ cup sugar
1 teaspoon vanilla
2 1.4-ounce chocolate-covered
  toffee bars, coarsely chopped
1 1.55-ounce white chocolate bar with
  crunchy chocolate cookie bits,
  coarsely chopped

Preheat the oven to 350°F. In a bowl, stir together the crushed cookies, graham crackers, and melted butter. Press over the bottom and up the sides of a 14x4x1-inch rectangular tart pan, or a 9-inch round tart pan, both with a removable bottom. (If using the 9-inch pan, increase the crushed cookies to 1 cup, the graham crackers to ⅓ cup, and the melted butter to ¼ cup.) Bake the crust for 10 minutes or until lightly browned. Remove from the oven and set aside.

Combine the cream cheese, softened butter, cream, eggs, sugar, and vanilla in a blender or food processor and process until smooth. Combine the chopped candy in a mixing bowl. Set aside ¼ cup. Stir the cream cheese mixture into the remaining candy. Place the tart pan on a rimmed baking sheet. Carefully pour the filling into the crust (the crust will be full). Bake for 30 to 35 minutes or until the edges of the tart are puffed and golden, and the center is almost set.

Remove the tart from the oven and sprinkle with the reserved candy. Transfer the tart to a rack and cool for 1 hour. Cover and chill for at least 4 hours before serving.

Serves 12

Banana Cream Crunch Pie

This easy version of the old-fashioned favorite is all spruced up with a chocolate-graham cracker crust and toffee bits.

1 small box (3.4 ounces) banana cream
   flavored instant pudding mix
1 cup milk
5 tablespoons coffee liqueur
1 8-ounce container frozen whipped
   topping, thawed

2 bananas, sliced
1 6-ounce chocolate graham cracker
   crumb pie crust
3 chocolate-covered toffee bars
   (1.4 ounces each), chopped

Combine the pudding mix, milk, and 4 tablespoons of the liqueur in a medium bowl. Stir with a wire whisk until smooth. Gently fold in 1 cup of the whipped topping.

Toss the banana slices in a small bowl with the remaining tablespoon of liqueur and arrange them over the crust. Sprinkle with half the chopped toffee and top with the pudding mixture. Cover and chill for 1½ hours or until set. Just before serving, spread the remaining whipped topping over the pie and sprinkle with the remaining toffee.

Serves 6 to 8

Faye's Strawberry Pie

This favorite summer pie is only as good as the quality of the berries. Make it when ripe, sweet strawberries are in season.

3 tablespoons cornstarch
½ cup cold water
1½ quarts (6 cups) ripe strawberries
½ cup sugar
1 teaspoon lemon juice

¼ teaspoon salt
Red food color (optional)
1 9-inch pre-baked pie shell
1 cup whipping cream
1 teaspoon confectioners' sugar

Dissolve the cornstarch in ¼ cup of the water. Puree 2 cups of the berries in a food processor. Pour the puree into a saucepan and add the cornstarch, sugar, lemon juice, salt, and the remaining ¼ cup water. Bring to a boil, stirring to dissolve the sugar. Lower the heat and simmer the puree until lightly thickened. Remove from the heat and add a few drops of food coloring. Cool to room temperature without stirring.

Wash, dry, and hull the remaining berries and stand them, stem ends down, in the pie shell. Cut larger berries in half and fit them into the empty spaces. Pour the puree over the berries. Chill the pie for 1 to 2 hours. In a bowl, whip the cream with the confectioners' sugar and spread it over the pie. Serve immediately, or chill for a few hours.

Serves 6 to 8

Frozen Kahlua Cream Pie

This rich dessert is worth every last calorie! Shaved or coarsely grated chocolate is a pretty touch atop the whipped cream garnish.

½ to ¾ box chocolate wafer cookies
6 tablespoons unsalted butter, melted
12 ounces semisweet chocolate chips
5 egg yolks

3 tablespoons Kahlua
1½ cups whipping cream, plus more
   for garnish

Preheat the oven to 400°F. Process the cookies in a food processor until reduced to fine crumbs (or place in a heavy plastic bag and crush with a rolling pin or the back of a small skillet). Combine the crumbs with the melted butter and pat over the bottom and sides of a 10-inch pie plate. Bake for 4 to 5 minutes and cool completely.

In a blender, process the chocolate chips and egg yolks until smooth. Pour the mixture into a bowl and stir in the Kahlua. Heat 1½ cups of whipping cream to just under the boiling point. Do not allow the cream to boil. Gradually stir ½ cup of the hot cream into the chocolate mixture. Add the remaining cream in a thin stream, stirring constantly. Pour the mixture into the pie shell and freeze. Let the pie stand at room temperature for several minutes before slicing. Garnish each slice with whipped cream.

Serves 8

Grandmother's Pumpkin Pie

This family recipe has been passed down for over sixty years. The grandson who sent us the recipe helped his father make the pies on Thanksgiving mornings when he was a child. Later, his own daughters helped him prepare them.

1½ cups unsweetened pumpkin puree
1 cup firmly packed brown sugar
½ teaspoon salt
1 teaspoon cinnamon
1 teaspoon ground ginger
⅛ teaspoon allspice

2 tablespoons molasses
3 eggs, slightly beaten
1 cup evaporated milk
1 unbaked 9-inch pie shell
Whipped cream

Preheat the oven to 425°F. In a large bowl, combine the pumpkin, brown sugar, salt, spices, and molasses and mix well. Add the eggs and milk and incorporate completely. Pour the mixture into the unbaked pie shell and bake for 15 minutes. Reduce the temperature to 325°F and bake for 35 to 45 minutes, or until the filling is set and a knife inserted near the center comes out clean. Cool completely. Serve with whipped cream.

Serves 6 to 8

Kentucky Derby Pie

A Derby-time favorite from Kentucky, this heavenly pecan pie is traditionally served warm with bourbon-spiked whipped cream.

2 eggs, slightly beaten
1 cup sugar
½ cup all-purpose flour
1 cup butter, melted and cooled
1 cup chopped pecans
1 6-ounce package semisweet
   chocolate morsels

1 teaspoon vanilla
1 unbaked 9-inch pastry shell
1 cup whipping cream
1 tablespoon bourbon
¼ cup confectioners' sugar, sifted

Preheat the oven to 350°F. Combine the eggs, sugar, flour, and cooled butter in a medium bowl. Beat with an electric mixer just until blended. Stir in the pecans, chocolate morsels, and vanilla. Pour the filling into the pastry shell and bake for 45 to 50 minutes. Transfer to a rack and cool for about 30 minutes.

In a bowl, beat the whipping cream with the bourbon. Gradually add the confectioners' sugar, beating until soft peaks form. Serve the pie warm with the bourbon cream.

Serves 6 to 8

Lemon Pie with Pecan Crust

So very simple and so very good!

CRUST
1 cup butter
2 cups all-purpose flour
2 cups chopped pecans

FILLING
1 14-ounce can sweetened
   condensed milk
1 6-ounce can frozen lemonade
   concentrate, thawed

1 9-ounce container whipped topping
Whipped cream
Thin slices of lemon

Preheat the oven to 300°F. In a bowl, cut the butter into the flour with a pastry blender or 2 knives. Add the pecans and mix well. Divide the dough in half and press into two 9-inch pie plates. Bake for 30 to 40 minutes. Cool completely on wire racks.

In a bowl, combine the condensed milk with the lemonade concentrate and blend well. Fold in the whipped topping. Pour the filling into the cooled pie shells and chill well. Garnish with whipped cream and lemon slices before serving.

Makes 2 pies (Serves 12)

Mother's Graham Cracker Pie

"This was my mother's special dessert" was the note added to this recipe. You'll agree that this silky, old-fashioned custard pie is indeed special. Make it the day before you plan to serve it.

CRUST
>   2 cups graham cracker crumbs
>   ½ cup sugar
>   ½ cup butter, melted

FILLING

>   2 cups milk
>   ½ cup sugar
>   3 tablespoons cornstarch

>   3 eggs, separated
>   ½ teaspoon vanilla

Preheat the oven to 400°F. Combine the graham cracker crumbs, sugar, and melted butter in a bowl and mix well. Set aside ½ cup for the topping. Pat the remaining crumbs over the bottom and sides of a 10-inch pie plate. Bake for 8 to 10 minutes until lightly browned. Cool completely.

In a saucepan, scald 1¾ cups of milk and remove the pan from the heat. Combine the sugar and cornstarch in a small bowl. Add the remaining ¼ cup of cold milk and stir to make a paste. Add the mixture to the hot milk, stirring constantly until smooth. Lightly beat the egg yolks. Gradually add ½ cup of the hot milk, beating constantly. Gradually stir the warmed eggs into the saucepan. Stir the mixture over moderate heat until it thickens. Transfer to a bowl and set aside until cool. Stir in ½ teaspoon of vanilla and pour the filling into the pie shell.

Preheat the oven to 400°F. In a bowl, beat the egg whites with an electric mixer until soft peaks form. Spoon the meringue over the pie and spread to cover it completely, sealing the edges. Sprinkle the reserved crumbs over the top and bake until the top is golden brown, about 5 to 10 minutes. Cool and refrigerate overnight before slicing.

Serves 8

Peach and Raspberry Cobbler

Peach cobbler is synonymous with summer. The drop-biscuit topping makes this favorite cobbler a breeze to put together. Make it with apples or pears in the autumn.

1 teaspoon cornstarch (increase to 2 teaspoons if the peaches are very juicy)
¼ cup sugar

7 to 8 ripe peaches, peeled and sliced into ½-inch-thick wedges
1 tablespoon fresh lemon juice
½ pint fresh raspberries

BISCUIT TOPPING
1 cup bleached all-purpose flour
½ cup sugar
1 teaspoon baking powder
½ teaspoon salt

6 tablespoons (¾ stick) cold, unsalted butter, cut into small pieces
¼ cup boiling water

Position a rack in the center of the oven and preheat to 425°F. Place the sliced peaches in a bowl. Combine the cornstarch and sugar and sprinkle over the peaches. Add the lemon juice and toss to coat. Transfer the fruit to a 2-quart glass or ceramic baking dish. Cover the dish tightly with foil, and bake until bubbling, about 15 minutes.

Stir the flour, sugar, baking powder, and salt together in a bowl. With your fingertips, quickly rub in the butter until the mixture resembles coarse meal. Set aside.

Remove the peaches from the oven. Stir the boiling water into the flour with a fork. Scatter the raspberries over the peaches. Drop 8 evenly spaced spoonfuls of topping over the fruit. The dough will spread as it bakes. Bake until the topping is golden brown, about 20 to 25 minutes. Serve warm with ice cream or a pitcher of cream.

Serves 6 to 8

Strawberries Balsamico

This simple dessert of sweet strawberries and balsamic vinegar is a fabulous Italian invention. The berries and deep red juices look beautiful in stemmed glasses. Vary the amounts of sugar and vinegar to suit your personal preference.

1 quart ripe strawberries
3 to 4 teaspoons good-quality balsamic vinegar
1 to 2 tablespoons granulated sugar

Wash, dry, hull, and slice the strawberries into a bowl. Add the vinegar and sugar and toss to combine. Let stand for at least 30 minutes and up to 2 hours, turning the fruit over occasionally with a large spoon, before serving.

Serves 4 to 6

Pear and Almond Tart

This elegant and utterly delicious tart needs no crust and no adornments. Make it on the day you plan to serve it. The glaze is pretty, but optional.

6 ounces blanched almonds, finely ground
½ cup plus 1½ tablespoons sugar
⅓ cup all-purpose flour
⅛ teaspoon salt
2 eggs, at room temperature
¼ cup milk

4 tablespoons unsalted butter, melted
4 medium, firm but ripe Bartlett or Bosc pears, evenly sized (about 6 ounces each)
1 tablespoon unsalted butter, cut in small pieces

GLAZE (Optional)
1 jar apricot preserves

Position an oven rack in the upper third of the oven and preheat to 350°F. Butter a round 10x1-inch ceramic or glass baking dish. Combine the ground almonds, ½ cup sugar, the flour, and the salt in a bowl. In another bowl, whisk the eggs until frothy. Whisk in the milk and melted butter. Add to the dry ingredients, stirring to blend. Spread the mixture evenly in the prepared dish.

Peel the pears, cut them lengthwise in half, and remove the cores. Working with one at a time, thinly slice each half crosswise, keeping the slices together. Beginning at the rounded end, slide a narrow metal spatula under the sliced pear, and place it on top of the batter in a spoke-like fashion with the narrow end pointing toward the center. Repeat with the remaining pears, spacing them evenly around the tart. Ideally, each slice will be topped with a pear half. Press the pears into the batter, fanning them toward the larger end, so that only the tops are showing. Sprinkle the tart with the remaining 1½ table-spoons of sugar and dot with the butter. Bake for 40 to 45 minutes, or until the tart is puffed and golden brown. Transfer to a cooling rack and cool for 10 minutes before glazing.

To prepare the glaze, place the preserves in a saucepan and warm over medium heat, stirring frequently, until melted. Strain out the solids and brush the top of the tart with the warm glaze. Serve the tart warm or at room temperature.

Serves 8

Rum Chiffon Pie

Make this luscious pie a day ahead. The bittersweet chocolate and pistachio topping is a perfect accent to the rum flavoring. If you like, serve it with a dollop of whipped cream.

CRUST
  1½ cups graham cracker crumbs
  ¼ cup sugar
  ½ cup (1 stick) unsalted butter, melted

FILLING
  1 tablespoon gelatin
  ½ cup cold water
  6 extra large egg yolks

  1 cup sugar
  ½ cup white Jamaican rum
  1 pint whipping cream

GARNISH
  Shaved bittersweet chocolate
  Ground unsalted pistachio nuts

In a bowl, combine the graham cracker crumbs, sugar, and melted butter. Reserve a tablespoon or two for the topping and press the remaining mixture over the bottom and up the sides of a 9-inch pie plate. Chill while preparing the filling.

In a small saucepan, sprinkle the gelatin over the cold water and set aside to soften. In a large bowl, beat the egg yolks on medium speed with an electric mixer and gradually add the sugar. Beat until the mixture is thick and pale and falls back on itself in a ribbon when the beater is lifted. Heat the gelatin over low heat, stirring constantly, until it dissolves completely. Do not allow it to boil. On low speed, slowly beat the hot gelatin into the eggs. Add the rum. In a medium bowl with clean beaters, beat the cream until stiff and fold it into the filling. Let stand for 10 minutes. Pour the filling into the chilled pie shell. Refrigerate, uncovered, for several hours. Cover the pie with foil and refrigerate overnight. Up to several hours before serving, sprinkle the pie with the reserved crumbs, shaved bittersweet chocolate, and ground pistachios. Serve chilled.

Serves 6 to 8

Chefs' Favorites

Bouridde
(Provençale Fish Stew)

Executive Chef Francois de Melogue, Pili Pili Restaurant, Chicago, sent us his recipe for the traditional seafood stew served in the south of France. Pour a wine from Provence, such as a white Cassis or a Bandol rosé.

1 pound cockles or manila clams
1 pound mussels
12 large shrimp, peeled and deveined
12 ounces salmon, cut in 4 pieces
12 ounces monkfish, cut in 4 pieces
12 ounces cod, cut in 4 pieces
2 small heads fennel
1 cup olive oil
2 tablespoons Pernod
2 teaspoons saffron threads
Chopped garlic
1 large onion
1 large carrot
3 large tomatoes, peeled and seeded

2 cups dry white wine
1 quart shellfish stock
4 drops orange oil, or 2 to 3 strips orange zest (no white pith)
1 bay leaf
2 tablespoons minced fresh thyme
¼ cup chopped basil
Sea salt and freshly ground pepper
2 egg yolks, lightly beaten
1 cup Rouille
4 large potatoes, boiled
8 garlic croutons*
Rouille for service

Scrub the mollusks under cold water, discarding any that will not close. Place all of the seafood in a nonreactive container. Chop the fennel tops and spread them over the seafood. Add ¾ cup of olive oil, 1 tablespoon of Pernod, a pinch of the saffron, and lots of chopped garlic. Refrigerate uncovered for 6 hours.

Julienne the fennel bulb, onion, carrot, and tomatoes. Heat ¼ cup of olive oil in a large, non-aluminum pot. Add the vegetables and sauté until softened. Add the remaining Pernod and the white wine. Bring to a simmer and add the stock, the remaining garlic and saffron, the orange oil, bay leaf, thyme, basil, salt, and pepper. Bring to a boil. Add all of the seafood to the broth and simmer until the fish and shrimp are just done and the mussels and clams are open. Discard any unopened mollusks. With a slotted spoon, remove the seafood to a large tureen. Slowly whisk ½ cup of broth into the egg yolks to warm them. Gradually whisk the egg yolks and 1 cup of rouille into the broth. Do not allow the broth to boil. Pour the broth over the seafood. Serve with boiled potatoes, garlic croutons, and more rouille.

*To make the croutons, toast 8 slices of French bread and rub one side of the warm toast with the cut side of a garlic clove.

ROUILLE
3 egg yolks
1½ tablespoons freshly squeezed lemon juice
3 teaspoons salt
Pinch pepper

3 pinches saffron threads
9 cloves garlic
4 to 5 tablespoons Sriracha Hot Chili Sauce
1½ cups olive oil

Blend all the ingredients except the olive oil in a blender or food processor. With the machine running, dribble in the oil until the mixture emulsifies. Add the remaining oil in a thin stream. Refrigerate overnight to allow the flavor to develop. The rouille should be garlicky and spicy. Makes about 1½ cups.

Serves 4

Ca Chien Saigon
(Thai Fried Whole Red Snapper)

This dish is a great favorite at Le Colonial restaurant in Chicago which generously shared the recipe. Garnish the serving platter with fresh cilantro, scallions, fresh red chilies, and orange slices. The dipping sauce can be served with grilled meats or on noodles, rice, and salads.

1 whole red snapper, 1½ to 2 pounds, dressed
Salt and freshly ground pepper
2 to 3 cups vegetable oil
Flour for dredging
2 tablespoons chili-garlic fish sauce (available at Asian markets)
Nuoc Cham for service

Rinse and dry the fish. Make two diagonal slashes to the bone on each side of the fish and season with salt and pepper. In a large wok or braising pan, heat the oil over medium-high heat to 375°F. Lightly coat the fish with flour and shake off the excess. Carefully lower the fish into the oil, head first. The oil will bubble vigorously. Ladle the oil over the fish and cook for 4 minutes or until golden brown. Lower the heat if necessary to avoid burning. Carefully turn the fish with two spatulas and cook the second side until golden, about 3 or 4 minutes. Remove the fish and check inside the scores for doneness. Transfer the fish to a platter and present it at the table. Pour the chili-garlic sauce over the fish. Filet and serve with small bowls of Nuoc Cham for dipping.

NUOC CHAM
½ cup Asian fish sauce
½ cup sugar
1 cup water
Juice from 1 lime
1 tablespoon chopped garlic
1 tablespoon chopped fresh chili pepper, or bottled chili paste

Combine the ingredients in a non-reactive container. The sauce can be refrigerated for 2 weeks.

Serves 2 as a main course, 4 as part of a multi-course Asian-style meal

Caramelized Fennel with Salt-Cured Capers and Thyme

Executive Chef John Coletta, Carlucci, Rosemont, Illinois, shared this unique recipe. The piquant capers heighten the sweetness of the fennel, and the unfiltered oil rounds out the flavors of the dish.

2 tablespoons olive oil
12 baby fennel bulbs, trimmed and
    halved lengthwise (or substitute 3
    small bulbs)
2 tablespoons salt-packed capers,
    well rinsed and drained
1 teaspoon fresh thyme leaves

2 bay leaves
2 cloves garlic, peeled
1½ cups vegetable broth
Kosher salt and freshly ground pepper
1 tablespoon unfiltered, extra-virgin
    olive oil

In a large, heavy skillet or sauté pan, heat 2 tablespoons of olive oil over medium heat. Add the fennel and cook until deep brown and caramelized on one side. Turn and caramelize the second side. Add the capers, thyme, bay leaves, garlic, and vegetable broth. Season with salt and pepper. Lower the heat and simmer slowly for 10 to 12 minutes, or until the fennel is tender. Remove the fennel to a warm platter. Spoon the capers and cooking juices over the top, drizzle with the unfiltered olive oil, and serve.

Serves 6

Cayuga Blue Cheese Parfait

Executive Chef John Reed, Food for Thought Catering, Lincolnwood, Illinois, serves this elegant dish as a combined cheese and dessert course with poached seasonal fruit, a small salad of petite bitter greens, and ginger biscotti.

3 tablespoons all-purpose flour
½ cup granulated sugar
8 ounces Cayuga Blue goat cheese,
    crumbled (substitute any other brand),
    or Stilton, Gorgonzola, or Danish
    Bleu cheese
1¼ pounds cream cheese, softened

3 eggs
8 ounces sour cream
4 tablespoons chopped crystallized
    ginger

Position a rack in the center of the oven. Preheat the oven to 300°F. Butter eight 4-ounce ramekins or molds. Bring a kettle of water to a boil. Sift together the flour and sugar.

In the bowl of an electric mixer, cream the blue cheese and cream cheese together until slightly smooth. Add the flour mixture and beat just until combined. Do not overwork. Add the eggs one at a time, beating after each addition just until incorporated. Fold in the sour cream and ginger. Pour the mixture into the prepared ramekins and place them in a shallow roasting pan. Transfer the pan to the oven rack. Carefully add boiling water to the pan until it reaches halfway up the sides of the molds. Bake until a toothpick inserted in the center of the parfaits comes out clean, about 30 minutes.

Remove the molds from the water bath, run the tip of a small, sharp knife around the inner edges, and cool on a wire rack for 30 minutes. Tip the parfaits out into your hand and place them on the plates, top side up. Serve warm.

Note: The parfaits can be cooled and refrigerated for several hours. Place the molds in a shallow pan of hot tap water for 10 minutes to reheat.

Serves 8

Carrot Cake with Cream Cheese Frosting

A perennial favorite from Executive Chef Abraham Aguirre, Grotto on State, Chicago.

CAKE

2 cups grated carrots
1 16-ounce can crushed pineapple
   packed in juice, undrained
½ cup golden raisins
½ cup chopped walnuts
3 cups cake flour
1½ teaspoons cinnamon

1 teaspoon salt
2 teaspoons baking powder
4 eggs
1 pound brown sugar (2¼ packed cups)
1 cup peanut oil
2 teaspoons vanilla

CREAM CHEESE FROSTING

1 pound confectioners' sugar
4 ounces unsalted butter, softened

8 ounces cream cheese, softened
Whole or chopped almonds or pecans

Preheat the oven to 350°F. Butter two 9-inch cake pans, line the bottoms with parchment, butter the parchment, and flour the pans. Combine the carrots, pineapple, raisins, and walnuts in a bowl and toss with ½ cup of flour. In another bowl, combine the remaining flour with the cinnamon, salt, and baking powder.

In a large bowl, beat the eggs with an electric mixer. Add the brown sugar and combine well. Slowly add the oil and vanilla and beat well. Stir in the flour and carrot mixtures. Pour the batter into the prepared pans and bake until the cakes are firm in the center and a tester comes out clean, about 30 minutes. Cool in the pans on wire racks. Turn the layers out and peel off the parchment.

For the frosting, combine the confectioners' sugar, butter, and cream cheese in a large bowl and mix well by hand. Fill and frost the cooled layers and garnish with nuts.

Makes one 9-inch layer cake

Chilean Sea Bass in Hoja Santa with
Warm Potato-Mushroom Salad and Corn and Chili Salsa

Executive Chef Edgar Rodriguez, Salbute Restaurant, Hinsdale, Illinois, serves this exciting dish. Used by the ancient Aztecs in rituals, anise-flavored Hoja Santa (sacred leaves) are used in Mexico today as wrappers for fish and tamales. They are difficult to find in the United States. Substitute banana leaves.

2 fresh or frozen banana leaves
(available in Asian and Hispanic
markets)
Salt and freshly ground pepper

4 Chilean sea bass fillets, about 6
ounces each (or substitute cod,
grouper, or halibut)
Micro greens

SALAD

1 cup sliced oyster mushrooms
1 cup sliced chanterelle mushrooms
½ cup halved pearl onions
½ cup sliced garlic cloves
2 tablespoons chopped basil leaves
3 tablespoons olive oil
¼ cup water or chicken stock

½ pound Peruvian Purple
fingerling potatoes
½ pound Banana fingerling potatoes
1 cup fresh corn kernels
2 jalapeño peppers, stemmed,
seeded and minced
Salt and freshly ground pepper

SALSA

6 ears fresh corn
2 tablespoons chopped onion
1 tablespoon ground cumin

2 canned chipotle peppers
in adobo sauce
Salt and freshly ground pepper

Wash the banana leaves with soapy water, rinse, and dry (thaw first if frozen). Cut away the hard stem that runs along one edge and cut the leaves into pieces large enough to wrap the fish. Soften by passing both sides of the leaves over a low gas flame or directly on an electric burner for a few seconds. Set aside.

Preheat the oven to 325°F. In a roasting pan, toss the mushrooms, pearl onions, and sliced garlic with 1 tablespoon of basil and 1 tablespoon of olive oil. Add ¼ cup of water or stock, cover, and bake until the mushrooms are tender, about 30 to 40 minutes. Cool in the cooking juices.

Raise the oven temperature to 400°F. Toss the potatoes and 1 cup of corn kernels with 1 tablespoon of olive oil and season with salt and pepper. Place on a baking sheet and roast until the potatoes are tender, about 20 to 25 minutes. Slice the potatoes into thick disks and combine with the corn, roasted vegetables, jalapeños, and remaining tablespoon of olive oil. Season with salt and pepper and fold in the remaining basil.

Meanwhile, place the ears of corn in a saucepan, cover with cold water by 2 inches and simmer for 30 minutes. In a small skillet, sauté the onions with the cumin until wilted. Add the onions to the corn along with the chipotle peppers. Force the mixture through a fine sieve, discarding the solids. Add salt and pepper and set aside.

Prepare a steamer. Season the fish with salt and pepper and steam for 5 minutes. Remove the fillets and wrap them in the leaves, leaving the ends of the fish slightly exposed. Secure with kitchen twine if necessary. Return the fillets to the steamer until the fish is just done, about 4 to 6 minutes. Remove the wrappers.

Portion the warm potato salad among 4 plates and top with the fish. Spoon corn salsa around the potatoes and garnish each fillet with a mound of micro greens.

Serves 4

Chicken Paupiettes Wrapped in Bacon
(Paupiettes de Volaille en Chemise de Potrine)

This wonderfully flavorful dish is from Chef Charlie Sochor, chef/owner of Café Matou in Chicago. The paupiettes can be refrigerated for a few hours before cooking, making this a perfect dish for entertaining. Serve the paupiettes with rice or orzo and a Pinot Noir.

4 boneless, skinless chicken
   breast halves
Salt and freshly ground pepper
3 ounces Gruyère cheese, grated
2 tablespoons capers, chopped
2 tablespoons chopped onion
Grated zest from 1 lemon

2 tablespoons chopped red bell pepper
4 large basil leaves
8 slices bacon
Extra-virgin olive oil
Fresh herb sprigs
Lemon and lime wedges

Preheat the oven to 450°F. Pound the chicken breasts between 2 sheets of plastic wrap until thin. Season with salt and pepper. Top each breast with cheese, capers, onions, lemon zest, bell peppers, and a basil leaf. Starting at the lower point, roll up the breasts. Wrap each breast with 2 slices of bacon and secure with toothpicks. Heat a large, heavy, oven-proof skillet over medium-high heat. Add the paupiettes and brown on one side, about 4 minutes. Turn them over and place the pan in the oven. Bake for 10 minutes, or until the chicken is cooked through. Transfer the paupiettes to plates and drizzle them with extra-virgin olive oil. Garnish with herb sprigs and lemon and lime wedges.

Serves 4

Chilled Avocado Soup with Shrimp and Mango Relish

Executive Chef Michael Garbin, Union League Club of Chicago, created this elegant and very pretty first course. Serve the soup with a glass of Chardonnay.

SOUP

6 ripe Hass avocados, cut into chunks
1 clove roasted garlic
Freshly squeezed juice from
   ½ lemon
2 tablespoons extra-virgin olive oil

3 cups chicken stock
¼ cup sour cream
Few drops Tabasco
Salt and freshly ground pepper

RELISH

2 ounces cooked bay shrimp
¼ cup ripe mango, in very
   small dice
2 tablespoons mixed bell peppers
   (red, yellow, green), in very
   small dice

2 tablespoons Roma tomatoes,
   in very small dice
1 teaspoon minced fresh cilantro
Pinch of grated lime zest
1 tablespoon extra-virgin olive oil
Salt and freshly ground pepper

Place all the ingredients for the soup in an electric blender and puree until smooth. Cover and chill well. Check the seasoning when the soup is cold. Combine the ingredients for the relish in a bowl. Cover and chill.

Pour the soup into chilled martini glasses. Garnish each serving with a spoonful of the relish.

Serves 4

Chocolate Fondant Cakes

Pastry Chef Nathan Brown, Spago, Maui, Hawaii, offers his version of these fabulous little cakes with molten centers. A small scoop of vanilla ice cream, a little pool of raspberry coulis, and a few fresh raspberries are nice accompaniments. The cakes are sensational with a glass of Banyuls.

9 ounces dark chocolate
   (64 percent cocoa butter, such as
   Valrhona), shaved or finely chopped
9 ounces unsalted butter

5 large whole eggs
5 large egg yolks
¾ cup sugar
5 tablespoons plus 1 teaspoon flour

Preheat the oven to 400°F. Butter and flour eight 4-ounce muffin cups. In a saucepan, melt the chocolate and butter together over low heat, stirring occasionally. Remove the pan from the heat.

In the bowl of an electric mixer, whip the whole eggs, egg yolks, and sugar until tripled in volume. Reduce the speed and add the warm chocolate. Sift the flour over the batter and fold it in, scraping the bottom and sides of the bowl to incorporate thoroughly.

Fill the prepared muffin cups and bake until the tops and edges are firm but the centers are still liquid, about 8 minutes. Unmold and serve immediately.

Serves 8

Desmond Hotel Bread Pudding

Hot dog rolls? Yes, hot dog rolls! You really must try this signature recipe from Executive Chef Tom Makrina, the Desmond Hotel, Malvern, Pennsylvania.

PUDDING

12 hot dog rolls
1 quart heavy cream
5 extra large eggs

2 cups sugar
2½ teaspoons vanilla

SAUCE

5 eggs, well beaten
½ cup sugar
1 cup whipping cream

Preheat the oven to 350°F. Spray a 9x13-inch pan with cooking spray. Tear the rolls into the pan. Scald the cream in a saucepan (do not allow it to boil). Beat the eggs in a large mixing bowl. Add the sugar and combine well. Whisking constantly, slowly add the scalded cream. Add the vanilla. Pour the mixture over the rolls and let stand until absorbed. Cover the pan with foil and bake for 1 hour. Uncover and bake until the top browns.

To make the sauce, beat the eggs in a bowl with half the sugar. Combine the cream and the remaining sugar in a saucepan and bring it to a boil. Slowly add the scalded cream to the eggs, whisking constantly. Transfer the mixture to the top of a double boiler and cook, whisking constantly, until thickened. Place the pan with the sauce into an ice bath and continue whisking until the sauce is cool.

Cut the pudding into serving pieces and serve warm with the sauce.

Serves 8 to 10

Crispy Game Hens with Quinoa Pilaf

This sophisticated dish is from Executive Chef Daniel J. Scannell, Oak Hill Country Club, Rochester, New York. The flavored brine makes for moist, flavorful meat. Dipping the hens in the boiling vinegar solution and drying them overnight ensures crispy skin.

2 Cornish game hens, 1¼ to 1½ pounds each	1 cinnamon stick
¾ cup kosher salt	½ cup brown sugar
½ gallon cold water	3 cups balsamic vinegar
1 tablespoon pickling spice	1 cup low-salt soy sauce
2 cups honey	1 cup molasses
	1 sprig thyme

Rinse and dry the hens, sprinkle them with kosher salt, and truss. Refrigerate. In a stainless pan, combine the cold water, pickling spice, 1 cup of the honey, the cinnamon stick, remaining kosher salt, and brown sugar. Bring to a boil, skimming off any foam. Cool and pour over the hens. Refrigerate for 3 hours.

In a large, non-aluminum pot, combine the vinegar, soy sauce, molasses, 1 cup honey, and the thyme. Bring to a boil. Drain the hens and dip each in the boiling solution 4 times. Drain well. Place the hens on a wire rack set in a shallow pan and refrigerate uncovered for 24 hours.

Preheat the oven to 375°F. Place the pan in the oven and roast the hens until they are golden brown and cooked through, about 45 minutes to 1 hour, basting with the pan drippings every 15 minutes. Let the hens rest for 5 minutes and cut them in half. Serve with Quinoa Pilaf.

QUINOA PILAF WITH BLACK TRUMPET MUSHROOMS

1 cup quinoa (available in health food stores and some supermarkets)	2 teaspoons minced garlic
½ cup dried black trumpet mushrooms (or substitute dried morels or porcini)	1 teaspoon crushed red pepper flakes
3 tablespoons extra-virgin olive oil	1 cup dry white wine
1 tablespoon unsalted butter	1 cup chicken stock
¾ cup diced onions	2 tablespoons Dried Chili Marmalade
	1 tablespoon chopped fresh cilantro
	Salt and freshly ground pepper

Place the quinoa in a fine mesh sieve and rinse it well under cold water. Drain. Spread the grains on a flat surface and let stand until completely dry, about 1 hour. Soak the black trumpets in ½ cup of cool water until softened. (Use hot water for morels or porcini.) Drain and set aside. Place the quinoa on a baking sheet and toast in a 375°F oven until golden brown. Transfer to a bowl and set aside.

In a medium saucepan, heat 1 tablespoon of olive oil and 1 tablespoon of butter. Add the onions and sauté until golden. Add the garlic, crushed red pepper flakes, drained mushrooms, and quinoa. Stir well. Add the wine in 2 or 3 additions, stirring until it is absorbed before adding more. Add the stock and simmer until the quinoa is tender. Do not overcook. Transfer the pilaf to a bowl and add the chili marmalade, remaining olive oil, and cilantro. Season with salt and pepper and serve hot.

DRIED CHILI MARMALADE

2 dried Ancho chilies	1 ounce raisins
Kosher salt and freshly ground pepper	Dash sherry vinegar
1 ounce brown sugar	3 ounces orange juice

Preheat the oven to 275°F. Rinse the chilies. Place them on a baking sheet and toast them in the oven for 5 minutes. Transfer them to a bowl. Add 1 cup of boiling water and ¼ teaspoon of kosher salt and steep the chiles for 10 minutes or until softened. Drain and cool. Reserve the soaking liquid. Remove the stems, cut the chilies in half, and rinse them in the chili water to remove the seeds. Set aside.

Strain the chili water into a medium-size stainless saucepan. Add the brown sugar and simmer until reduced to a syrup. Remove from the heat and add the raisins, salt, pepper, and a dash of vinegar. Simmer the orange juice in a small pan until reduced by ¾, or until syrupy. Place the chilies in a food processor and pulse 2 or 3 times. Add the chili and orange syrups and process until the marmalade has a coarse texture.

Note: Quinoa (keen-wah), a grainlike seed, has been cultivated in the Andes for five thousand years and sustained the ancient Incas. Highly nutritious, it has a delicious nutty flavor that is enhanced by toasting.

Serves 4

Rigatoni with Vodka-Tomato Cream Sauce

Chef Debbie Dunnewold, the Windy City Chef, shared her recipe for this creamy, spicy dish. The vodka adds a "certain something" without being really discernable. Pour a Chianti or a red Zinfandel.

6 tablespoons olive oil	1½ pounds rigatoni or penne
1¼ cups finely chopped shallots	6 ounces prosciutto, sliced ⅛-inch thick
¾ teaspoon crushed red pepper flakes	½ cup freshly grated Parmesan cheese
¼ cup vodka	6 tablespoons chopped flat leaf parsley
2¼ cups heavy cream	Salt and freshly ground pepper
2¼ cups tomato sauce	

In a large skillet, heat the oil over medium-high heat. Add the shallots and crushed red pepper flakes and sauté until the shallots soften. Add the vodka, avert your face, and ignite. When the flames subside, increase the heat to high, add the cream, and boil until it thickens. Add the tomato sauce and boil until the sauce thickens, about 2 minutes. (The sauce can be refrigerated.)

Boil the pasta in 4 quarts salted water until al dente. Cut the prosciutto into thin sticks. Scoop out some of the pasta cooking water and drain the pasta. Add the pasta, prosciutto, cheese, and parsley to the sauce and toss. Add cooking water if the pasta seems dry. Season with salt and pepper and serve.

Serves 6

Endive Salad with Warm Goat Cheese Fritter, Toasted Almonds, and Pomegranate Seeds

(Salade d'Endive au Fromage a l'Anglaise)

The recipe for this colorful salad is from Chef Charlie Socher, chef/owner of Chicago's Café Matou. It's a very impressive first course, but not difficult to make.

VINAIGRETTE

1 teaspoon Dijon mustard
1 teaspoon minced garlic
2 tablespoons white wine vinegar

Salt and freshly ground pepper
6 tablespoons olive oil

FRITTERS

4 ounces fresh goat cheese
Flour
1 egg, beaten in a small bowl

1 cup bread crumbs, spread
   on a plate
Olive oil

SALAD

3 heads Belgian endive, julienned
   lengthwise
½ pomegranate, seeded (See page 77)
16 grape or cherry tomatoes,
   halved if large
1 small roasted red pepper, cut into
   strips or diced

2 small green onions, thinly sliced
2 tablespoons sliced almonds,
   toasted
20 whole cloves roasted garlic
6 tablespoons chopped mixed
   fresh herbs
4 large basil leaves, chopped or torn

In a small bowl, whisk together the mustard, garlic, vinegar, salt, and pepper. Slowly whisk in the oil until the dressing emulsifies. Set aside.

Form 4 silver dollar-sized goat cheese cakes and dust them with flour. Dip the cakes in the beaten egg and coat them with bread crumbs. In a small skillet, heat 1 to 2 tablespoons of olive oil over medium-low heat. Add the goat cheese cakes and sauté until lightly browned and warmed through, about 2 minutes per side. Do not allow the cheese to melt. Remove the cakes to a plate and keep warm.

Fan equal amounts of the endive on 4 plates. Place a goat cheese fritter at the base of each fan. Scatter the remaining ingredients over the salads and drizzle with vinaigrette.

Serves 4

Flourless Chocolate Cake

Chef Debbie Dunnewold, the Windy City Chef, Chicago, makes this decadent cake. Serve it with a few fresh cherries or berries and a glass of port or Banyuls—perfection!

8 eggs	1 tablespoon vanilla
½ pound butter	¼ cup confectioners' sugar
1 pound dark chocolate	

Preheat the oven to 350°F. Butter a 9-inch springform pan. Using a stand mixer with the whisk attachment, whisk the eggs in a bowl until they triple in volume, about 5 minutes. Melt the butter and chocolate together in the top of a double boiler. Remove the pan from the heat and add the vanilla. Stir until the chocolate is completely smooth and pour it into a large bowl. With a rubber spatula, fold one-third of the eggs into the chocolate. Fold in the remaining eggs in two additions. Pour the batter into the prepared pan and bake for 20 minutes or until an instant read thermometer inserted into the center of the cake registers 140 degrees. The cake will be loose in the center. Transfer the pan to a wire rack and cool the cake to room temperature. Cover and refrigerate for at least 4 hours or overnight. Sift confectioners' sugar over the top before serving.

Serves 12

Gibsons Pepper Steak

This quick and delicious sauté is a favorite at Gibsons Steakhouse Restaurant, Chicago. The recipe is from Executive Chef/Partner Audry Triplett. Pour a dry, full-bodied red wine.

Olive oil or vegetable oil	1 large Spanish onion, sliced
2 pounds beef tenderloin, cut into 2-ounce medallions	⅓ cup flour
Salt and freshly ground pepper	1 cup dry red wine
2 red bell peppers, cut into strips	2 cups veal or beef stock, or low-salt broth
2 yellow bell peppers, cut into strips	

Heat 3 tablespoons of oil in a large, heavy skillet over medium-high heat. Season the medallions with salt and pepper. In batches, sauté the medallions until browned on both sides, about 2 to 3 minutes. Do not crowd the pan. Remove the meat to a plate. Add the peppers and onions to the skillet and sauté until crisp-tender. Return the meat to the pan and sprinkle with the flour. Toss to coat. Cook, stirring constantly, for about 1 minute. Deglaze the pan with the wine and simmer until the wine is reduced by three-quarters. Add the stock and simmer until it reduces and the sauce thickens. Check the seasoning. Serve immediately with rice or buttered noodles.

Serves 4 to 6

Braised Sea Bass with Lentil and Mushroom Ragout and Fennel and Orange Nage

This delectable dish is from Executive Chef John Ferguson, the Fortnightly of Chicago. "Nage" (French for "swim") is often used in fish recipes to indicate a light sauce. Pour a Chardonnay.

LENTIL RAGOUT

2 tablespoons olive oil
1 small Spanish onion, diced
1 teaspoon minced garlic
½ pound assorted mushrooms
1 tablespoon fresh chopped thyme

1 cup French green lentils (lentils de Puy)
2 cups chicken stock
2 plum tomatoes, peeled, seeded, diced
½ cup good quality balsamic vinegar
Salt and freshly ground pepper

FISH

4 skinless fillets Chilean sea bass
   (or cod, halibut, or grouper),
   about 6 ounces each
1 to 2 tablespoons olive oil

Kosher salt and cracked black pepper
1 teaspoon grated orange zest
½ cup dry white wine
Arugula leaves, cut into chiffonade

FENNEL AND ORANGE NAGE

1 tablespoon olive oil
1 medium fennel bulb, diced
2 shallots, finely diced
½ teaspoon minced garlic
2 ounces fresh orange juice

1 cup white wine
½ cup heavy cream
6 tablespoons butter, softened
Salt and freshly ground pepper

For the ragout, heat the oil in a 2-quart saucepan over medium heat. Add the onions and sauté until tender. Add the garlic, mushrooms, and thyme, and sauté for 2 to 3 minutes. Add the lentils and chicken stock. Reduce the heat, cover, and simmer until the stock is absorbed and the lentils are tender, about 30 minutes. Add the tomatoes and vinegar and simmer until most of the liquid has been absorbed, 5 to 10 minutes. Season with salt and pepper. (The ragout may be pepared several hours ahead.)

Preheat the oven to 300°F. Heat a heavy, ovenproof skillet over high heat. Brush the fillets with olive oil and sprinkle with kosher salt, pepper, and orange zest. Sear the fish, skinned side up, until lightly browned. Turn the fillets and add the wine. Place the pan in the oven and braise until just cooked through, about 15 to 20 minutes.

While the fish cooks, prepare the nage. Heat the oil in a saucepan over low heat. Add the fennel, shallots, and garlic and sauté gently until softened. Add the orange juice and wine and cook over medium heat until the liquid is syrupy. Add the cream and simmer until the sauce coats the back of a spoon. Whisk in the butter 1 or 2 tablespoons at a time, beating constantly. Remove the pan from the heat and season with salt and pepper. If necessary, keep the sauce warm over a pan of hot, not simmering, water.

To serve, reheat the lentils if necessary. Spoon the ragout into the centers of four warm soup plates and top with the fish and the nage. Garnish with the arugula chiffonade.

Serves 4

Grilled Gulf Grouper with Charred Melon Relish

Executive Chef Mark Baker, the University Club of Chicago, contributed the recipe for this elegantly simple dish, which he serves with a petite herb salad.

RELISH

4 ounces grapeseed oil
1 red onion, diced
1 yellow pepper, diced
1 red bell pepper, diced
1 cup apple juice
½ cup watermelon in
  medium dice

½ cup honeydew in
  medium dice
½ cup cantaloupe in
  medium dice
2 tablespoons cider vinegar
1 tablespoon julienned basil
1 tablespoon finely cut chives

FISH

¼ cup olive oil
4 tablespoons fresh lemon juice
Grated zest from 1 lime

Freshly cracked pepper
4 grouper fillets, about
  6 ounces each

For the relish, film the bottom of a nonstick pan with grapeseed oil and place over high heat. Add the onion and bell peppers and cook until lightly colored. Deglaze the pan with apple juice and simmer until reduced to about ¼ cup. Add the diced melon and cook for 30 seconds. Remove the pan from the heat and add the cider vinegar. Transfer to a bowl and cool. Fold in the basil and chives, cover, and refrigerate overnight.

Combine the olive oil, lemon juice, lime zest, and cracked pepper in a glass bowl or plastic bag. Add the fish and refrigerate for up to 1 hour, turning once. Prepare a grill or preheat a nonstick skillet. Cook the fish for about 7 minutes per inch of thickness, turning once. Spoon the relish into the center of each plate. Top with a fillet of fish. If desired, mound a petite herb salad over each fillet.

Serves 4

Grilled Quail with Ancho Chili and Honey Salsa
(Codornices en Salsa de Chile Ancho con Miel)

Chef Priscila Satcoff, chef/owner of Salpicón! restaurant in Chicago, sent us the recipe for these spicy little gamebirds. Chef Satcoff was a host on the Food Network's show, Melting Pot, *and demonstrated the preparation of the quail and the delectable sauce.*

QUAIL

4 semi-boneless quail with skin, butterflied
4 large cloves garlic, chopped

⅓ cup olive oil
1 tablespoon Ancho chili powder

SALSA

3 dried Ancho chili pods
1 cup boiling water
1 tablespoon canola oil
¼ medium-size onion, finely chopped

¼ cup honey
Salt
Pinch cinnamon
Pinch ground cloves

In a glass bowl, combine the quail with the garlic, olive oil, and chili powder. Refrigerate for at least 12 but preferably 24 hours.

For the sauce, stem and seed the chilies and remove any thick veins. Preheat a heavy skillet over medium-high heat. Add the chilies and toast, turning them over frequently and pressing them against the pan, until they puff slightly and become pliable, about 1 minute. Transfer them to a bowl and cover with boiling water. Soak for 20 minutes.

Meanwhile, heat the oil in a large saucepan over medium heat. Add the onion and cook gently until it turns golden, stirring frequently. Set aside.

Strain the chilies and reserve the soaking liquid. Puree them in a blender with ½ cup of the reserved liquid. Force the puree through a medium mesh strainer into the pan with the onion. Add the honey, salt, and spices. Bring to a boil, reduce the heat, and simmer gently until lightly thickened, about 8 minutes.

Drain the quail and place them skin side down over a hot grill or in a well-seasoned cast-iron skillet (do not add additional oil to the skillet). Cook for about 4 minutes. Turn and cook the second side until the breasts feel fairly firm, about 2 to 3 minutes longer. The meat should be juicy and tinged with pink.

Spoon some of the sauce on each plate and top with a quail.

Serves 4 as an appetizer, 2 as a main course

Hugo's Crab Cakes with Hot Pink Mayo

Executive Chef Laura Piper, Hugo's Frog Bar & Fish House, Chicago, graciously shared this recipe for Hugo's terrific crab cakes. The Hot Pink Mayo is wonderful with cracked crab or cold shrimp.

1 small red onion, chopped
2 green onions, chopped
1 rib celery, chopped
2 tablespoons sour cream
2 tablespoons mayonnaise
1 tablespoon hot sauce
2 tablespoons Worcestershire sauce
2 tablespoons lemon juice
4 eggs

½ teaspoon salt
½ teaspoon freshly ground pepper
2 pounds fresh lump crabmeat
8 ounces (by weight) coarse
   bread crumbs (See note)
1 egg yolk, beaten
Unsalted butter for frying
Lemon wedges for garnish

Combine all the ingredients except the crabmeat, bread crumbs, and egg yolk in a large bowl, and mix well. Add the crabmeat and toss gently. Add the bread crumbs gradually until the mixture just holds together. Gently form 10 cakes. Lightly brush the cakes with the egg yolk and dip each into the remaining crumbs. (The crab cakes can be refrigerated for several hours.) Heat 3 tablespoons of butter in a heavy skillet until foaming. Add as many crab cakes to the pan as will fit without touching. Brown well on both sides, turning once. Cook any remaining crab cakes, adding more butter as necessary. If the cakes have been refrigerated, finish them in a preheated 350°F. oven until heated through, about 5 to 7 minutes. Serve with Hot Pink Mayo and lemon wedges.

Note: To make coarse bread crumbs, remove the crust from slightly stale Italian, French, or dense bakery bread; tear the bread into pieces, and whirl in a food processor.

HOT PINK MAYO

6 ounces mayonnaise
6 ounces sour cream
3 ounces chili sauce
2 ounces hot sauce

½ small red onion, cut into small dice
1 teaspoon lemon juice
Salt and freshly ground pepper

Combine the ingredients in a bowl and refrigerate for several hours. Makes 1 pint.

Makes 10 crab cakes

Kokopelli Berry Crumble

This delightful dessert comes from Chef Stephanie Schifrin, Kafe Kokopelli, Hinsdale, Illinois. Bramley apples are the cooking apples of choice in Britain. Substitute your favorite cooking apple.

1 Bramley apple, quartered, cored, and finely chopped	Small handful fresh basil leaves, chopped
2 pints blackberries	5 heaping tablespoons sugar
1 tablespoon balsamic vinegar	4 heaping teaspoons flour
	¼ pound unsalted butter

Preheat the oven to 400°F. Toss the fruit with the balsamic vinegar, basil, and 2 tablespoons of sugar in a medium bowl. Set aside to macerate.

Using your fingers, blend together the flour, butter, and the remaining sugar until the mixture is crumbly (or use on-off turns in a food processor). Place the fruit in a baking dish or individual dishes. Sprinkle the topping over the fruit, mounding it in the center. Bake for 30 minutes, or until the topping is golden in the center and the fruit has started to bubble around the edges. Serve warm with ice cream or a pitcher of cream.

Serves 4

Pan-Seared Scallops with Tomato-Kalamata Olive Relish

The recipe for this lovely dish comes from Executive Chef Laura Piper, Hugo's Frog Bar & Fish House, Chicago. The relish is excellent with sautéed shrimp, fish, chicken, or veal.

RELISH

2 large vine-ripened tomatoes, seeded and chopped	1 teaspoon dried oregano
2 ounces Kalamata olives, pitted and chopped	1 teaspoon dried thyme
2 tablespoons capers	Red or white wine vinegar
½ small red onion, cut into small dice	Extra-virgin olive oil
1 to 2 tablespoons chopped fresh basil	Salt and freshly ground pepper
	2 pounds jumbo sea scallops (dry pack preferred)

Combine the tomatoes, olives, capers, onion, and herbs in a bowl. Add wine vinegar, olive oil, salt, and pepper to taste. Toss gently and chill.

Heat a large skillet over medium-high heat. Add 4 tablespoons of olive oil. Season the scallops with salt and pepper. Add as many scallops to the pan as will fit comfortably without touching and cook until golden brown. Turn and cook the second side. When done, the scallops should be slightly opaque in the center. Serve with the relish.

Serves 4

Porcini Crusted Ahi Tuna
with Peperonata and Shaved Celery Salad

The recipe for this superb first course is from Executive Chef John Coletta, Carlucci, Rosemont, Illinois.

PEPERONATA

- 3 tablespoons olive oil
- 2 tablespoons each green, yellow, and red bell peppers in small dice
- 1 tablespoon salt-packed capers, well rinsed and drained
- 2 tablespoons dry white wine
- 1 teaspoon finely minced garlic
- 2 basil leaves, torn
- 1 tablespoon tomato sauce
- 1 teaspoon finely chopped flat leaf parsley
- Fresh lemon juice to taste
- Salt and freshly ground pepper

SHAVED CELERY SALAD

- 12 stalks celery hearts, sliced paper thin
- 2 cups ice cubes
- 1 cup cold water
- 1 tablespoon extra-virgin olive oil
- 1 teaspoon lemon juice, freshly squeezed
- Kosher salt and freshly ground pepper
- ⅛ cup celery leaves, yellow and green

TUNA

- 3 pieces Ahi tuna loin cut into 1x1x4-inch logs (4 to 5 ounces each)
- Kosher salt and freshly ground pepper
- Porcini powder (See note)
- 2 tablespoons olive oil
- 12 fresh basil leaves, torn

For the peperonata, heat 1 tablespoon of olive oil in a heavy, nonreactive saucepan over medium heat. Add the peppers and capers and cook for 3 minutes, stirring with a wooden spoon. Add the wine, garlic, and basil and cook for 3 minutes. Add the tomato sauce and simmer for 3 minutes. Remove the pan from the heat and add the remaining 2 tablespoons of oil. Stir in the parsley and season with lemon juice, salt, and pepper. Set aside. (The peperonata can be refrigerated for 2 days. Bring to room temperature before using.)

Place the shaved celery hearts in a container and add ice and water. Cover and refrigerate overnight. The celery will curl into unique shapes. Drain the curls and pat them dry. Place them in a bowl, drizzle with the olive oil and lemon juice, and season with salt and pepper. Toss gently and add the celery leaves. Set aside while preparing the tuna.

Season the tuna with salt and pepper and dredge in the porcini powder, covering completely. Heat the oil over high heat until very hot but not smoking. Add the tuna and sear for 1 to 2 minutes per side (the tuna will be rare). Remove the tuna from the pan and allow it to rest for 5 minutes. Place the celery salad in the center of a serving platter. With a sharp knife, slice the tuna and arrange it around the salad. Drizzle the peperonata over the slices and garnish with basil leaves.

Note: Porcini powder is available in some gourmet markets or from Internet sources. To make your own, grind dried porcini mushrooms to a powder in a spice grinder or coffee mill.

Serves 6 as a first course

Prawns Sambuca

This fresh and original first course comes from Chef Bert Cutino, co-founder of the Sardine Factory Restaurant in Monterey, California. Chef Cutino is a member of the Union League Club.

16 raw Monterey Bay prawns or
   jumbo shrimp (about 1 pound)
1 cup olive oil
1 tablespoon chopped shallots
1 tablespoon chopped garlic
3 ounces Chardonnay or other
   dry white wine
2 ounces Sambuca liqueur

¼ cup diced fresh tomato
1 tablespoon finely chopped
   fresh tarragon
2 teaspoons salt
Freshly ground pepper
4 ounces unsalted butter
12 ounces hot angel hair pasta,
   cooked and drained

Peel and devein the prawns. Heat the olive oil in a large, heavy sauté pan over medium-high heat. Add the shallots, garlic, and prawns and cook for 1 to 2 minutes, turning once. Standing back, add the wine and Sambuca and flambé. Add the tomatoes, tarragon, salt, and pepper and cook for 2 minutes. Add the butter and cook until the sauce has reduced and thickened. Portion the pasta into 4 soup plates and top with the prawns and sauce.

Serves 4 as a first course

Roasted Corn Soup with Tomato-Onion Confit and Red Pepper Cream

Executive Chef Matthew Koury, Rivers, Chicago, serves this richly flavored soup. The creative garnish really puts it over the top, but the soup is fabulous with nothing more than a sprinkling of chives.

6 ounces unsalted butter (1½ sticks)
1 pound corn kernels
1 cup flour
1 quart chicken stock
1 pint heavy cream
1 pint half & half

2 tablespoons light brown sugar
Salt and freshly ground pepper
Red Pepper Cream
Tomato and Onion Confit
Chopped chives

Heat 4 tablespoons of butter in a heavy skillet over medium-high heat. Add the corn and sauté until light brown and crispy, about 10 minutes. Remove from the pan and cool. Melt the remaining butter in the pan over medium heat. Add the flour and stir until smooth. Cook the roux for 5 to 7 minutes, stirring frequently, until light brown. Transfer the roux to a bowl and cool.

In a large, heavy saucepan, heat the stock with half of the roasted corn and simmer for 5 minutes. Transfer the mixture to a blender and puree. (Do not fill the blender more than ⅓ full; hold the lid slightly askew to allow steam to escape.) Pass the puree through a fine sieve and return it to the pan. Discard the solids. Reheat the soup over medium heat. Add the cream, half & half, brown sugar, and half of the roux. Bring the soup to a simmer. Add more roux until the desired consistency is reached. Season the soup with salt and pepper and add the remaining roasted corn. (The soup can be refrigerated overnight. Reheat gently.)

Ladle the soup into bowls and drizzle with Red Pepper Cream. Place 2 tablespoons of warm confit in the center of each serving and garnish with chives.

RED PEPPER CREAM

1 roasted red bell pepper
2 tablespoons mayonnaise

2 tablespoons sour cream
Salt and freshly ground pepper

Peel and seed the pepper. Puree in a blender with 2 tablespoons of water. Transfer the puree to a bowl. Whisk in the mayonnaise and sour cream. Season with salt and pepper and reserve.

TOMATO AND ONION CONFIT

2 large tomatoes
Olive oil
Salt and freshly ground pepper
½ red onion, julienned

½ yellow onion, julienned
¼ cup balsamic vinegar
¼ cup honey
½ cup minced green onions

Seed the tomatoes and cut them into 1-inch dice. Toss with a little olive oil and season with salt and pepper. Spread them on a baking sheet in one layer and broil for 5 to 7 minutes or until lightly browned and caramelized. Remove from the pan and cool.

Heat ¼ cup of olive oil in a heavy sauté pan over medium-high heat. Add the red and yellow onions and sauté until lightly browned, about 10 minutes. Stir in the vinegar and honey and remove the pan from the heat. Add the green onions and roasted tomatoes. Season with salt and pepper and reserve.

Note: The confit is a delicious condiment for fish and poultry.

Serves 6

Salmon Napoleon with Stir-Fried Vegetables and Chinese Noodles

Created by Union League Club of Chicago Executive Chef Michael Garbin, this superb dish is a study in contrasting tastes and textures. Although it may look daunting at first glance, the dish is easier to put together than you might think. Uncork a good Pinot Noir.

HOISIN ESSENCE (1½ CUPS)

- 1½ teaspoons Asian sesame oil
- 1½ teaspoons minced garlic
- 1½ teaspoons minced ginger
- ¼ cup soy sauce
- ¼ cup hoisin sauce
- 1 cup chicken stock
- ¾ teaspoons fresh lime juice
- Cornstarch slurry (2 tablespoons cornstarch dissolved in 3 tablespoons cold water)

CRISP SALMON NAPOLEON

- 4 square-shaped, skinless salmon medallions, pin bones removed, 5 ounces each
- Salt and freshly ground pepper
- Olive oil
- 6 ounces shitake mushroom caps, sliced
- 1 clove, garlic
- 2 green onions, sliced
- 1 teaspoon soy sauce
- 4 rice paper wrappers (Banh Trang)
- White and/or black sesame seeds, toasted

STIR FRIED VEGETABLES AND CHINESE NOODLES

- 2 ounces Asian sesame oil
- 1 tablespoon minced garlic
- 1 tablespoon minced fresh ginger
- 4 green onions, thinly sliced
- 1 cup Napa cabbage, shredded
- ½ cup sliced bok choy
- ½ cup carrots, thinly sliced on the bias
- 1 cup snow peas, sliced on the bias in ½-inch pieces
- ½ cup fresh bean sprouts
- Salt and freshly ground pepper
- 4 ounces Chinese egg noodles, fresh or dried, cooked
- 1 cup Hoisin Essence

For the Hoisin Essence, heat a saucepan over medium-high heat. Add the sesame oil, garlic, and ginger and sauté briefly. Add the soy sauce, hoisin, chicken stock, and lime juice. Bring to a boil, lower the heat, and simmer for 5 minutes. Add enough of the slurry to thicken the mixture lightly. Strain and set aside.

Slice each salmon medallion horizontally into 3 pieces. Season each slice with salt and pepper and sear quickly in a little hot olive oil, turning once. Cool.

Heat 2 tablespoons of olive oil in a skillet. Add the mushrooms and sauté until tender. Add the garlic and green onions and sauté until the garlic is fragrant. Stir in the soy sauce and remove the pan from the heat. Season with pepper and cool.

Reassemble the salmon medallions spreading the mushroom filling between the layers. Set aside.

Preheat the oven to 375°F. Soak a rice paper wrapper in a bowl or shallow pan of warm water for a few seconds until softened. Lay the wrapper on a kitchen towel to drain. Place a napoleon in the center of each wrapper and neatly fold the edges over to enclose it completely. Remove to a plate and cover with a damp towel or plastic wrap. Repeat with the remaining napoleons. Heat a heavy, oven-proof skillet over medium-high heat. Add enough olive oil to film the bottom of the pan. Add the napoleons and cook until lightly browned and crisp. Turn and cook the second sides until lightly browned, adding more oil if necessary. Transfer the skillet to the oven and bake for 6 minutes. Remove the napoleons from the oven and keep warm.

Meanwhile, heat a large skillet over medium-high heat and add the sesame oil. Add the garlic and ginger and stir-fry for 15 seconds. Add the vegetables and stir-fry until crisp-tender. Season to taste and add the noodles and 1 cup of Hoisin Essence. Toss until the ingredients are combined and the noodles are hot.

Divide the vegetables and noodles among 4 warm plates. Top with the napoleons and garnish with toasted sesame seeds. Serve immediately.

Serves 4

Tournedos of Veal Chester County

Executive Chef Tom Macrina, the Desmond Hotel, Malvern, Pennsylvania, offers this simple and elegant dish. Pair it with a red Burgundy.

1 stick unsalted butter	2 ounces white mushrooms, sliced
2 shallots, chopped	8 veal tournedos, 3 ounces each
3 ounces hedgehog mushrooms, sliced	Salt and freshly ground pepper
	Flour for dredging
3 ounces oyster mushrooms, sliced	3 ounces tawny port
	5 ounces veal demi-glacé

Heat a sauté pan over medium-high heat until hot. Add 3 tablespoons of butter. Add the shallots and sauté briefly. Add the mushrooms and sauté until they brown. Remove the mushrooms from the pan and keep warm. Season the tournedos with salt and pepper, lightly dredge them in flour, and shake off the excess. Add 3 tablespoons of butter to the pan and heat until foamy. Add the tournedos and sear until browned, turning once, about 2 to 3 minutes per side. If necessary, add the remaining 2 tablespoons butter before turning. Deglaze the pan with port and boil, shaking the pan and scraping up all of the browned juices, until the liquid reduces and is syrupy. Stir in the demi-glacé. The tournedos should be done to medium at this point and should feel fairly firm, but still have some "give," when pressed. Divide the tournedos and mushrooms among 4 plates. Spoon sauce over and around the veal and serve.

Serves 4

Salmon Sweet, Tart, and Spicy with Summer Succotash

Executive Chef Jack Kennedy serves this all-American dish at the Chicago Firehouse, owned by Union League Club member Matthew O'Malley. Try it with an Oregon Pinot Gris.

HOMESTYLE BBQ SAUCE

- 2 cloves garlic
- 1 red bell pepper
- 1 green bell pepper
- 1 medium Spanish onion
- 1 or more jalapeño peppers stemmed and seeded (optional)

- 1 tablespoon olive or vegetable oil
- 1 12 to 16 ounce jar chili sauce
- 1 10-ounce jar sweet chili sauce
- 1 12 to 16 ounce can crushed tomatoes
- Salt and freshly ground pepper

SUCCOTASH

- 2 teaspoons olive or vegetable oil
- 1 clove minced garlic
- 2 cups diced fresh tomatoes
- 2 cups fresh corn kernels
- 1 cup lima beans

- Generous pinch each, chopped basil, chives, parsley, and cilantro
- Salt and freshly ground pepper
- 1 tablespoon unsalted butter

SALMON

- 4 skinless salmon fillets, pinbones removed, 6 ounces each

- 6 ounces Homestyle BBQ Sauce
- Fresh herb sprigs

For the sauce, cut the garlic, bell peppers, onion, and jalapeño pepper into small dice. Heat the oil in a large saucepan over moderate heat. Add the vegetables and sauté until soft. Add the chili sauces and tomatoes and simmer for 30 minutes. Puree the mixture in a blender. (Do not fill the blender more than ⅓ full; hold the lid slightly askew to allow steam to escape.) Season with salt and pepper and set aside.

For the succotash, heat a large skillet over medium-high heat. Add the oil and garlic. Sauté for a few seconds. Add the tomatoes and simmer until most of the juices have evaporated. Add the corn, lima beans, and fresh herbs and simmer just until the corn is tender, about 2 to 3 minutes. Remove from the heat and season with salt and pepper. Add the butter and stir to combine. Set aside.

Preheat the oven to 400°F. Place the salmon fillets on a foil or parchment-lined baking sheet, skinned sides down, and brush with BBQ sauce. Roast for about 12 minutes, or until the fish is done but still slightly translucent in the center.

Spoon the succotash onto 4 plates and top with the salmon. Garnish with fresh herbs and serve.

Serves 4

Savory Potato Waffle with Cabernet-Orange Butter

This sophisticated appetizer is from Executive Chef Daniel J. Scannell, Oak Hill Country Club, Rochester, New York. The waffle would also be delicious topped with smoked salmon, a dollop of crème fraîche, and caviar or salmon roe.

1 pound Yukon Gold potatoes
2 sticks unsalted butter, melted
2 teaspoons salt
1 teaspoon fresh ground pepper

2 teaspoons white truffle oil (optional)
2 tablespoons Parmesan cheese
Melted butter

Peel and rinse the potatoes. Place them in a saucepan with 3 quarts of salted water. Bring to a simmer and cook until the potatoes are tender but still firm. Drain and let the potatoes air-dry until completely cool. Grate the potatoes on the large holes of a box grater. Place them in a bowl and add the butter, salt, pepper, truffle oil, and cheese. Mix gently just until combined. Do not overmix or the potatoes will be gluey. Preheat a round waffle iron and brush both sides liberally with melted butter. Spread an ample amount of the potato mixture evenly in the waffle iron. Close the lid and gently press shut. Bake until the waffle is golden brown, about 15 minutes. (Allow the waffle to bake for at least 10 minutes before raising the lid to check for doneness.) Meanwhile, preheat the oven to 200°F. Keep the cooked waffle warm in the oven while making the second waffle. Cut each waffle into quarters and serve hot with Cabernet-Orange Butter.

CABERNET-ORANGE BUTTER

¼ bottle Cabernet Sauvignon
1 teaspoon sugar
3 ounces (¾ stick) unsalted butter, softened

1½ teaspoons chopped fresh tarragon
1 teaspoon grated orange zest
¼ teaspoon kosher salt
¼ teaspoon freshly ground pepper

Combine the wine and sugar in a small stainless saucepan. Reduce gently over medium heat until syrupy. Do not boil. Set aside until cool. In a small bowl, beat the butter with an electric mixer. Beat in the syrup and add the remaining ingredients. The butter can be refrigerated. Let soften before serving.

Serves 8

Summer Turkey Pasties

Renowned Chicago caterer George L. Jewell, Jewell Events Catering, offers these savory English-style pastries. Serve them with a green salad and a chilled, dry white wine.

PASTIES

3 17-ounce packages frozen
   puff pastry
¼ pound cream cheese, softened
½ cup cream
1¼ to 1½ pounds diced, uncooked
   turkey breast
½ cup rutabaga in ½-inch cubes
2½ cups potatoes in
   ½-inch cubes

1 cup carrots in ½-inch cubes
1 cup thinly sliced leek (white and
   light green parts only)
½ cup chopped onions
½ cup corn kernels, thawed
   if frozen
Salt and freshly ground pepper
1 teaspoon chopped fresh
   thyme leaves

SAUCE

½ cup mayonnaise
½ cup honey mustard

Thaw the pastry according to package directions. Line a baking sheet with kitchen parchment. In a large bowl, beat the cream cheese and the cream with a wooden spoon until smooth. Stir in the remaining filling ingredients.

Remove a sheet of pastry from the refrigerator and roll it out slightly with a rolling pin. Using a cake pan as a guide, cut out two 8-inch rounds. Spoon filling onto half of each round, leaving a 1-inch exposed border. Working with one at a time, fold the top half of the dough over and tuck it under. Moisten the exposed bottom edge with water and fold it over the top edge, pressing lightly. Press the tines of a fork around the edge of the pasty to seal, transfer to the baking sheet, and refrigerate. Repeat with the remaining dough. Refrigerate the completed pasties for 30 minutes.

For the sauce, combine the mayonnaise and mustard and chill until needed.

Preheat the oven to 300°F. Cut a slit in the top of each pasty and bake until golden, 50 to 60 minutes. Cover with foil or parchment if they are browning too quickly.

Remove the pasties from the oven and cool for several minutes. Serve warm or at room temperature with the sauce.

Serves 6

Vietnamese Grilled Shrimp Rice Paper Rolls
with Citrus Shoyu Sauce

This stylish version of Vietnamese salad rolls is from Executive Chef Mark Baker, the University Club of Chicago. The cool, refreshing rolls go together quickly and are fun to make.

⅓ to ½ cup olive oil
Juice from 1 large lime
Several sprigs cilantro, torn
1 tablespoon coarsely chopped
    fresh ginger
12 large raw shrimp, peeled
    and deveined
Warm water and rice wine vinegar
12 rice paper wrappers (Banh Trang)
Boston lettuce leaves, torn in half

Cellophane noodles, cooked and
    drained well (optional)
4 ounces carrots, cut into fine julienne
1 papaya, cut into small strips
1 cucumber, cut into small strips
4 ounces shitake mushroom caps,
    thinly sliced
Fresh cilantro sprigs
Fresh mint leaves, torn if large
Assorted baby greens (optional)

Combine the olive oil, lime juice, cilantro, and ginger in a glass bowl and add the shrimp. Marinate for 30 minutes at room temperature. Drain and grill the shrimp on an outdoor grill or indoors on a hot, ridged grill pan until just cooked through. Cool and cut the shrimp in half lengthwise.

Have all of the remaining ingredients at hand. Fill a large bowl or shallow pan with very warm (not hot) water and add a touch of rice wine vinegar. Immerse a sheet of rice paper in the water for a few seconds until softened. Lay the wrapper on a dry kitchen towel to drain. Place a lettuce leaf over the bottom portion of the wrapper leaving about 1½ inches of the sides uncovered. Place a small amount of noodles across the lettuce and, in this order, add carrots, papaya, cucumber, and mushrooms. Lay 2 shrimp halves, end to end, over the mushrooms and top with cilantro sprigs and mint leaves. Fold the bottom of the wrapper over the filling and tuck it under. Fold the sides in and roll up tightly, eggroll-fashion. Place the salad roll on a plate, seam side down, and cover with a damp towel. Repeat with the remaining wrappers. The finished rolls can be covered with a damp towel or plastic wrap and refrigerated for up to 3 hours. Serve them whole or slice them in half on a severe bias. Serve with Citrus Shoyu Sauce for dipping as an appetizer, or arrange them on baby greens and serve with the sauce as a first course.

CITRUS SHOYU SAUCE

1 tablespoon shoyu sauce (Japanese soy)
3 tablespoons sake
1 tablespoon mirin (sweetened
    Japanese rice wine)
Dash sugar

Zest and juice from 1 yuzu
    (Japanese citrus), or substitute the
    zest and juice from ½ lemon
Chinese chili and garlic paste
    to taste (optional)
Touch of olive oil (optional)

Combine the ingredients in a non-reactive container at least 4 hours in advance.

Serves 12

COOKBOOK COMMITTEE

Co-Chairs and Recipe Editors

Barbara Barker   Lee Karton

Archives Research

Marguerite Carington   Dorothy O'Malley   Elaine Roth

Christine M. Brown
Cecelia Bull
Pamela K. Bull
Kathleen Fox
Margaret Lemker
Paula Maguire

Florine McKay
Mary Ellen Niederman
Christina Norton
Terri Ryan
Melanie Shannon
Jackie Thompson

RECIPE CONTRIBUTORS

John Alberts
Christine Babb
Ann Baise
Barbara Barker
Lois C. Beh
Carol Beilfuss
Joan Blumenthal
Jack Bolling
Alice Bowers
Rufus Broadaway
Ann Marie Brown
Katie Brown
Karen Brumund
Guy Buffet
Cecelia Bull
Lois Bull
Rick Bull
Barbara Bush
Stephanie Butler
Marguerite Carington
Cat Carpenter
Ellen Carson
Katherine Chiara
Mary Ann Childers
Lynda Chioros
Serena Cole
Kathryn Cooper
Pat Covey
Peggy Darr
Anne Megan Davis
Joanne Dempsey

Abbie Deneen
Tom Deneen
June Dienes
Mike Donatelli
Billye Dvorak
Virginia Edwards
Carrie Erzinger
Betty Feltes
Marsha Fischl
Marcia Flanagan
Carolyn Friedman
Nancy Friedman
Kathleen Fox
Sandra Ganakos
Lisa Gerkin
Dona Gester
Heidi Gleason
Allison Greene
Fr. William Gros
Karen Hagberg
Stephanie Hammer
Dan Healy
Mary Healy
Marietta Hipskind
Beverly Hogan
Nancy Holz
Muffy Hunt
Linda Ingram
Ginny Istnick
Linda Jakubs
Lee Karton

Robert Karton
Susan Keenan
Lois Kendellen
Jane Kirk
Bonnie Kraska
Judy Krotky
Greg David Laka
Helen Laka
Christy Lampa
Jeanne Lanphier
Barbara LaPointe
Margaret Lemker
Marilyn Lennon
Lois Long
Julianne Lovejoy
Jori Maguire
Paula Maguire
Mary Ann Mahon-Huels
Frank Matkovich
Carol McCabe
Jonathon McCabe
Lois McCullagh
Colleen McElligott
Florine McKay
Louise Nicol Meier
Corinne Morrissey
Sheila Murphy
Mary Ellen Neiderman
Christina Norton
Mary O'Connor
Dorothy O'Malley

Amy Owen
Dorothy Parrot-Hughes
Sharon Prior
Barbara Reed Perkaus
Anne Rigazio
Solvig Robertson
Elaine Roth
Judie Roth
Alan Rubin
Winifred Rubin
G. E. "Russ" Russell
Suzie Russell
Terri Ryan

Sheila Seaborg
Bette Schlegel
Bill Schneider
Lorrie Schneider
Barbara Schuld
Judy Scully
Diane Siaroff-Jacobson
Leslie Smart
Elaine Smith
Elizabeth Smith
Scott Smith
Candy Strom
Michele Sullivan

Jacqueline Thompson
Jean Topinka
Judy Baar Topinka
Jutta Tragnitz
Julie Tucek
Martin von Walterskirchen
Ursula von Walterskirchen
Edye Wagner
Dianna Whetsell
June Taylor Wolcott
Theresia Wolf-McKenzie
Lori Woodland

CONTRIBUTING CHEFS

Abraham Aguirre
Executive Chef
Grotto on Rush
Chicago, Illinois

Mark Baker
Executive Chef
University Club of Chicago
Chicago, Illinois

Nathan Brown
Pastry Chef
Spago
Maui, Hawaii

John Coletta
Executive Chef
Carlucci's
Rosemont, Illinois

Bert P. Cutino, CEC, AAC
Chef/Owner
Sardine Factory Restaurant
Monterey, California

Debbie Dunnewold
Windy City Chef
Chicago, Illinois

John Ferguson
Executive Chef
Fortnightly of Chicago
Chicago, Illinois

Michael Garbin, CEC, AAC
Executive Chef
Union League Club of Chicago
Chicago, Illinois

George L. Jewel
Jewel Catering Events
Chicago, Illinois

Jack Kennedy
Executive Chef
Chicago Firehouse
Chicago, Illinois

Matthew Koury
Executive Chef
Rivers
Chicago, Illinois

Le Colonial Restaurant
Chicago, Illinois

Tom Macrina, CEC, AAC
Executive Chef
Desmond Hotel
Malvern, Pennsylvania

Francoise de Melogue
Executive Chef
Pili Pili
Chicago, Illinois

Laura Piper
Executive Chef
Hugo's Frog Bar & Fish House
Chicago, Illinois

John Reed
Executive Chef
Food for Thought Catering
Lincolnwood, Illinois

Edgar Rodriguez
Executive Chef
Salbute
Hinsdale, Illinois

Priscila Satcoff
Chef/Owner
Salpicón!
Chicago, Illinois

Daniel J. Scannell, CEC, CMC
Executive Chef
Oak Hill Country Club
Rochester, New York

Stephanie Schifrin
Chef
Kafe Kokopelli
Hinsdale, Illinois

Charles Sochor
Executive Chef/Owner
Café Matou
Chicago, Illinois

Audry Triplett
Executive Chef/Partner
Gibsons Steakhouse Restaurant
Chicago, Illinois

WOMEN'S BOARD

INDEX

Join the Celebration!
A COLLECTION OF FAVORITE RECIPES

Send to:

Women's Board
Union League Boys and Girls Clubs
65 W. Jackson Boulevard, Chicago, IL 60604
Telephone: (312) 588-1863   Fax: (312) 583-0320
Website: www.ulbgc.org   E-mail: cookbook@ulbgc.org

All proceeds from the sale of
Join the Celebration! will benefit
the Union League Boys and Girls Clubs.

Please send _____ copies @ $29.95 each $ _____

(10% off with order of 3 or more books) $ _____

Illinois residents add 8.75% sales tax $ _____

Shipping and handling
$5.00 for first cookbook $ _____
$2.00 for each additional cookbook shipped to same address $ _____
$5.00 for each additional cookbook shipped to different address $ _____

Total $ _____

Prices subject to change without notice.

Order date _____

Ship to (Please check here if billing address is different from shipping address) _____

_____
Name, Telephone

_____
Address

_____
City, State, Zip Code

Sold to (If different from shipping address)

_____
Name, Telephone

_____
Address

_____
City, State, Zip Code

Payment method ___ Check (Payable to Union League Boys and Girls Clubs)
___ Visa   ___ MasterCard

_____   _____
Account Number   Exp. Date

_____   _____
Cardholder Name (Please print)   Signature

_____
Telephone